Flying High

To . Jacqui

Keep laughing!

Don Maclean

DON MACLEAN

Flying High

MY AUTOBIOGRAPHY

Hodder & Stoughton
LONDON SYDNEY AUCKLAND

Copyright © 2003 Don Maclean and Chris Gidney

First published in Great Britain in 2003
This paperback edition first published in 2004

The right of Don Maclean to be identified as the Author
of the Work has been asserted by him in accordance with
the Copyright, Designs and Patents Act 1988.

10 9 8 7 6 5 4 3 2 1

British Library Cataloguing in Publication Data
A record for this book is available from the British Library

ISBN 0 340 78691 4

Typeset in BaskervilleBERegular by Avon DataSet Ltd,
Bidford-on-Avon, Warwickshire

Printed and bound in Great Britain by
Clays Ltd, St Ives plc

The paper and board used in this paperback are natural recyclable
products made from wood grown in sustainable forests.
The manufacturing processes conform to the environmental
regulations of the country of origin.

Hodder & Stoughton
A Division of Hodder Headline Ltd
338 Euston Road
London NW1 3BH
www.madaboutbooks.com

Contents

Hello Reader,

If you're one of those people who enjoy sex, drugs and rock and roll, this book is definitely not for you. If you enjoy autobiographies in which the writer slags off his contemporaries, you'll not get that either. I've only encountered one person in showbiz whom I found detestable and I wouldn't afford him publicity by mentioning him in these pages.

I've met many people in showbusiness of whom I've disapproved but that's probably because I'm a self-righteous old prude. No, this is rather the story of a life incredibly blessed. OK, I could have been more successful if only two or three of the television opportunities I had had materialised, but it obviously wasn't to be and I emerged older, wiser and more content.

This is not one of those self-effacing autobiographies either. While not being totally self-satisfied, it was once said of me, 'Don's had a humility by-pass', and I think that just about sums things up.

If none of these warnings put you off, please read on and hopefully enjoy these ramblings; and, as He's done with me, may the Lord walk with you and keep you safe.

1

Making an Entrance

I was born at an early age, of mixed parents – one male, one female, which was the norm in those days though things have since changed. I first saw the light of day in the Sorrento Maternity Home, Moseley, where my mother had been in labour for three weeks. 'If I'd been in a proper hospital they'd have given me a caesarean,' she would say. I'm grateful they didn't, I might have been named Stanley after the knife. Mom's difficult pregnancy, her interminable labour, the 300 stitches needed to reconstruct her and the fact that the doctor had afterwards told Dad, 'Don't let her have another, it could be fatal', meant that I grew up with a deep sense of gratitude, and rightly so! I had a wonderful start in life. Apart from two doting parents, I was born in Birmingham and I was a Roman Catholic, two facts that more than anything else made me what I am.

There was apparently only one major air raid after I was born, the BSA (Birmingham Small Arms) factory once again being the intended target. I was in no danger because Dad was an air-raid warden. At the outbreak of hostilities, he had applied to join the Fleet Air Arm but was turned down because he was in a 'reserved occupation' – the work he was doing at George Ellison Ltd in Perry Barr was essential to the war effort, and he couldn't be spared. He harboured dreams of looking down on the Bismarck from the rear seat of a Fairy Swordfish but had to make do with putting out fires. He did get a war medal, being the ARP table tennis champion, and he became something of an ARP legend for a different reason. One summer night when on fire watch, all

1

civilians having taken refuge in their shelters, Dad found a deck-chair in a garden. He sat in it and dropped off. The Luftwaffe duly paid their visit, bombs fell just a few streets away but Dad never woke up, slept right through it.

Yes, Dad could sleep! If sleeping had been an Olympic event, Dad would easily have made the British team. He was calm and unruffled; Mom described him as 'a steady chap'. She, on the other hand, was volatile, quick-tempered and did everything at a hundred miles an hour – I'm like my Mom! They'd been married eight years by the time I came along. When I questioned Mom about this in later life, she said, 'Don't blame me, you'd have been a lot older if your Dad had managed to stay awake a bit longer.' Bless him!

I don't remember the war though one of my first recollections is of VE Day – come to think of it, it was more likely VJ Day. A string of triangular flags was strung from our front bedroom window to the corresponding window on the opposite side of the road. There were long tables in the middle of the road for as far as the eye could see. Everyone was deliriously happy and the weather was so good that I was forced to wear a sun hat.

Growing up in Birmingham after the war was idyllic. We lived in a three-bedroomed terraced house with an outside loo, no bathroom and a front room which opened straight on to the pavement. Written in pencil on the brickwork of each doorway in the street was a six-figure number. That was the Co-op number of the occupants and it enabled the milkman and the breadman and the coalman to write your number on the bill before you'd managed to get the door open. One of the first things you learned was your mom's Co-op number – 176841 – there, it just slipped out after all these years. Women were house-proud. The front window gleamed; the net curtains were as white as an angel's wing and the front step – well!! The doorstep was washed at least once a day and then attacked with pumice. Most steps were worn away from constant ministration. The cleanest woman in the street was the one with the most dangerous step. Small boys too came in for excessive cleaning. Before bed each night, I would sit on a kitchen chair while Mom scrubbed my knees with a scrubbing brush and red carbolic soap. The whole house had a clean smell made up of carbolic soap, Cardinal floor polish and lavender furniture polish; you didn't need a mirror, it was possible to see yourself in every bit of furniture.

Dad was a metronome; you could set your watch by him. At the expected time, I would stand on the unsafe step to catch sight of him as he turned the corner at the bottom of Ombersley Road. At this point, I'd launch myself off the step and career towards him. He walked faster than most people run but slowed to my pace as I fell in beside him and took his hand. Once inside, the strict routine continued: a peck for Mom then, with shirt sleeves rolled up beyond the shoulder and shirt collar tucked right in, he'd attack his face, hands and arms with carbolic soap and cold water. Once clean, he'd relocate to the living room where his dinner was already on the table. He ate his dinner, always cleared the plate, and, as he took the last mouthful, he'd rise from the table to sit in his chair. Within minutes he'd be asleep. Sometimes he fell asleep in mid-chew. At ten o'clock precisely, by which time I was tucked up in bed, Mom would wake him with a cup of Cadbury's cocoa which he'd drink and then retire to bed. He worked ever so hard in a factory, building the metal frames which housed electrical switch gear, but his need to spend most of his life comatose still puzzles me.

Mom was a wide-awake woman who wore her Catholicism openly. She'd been in the Legion of Mary and had a great devotion to Our Blessed Lady. It was inevitable that I should be infected with her enthusiasm for her faith, as indeed I was from a very early age. She was also an accomplished amateur pianist and the most important piece of furniture in the house was an upright piano which stood proudly in the front room. Mom polished everything in the house daily, the piano being the last to receive her attention. Having buffed the rosewood to a rosy glow, she would then dust the notes and, as if forced to do so by some aeolian wind, her fingers would begin to play.

From the age of about two, I was taught to sing. First nursery rhymes then simple songs; by the time I was four I had quite a large repertoire. Family parties were frequent. Both of Mom's brothers, Uncle George and Uncle Frank, played piano too so music filled whoever's house we were gathered in. Mom would have rehearsed me prior to the event and I'd stand beside the piano giving full vocal vent for the benefit of cousins, uncles and aunts. There's a fine Brummagem word, 'poppy-show', which describes someone who can't wait to be the centre of attention – it fitted me perfectly.

I am a child of the wireless era. There were three choices for the wireless listener: the Home Service which was all talk, the Third Programme which was all classical music, and the magnificent Light Programme to which we were permanently tuned. While I was still very young, I became addicted to the laughter I heard on the wireless. The highlight of the week, for which I was allowed to stay up very late, was *Variety Bandbox*. Sunday night between nine and ten, the cream of variety acts came out of the speaker. There were three resident comedians who took it in turns to top the bill: Derek Roy, Arthur English and Frankie Howerd. I couldn't possibly have understood the jokes when I was four but I loved them all and picked up their catch phrases: 'Play the music, open the cage.' 'No don't, don't mock!' 'Naughty Francis!' 'What a funny woman!' There were dozens of them. I'm proud to say that I shared the stage with Derek Roy and Arthur English in pantomime and with Frankie Howerd in several radio and TV shows.

Mom was incredibly devoted to her own mom, who never seemed to appreciate the fact as far as I was concerned. My Nanny was crippled with arthritis. No doubt in this day and age she would have had both hips and both knees replaced and would have been a bionic gran. She owned a grocery shop in Belgrave Road and we visited her every afternoon. She sat by the fire in the living room behind the shop, able to walk only with the aid of two sticks and probably dreading the arrival of her extremely noisy grandson. An aspidistra in a brass pot stood in front of the only window, blocking out most of the light. My first act on entering the room would be to climb on a chair to reach the light switch. Nan always moaned that it was too expensive to have the 'lectric on during the day but a boy's gotta see. I was fascinated by two framed pictures, one of the Sacred Heart and one of the Blessed Virgin Mary, which hung on the wall. Nanny always said, 'You can have them when I've gone,' but when she eventually went so did they. I've no idea what happened to them. There was also a large family Bible with brass corners and coloured pictures

4

inside. I used to get very bored at the Shop but the walk there and back was OK.

Both Mom's sisters lived at the Shop. Doris, the youngest, was unmarried and none too keen on small boys. She always greeted me in the same way, 'Hello, Donald Duck!' and thereafter ignored me except for the occasional 'Don't touch that!' Rene was altogether different. She was the mother of cousin Norma who was almost exactly one year younger than me. Uncle Norman was away fighting Hitler, or Rommel if you want to split hairs. Auntie Rene served in the grocery shop which Nanny insisted on being 'open all hours'. Norma was a pretty child with pale skin, freckles and wonderful red hair sculptured into ringlets. She hated having her hair done and was probably the first little girl to offer the advice, 'If your mom's had a row with your dad, don't let her brush your hair.' She was chubby as a kid but grew up to be tall, slim and elegant. Nanny much preferred Norma to me but I accepted that with good grace. After all, I was noisy and got dirty incredibly quickly while Norma was quiet and always clean.

I was, however, about to acquire an ally. It must have been 1946. Since the war's end Sergeant Norman Owen of the Pioneer Corps had been detained in Cairo, rebuilding Egypt. We'd been expecting his return for a week; Auntie Rene was a nervous wreck. Every day as we approached the Shop I'd been told, 'Uncle Norman may be there.' One day he was. I walked into the back room where he was sitting by the fire polishing his black boots. His sleeves were rolled up and he had wide braces which were the same khaki as his shirt.

'Hello,' he said in a very friendly voice. I liked him straight away. I decided that I'd stand right next to him. I had my question ready.

'Did you kill any Germans?' I remember him laughing loudly.

'No, they only gave me a shovel,' he said.

I thought for a bit then said, 'Did you bury any Germans?' – not bad for three!

I liked Uncle Norman. He was always interested in me and in what I was doing. I liked my Uncle George too. He was Mom's elder brother, a big man with a bald head; male members of the Field family didn't grow hair. George always wanted to make people laugh – is that where I got it from? Fridays I couldn't wait to get to the Shop because I knew George would be there. He'd fight with me and I'd keep coming back for more.

'Gorra toughen him up,' George would say to Nanny's frequent requests to 'Stop turning that boy into a wild animal'. I slept well after seeing Uncle George, all my energy spent.

My early life was blighted by meat. I am one of nature's vegetarians. Apparently before I could talk I rejected it as food. In those days meat was rationed, and you're not gonna waste it on a kid who won't eat it. I hated the taste, the smell and most importantly the texture of the stuff. This caused great consternation. In the 1940s, everyone's idea of a meal was the leg of some animal on a plate usually surrounded by cabbage and potato swimming in gravy. No one could cope with me. I was perfectly happy living on Pom (dehydrated potato) and American dried egg, but the dried egg dried up once hostilities ceased and I was stuck with 'proper' food. Weekdays were fine, Mom didn't bother too much that her only son was a herbivore, but at the weekends things got unpleasant. Dad insisted that I ate bacon for breakfast. I could chew the stuff until it was white but there was no way I could swallow it.

'You'll sit there till you've eaten it,' said Dad like a broken record. My rescuer was a large ginger tomcat whom I had named Tiddles. He and I were partners on Saturday and Sunday mornings. As soon as Dad was diverted, I'd remove the bacon from my mouth and drop my hand to my side. Tiddles would be sat exactly on station. He'd slyly take the bacon from my hand and devour it. I continued to chew for Dad's benefit but if Dad looked at the cat, he stopped chewing immediately – what a star!

Apart from the assault on my digestive system, I looked forward to Sunday mornings. Mom and I would be up early for nine o'clock mass. Dad would stay in bed worshipping the great god Morpheus until we returned. It was a long way to St John's Church especially if you've only got little legs. As we got closer to our chosen place of worship Mom would invariably decide that her infant was not as clean as God would want him to be. Out would come the hankie which she would spit on and gleefully wipe all round my mouth – I hated that! The Church of St John the Evangelist had a hush about it. I became reverent the moment I entered the porch and, with the holy water still moist on my forehead, I genuflected crisply and slipped into the pew. I quickly learned when to stand, when to sit and when to kneel. The mass was in Latin but you did get a Bible story, the Gospel, in English, and also a sermon – not that I understood much of that though I never allowed myself to become bored. There was so much to look at: statues in their niches, no less than fourteen Stations of the Cross, each one different from the next, and, hanging above the altar, a huge crucifix. The cobweb-covered chains from which it was suspended were substantial but I always feared it would come loose and crash to the floor, or perhaps just one chain would break and the mighty crucifix would swing to one side before smashing through the stained glass window. The prospect of this defenestration occupied me during many an adult sermon. Occasionally we'd go to High Mass at eleven o'clock. This was even better, we sang the *Kyrie, Gloria, Credo*, etc. and by extending my nostrils I was able to overdose on incense. I embraced Catholicism with a passion which didn't go unnoticed. Churches were packed in those days and everyone knew everyone else. I was patted on the head by several members of my church family as well as the priest and regularly told what a well-behaved boy I was.

Every Saturday morning a little Irish chap would call at our house, my mother would open her purse and give him one shilling. This was towards the upkeep of Catholic schools. At the beginning of the century, Catholic parents had marched to Westminster from Birmingham, and indeed from many other places, to lobby the Director of the Board of Education, Reginald McKenna MP. Their cry was 'Catholic education by Catholic teachers for Catholic children in Catholic schools'. Catholic schools were still not wholly supported by the state and relied on parents to supplement them with one shilling per week. Mom was happy to pay because her son would shortly be educated in a Catholic school – or would he? Places were scarce. Our postal address said that we lived in Sparkbrook. St John's School was in Balsall Heath.

'He's not ours,' claimed St John's, 'he has to go to the English Martyrs in Sparkhill.' The Martyrs refused me too, claiming that I belonged to St John's. Mom was distraught. More than 250 shillings had left her purse since my birth, and for what? She tried her best but to no avail and eventually, at the age of five and a half, I was enrolled in Clifton Road Infants' School.

I suppose everyone remembers their first day at school. Half-way through the morning we were each given a bottle of milk. I'd never seen a straw, so I blew instead of sucked and the milk which should have been on my inside ended up on my outside. A little girl named Mary mopped me down with a large, clean hanky which she produced from up the leg of her bottle-green knickers. I stayed in Class 1 for exactly a week. The teacher's name was Miss Jones. She confiscated my gun, which no one had told me I shouldn't bring to school, and refused to let me play in the sand box – I dislike her even now. Class 2 beckoned but I didn't stay there long either, they kept moving me on. After two weeks of school I informed my mother that I was too big to be taken to school, I was capable of going on my own – she cried. How callous I'd become after just a fortnight in the real world.

Every morning we sat on the floor in a big circle and said prayers. I knew the Lord's Prayer, I said it every night before I went to sleep, but when I finished this lot carried on, something about 'power and glory'; I wasn't about to start saying that. I soon realised that if I stopped at the real end of the prayer, I could fit in the Hail Mary while the rest of the kids were still powering and glorying. We sang hymns at assembly, most of which I knew. When Christmas came, I knew all the carols plus a variety of Christmas songs. My teacher became quite excited to realise that she had a five-year-old who could sing loudly and in tune. I ended up being taken from room to room, stood in front of the class and invited to sing 'Rudolph the Red-nosed Reindeer'. My days as a performer had begun.

One Saturday morning, Dad took me out. I liked being on my own with my Dad, he smelled of carbolic soap and tobacco, he had a big hand that my hand disappeared into and arms covered in thick fur. He was excited and the excitement transmitted to me. We walked quickly and soon reached Stratford Road where we stopped at a small shop with nothing in the window. Dad signed some forms, then we went outside and got into a car. I was six but I'd never been in a car before. Dad was behind the wheel, the man sat next to him and I had the back seat to myself. It wasn't easy for Dad to learn to drive but he persevered. Before he passed his test he'd bought a car, a 1940 Ford Anglia de luxe – black, of course. WG 9440 was the registration and I can smell the leather upholstery even now; they didn't have real vinyl in those days. Houses in Sparkbrook didn't have garages so Dad hired a lock-up garage which was about two miles' walk away. It cost 3s.3d per week. When they put it up to 3s.9d there was a lengthy discussion about whether the family finances could afford the increase – we knew all about inflation even then.

There weren't that many cars about; we were one of only four families in Ombersley Road to own a car. The road was still referred to by grown-ups as 'the 'orse road' and milk and coal was delivered by horse-drawn transport. These gentle, hard-working creatures were the only animals we saw apart from dogs and cats and the occasional mouse in a trap. The kids would be out as soon as a horse was heard in the road, stroking and making a fuss of it. I feel sorry for today's kids; you can't feed carrots to a milk float can you?

Shortly after we got a car, Uncle Norman bought one too. It was an Austin 7 and I loved it. It screamed in top gear and rocked from side to side when cornering, probably because Uncle Norman still thought he was driving a jeep in the Western Desert. During the summer, we'd call at the Shop every Sunday afternoon, load Nanny into the car with a struggle, then set off for a local destination: Stratford, Bidford, Evesham, anywhere with a river. Once under way, I'd keep up a running commentary of what was going on around us. Sometimes the car was a tank, sometimes an aeroplane on a bombing raid, sometimes a racing car in a race. Mom and Dad were very indulgent but Nanny found me a bit of a strain. 'Doesn't he ever shut up?' She was always pleased if I opted to travel in Norman's Austin 7.

Once we arrived I was like a dog that'd been let off a lead. I'd charge about whichever field we'd parked in, delighting at the space on offer. Dad would spend hours pumping away at his primus stove. Why we wanted a cup of tea I'll never know, I never drank the stuff, but it became a matter of honour that the stove would be lit and the kettle with its collapsible handle would be boiled. That primus was a great source of fun for the whole family. Mom would delight in taking the mickey out of Dad's efforts to become a mobile café. He took it all in his stride.

Although I was making quite a mark at Clifton Road School, Mom was still smarting over my rejection from Catholic education – but help was at hand. I could read by now, I had my very own library ticket, and at mass I was more than occupied trying to relate the Latin words on the one page to the English words on the opposite page, so I missed the announcement the priest made from the pulpit. Apparently there were so many children attending non-Catholic schools that the nuns at St John's Convent were to start a religious education class on Saturday mornings. At the end of mass, we dashed into the sacristy and Donald Michael Maclean was the first name on the list.

St John's Convent comprised three very large houses on Park Road, Moseley. My shoes shone and so did my hair which was plastered to my head with Brylcreem. Mom mounted the steps and knocked on the door, which was opened by the biggest nun in the world. Nuns wore habits in those days and wimples, which must have been a danger when crossing the road, there was no way they could see to the side without turning their heads completely. I prefer nuns in habits, I must admit. Nowadays you can be talking to a nice woman in twin set and pearls only to discover after twenty minutes that she's one of the Little Sisters of Perpetual Motion – disconcerting to say the least. Sr Mary Annuncia was very tall and the voluminous habit gave no indication of the girth of the woman inside it but there was no way she was frightening. Her voice was so gentle; I remember thinking that it was like melted butter. I knew instantly that I was in the presence of holiness; without hesitation I took the hand she offered.

Sr Annuncia and Miss Freda King, the primary school teacher who assisted her, were to become very important in my life. Over the next four years they gave me knowledge of and grounding in the Roman Catholic faith that I would never have got at a Catholic school. We learned lots of prayers, often obscure ones, heard stories from the lives of the saints and studied catechism – we weren't too keen on that – for three hours every Saturday morning. We were encouraged to recruit other children. I made it my business to find other baptised Catholics in my school and tell them about Sr Annuncia. My cousin Norma, whom I've told you was a year younger than me, joined me each week. Pretty soon there were about fifty children attending and we had to expand into two rooms. Sr Annuncia called me her little disciple and the title caught on with the other nuns.

After a very short time, about six weeks, Sr Annuncia and Miss King took me into the Reverend Mother's office. She was a tiny woman, no bigger than me. She was French and I was fascinated by the way she spoke and moved her hands about all the time. She asked me several questions about the eucharist, the consecration, confession and penance. When we left the Reverend Mother, I remember both Sr Annuncia and Miss King being very pleased with me. I now realise that the main reason for starting the Saturday morning class was to enable those of us from non-Catholic schools to make our first Holy Communions. It had been decided that morning that I was ready to do just that. I would be their first 'first communicant', proving the scheme a success.

There have been several unforgettable days in my life; this was probably the first. I was up early, and dressed in my suit which was a navy blue jacket with short trousers to match. I wore shirt and tie and my hair had succumbed to a generous helping of Dad's Brylcreem. We were early for nine-o'clock mass but Sr Annuncia was there before us, I could see her tall figure outside the church as we turned the corner into George Street. She greeted me kindly as always then delved inside her habit to find a dark red sash. She placed this over my shoulder and pinned it with a large safety pin. It had dark red tassels which banged against my hip as I walked. Once in church we were ushered into the very front pew on the right-hand side. Reverend Mother was already deep in prayer, Sr Annuncia sat next to her and I was sandwiched between the large nun and my Mom, who was wearing her best hat. I looked beyond Mom and was comforted to see Miss King. The mass seemed interminable but eventually it became time for communion. Reverend Mother was always first to the rail to receive but this time she stood and allowed me to pass her. I knelt at the altar rail, Mom next to me and then Sr Annuncia. The altar server approached and placed the paten under my chin. The priest stood before me; the chalice in his hand looked enormous.

'*Corpus Domini Nostri Jesu Christi custodiat animam tuam in vitam eternam.*'

'Amen,' I responded and the body of Christ was placed on my tongue. A shudder passed over me causing me to raise my shoulders and arch my back. It's happened to me at various times since when I've received Holy Communion, though rarely; why not every time, I wonder? The receipt of the host during mass is very important to me, I feel unfulfilled if I attend mass without receiving communion; but I would never take communion if I considered that I was not in a state of grace. That day is still vivid in my memory. It was important and I was important; from now on I would be able to commune with God at every mass, I was a complete Catholic. A few months later, most of the other children, including my cousin Norma, were ready to make their first communion. As there were quite a few of them, the nuns put on a party for them afterwards at the convent. The following Saturday morning they went to great pains to point out that they'd had a party and I'd not following my first communion. I remember pointing out that the sacrament was the only worthwhile part of the day; receiving Jesus was far more important than receiving jelly and cake. Such 'profound' words further added to my standing at the convent.

Weekdays, I jogged along quite nicely at Clifton Road School where most of the teachers hailed from South Wales. There was a Miss Phillips and a Mrs Phillips, a Miss Pugh, a Mr Davies and a Miss Lewis – those two ended up marrying one another. Apparently, immediately post-war, the bright kids from the valleys were encouraged to take themselves off to teacher training college – better than going down the pit, mind, isn't it, look you, can't they? See, I told you it had rubbed off! I really feel that I got the best education available for a working-class kid at the time. Teachers were impressed with my imagination, which was really down to the fact that I was an only child. Not having anyone of my generation in the house meant that everything in the house took on an entity. Chairs, tables, animals, everything talked and I answered. I frequently got funny looks from grown-ups and often I heard the remark 'What is wrong with that boy?' but it all washed over me. I had my own music too, it went everywhere with me. I had monsters that lived in the wardrobe and dis-embodied hands that lived under the bed but they never got me because I ran from the door then jumped on to the bed from quite a distance out. Once on the bed, I had a cricket stump with which I'd beat the lower reaches of the bedclothes to ensure that there was no giant python under the covers waiting to swallow me whole.

Scary things weren't confined to my bedroom; even worse creatures lay in wait at the bend in the stairs. There was a door at the bottom of our stairs which opened straight into the living room. There was no electric light on the stairs so if that door was closed the stairway from the upstairs landing appeared to be a black void. There was a thin handrail down the left-hand side but I never touched it, I kept well to the right. As I reached the bend towards the bottom each stair broadened on the left and narrowed on the right. This was where the creatures struck. Vividly coloured, constantly changing their shape, they each had three fingers which plucked at my clothing and hair. You couldn't fight them off; you just had to run the gauntlet. Many's the time I've fallen headlong into the living room having launched myself, head first, at the closed door in an effort to reach safety.

'What's wrong with that boy?' Dad would say if he happened to be there.

2

A Growing Brummie

My imagination was further fed by weekly visits to 'the pictures'. Words such as 'cinema' and 'movies' had not yet entered the English language. There were no less than seven 'picture houses' within easy walking distance of our house. The Olympia was the nearest and that was the usual destination of the Maclean family on a Saturday night. On the way we'd pass the local barrow boy, Billy Bunk, so-called because each eye looked in a completely different direction – no kid ever attempted to steal from his barrow, he could see you even if you were behind him. One Saturday as we approached we could see a queue had formed at the barrow. That was unusual, we quickened our step.

'Pineapples,' said Dad. 'Billy Bunk's got pineapples.' Fresh fruit had been a scarcity during the war. If fruit didn't come out of a tin I didn't recognise it and I'd certainly never seen a pineapple before. Billy was restricting each customer to just one fruit, Dad paid his money and handed it on to me. 'Here y'are, son, a pineapple.' I opened my mouth and tried to bite into it, which all the grown-ups found hysterical. I was crying because I'd cut my lips on this ugly thing and they were laughing. I prefer my pineapple out of tins!

Once we reached the Olympia, we sat in the best seats which cost the princely sum of tenpence each. I became quite brilliant at stitching two halves of a film together. For some reason we always got in half-way through the main feature. Having enjoyed half of that, we sat through the adverts, Pathé News, travelogue and the support picture, then the main feature started again. The words I dreaded most on a Saturday were 'This is where we came in.' Mom and Dad would then get up and leave, with me walking backwards up the aisle to catch every last minute of celluloid wonderment.

If the film was a Western, I would often have to be dragged out of my seat. Roy Rogers and Hoppalong Cassidy were my real favourites. Gene Autry was a bit wet, he had a girl's name for a start and, when any self-respecting cowboy would have been punching cows and shooting Indians, he'd start singing. Whenever he sang, the Sons of the Pioneers would be sat on the fence behind him adding insult to harmony. No, Gene was not in the same street as Roy. Roy Rogers once came to the Birmingham Hippodrome with his famous horse, Trigger. Needless to say I was taken to see them both. I remember little about it except that I was in total ecstasy for the entire evening. Years later I visited the Roy Rogers Museum somewhere in the USA and there was Trigger – stuffed! What an undignified end for such a noble beast.

I tended to become whatever I'd seen on the pictures that week. Seeing a cowboy film meant I'd travel everywhere on an imaginary horse. When I saw *Cockleshell Heroes* I went every-where paddling an imaginary canoe. Can you wonder why I subscribe to the theory that we reflect what we see on TV and films? Experts would have us believe that films and TV reflect life but I'd disagree; the opposite is true. That's why young people now live in a violent society obsessed with sex. I thank God that when I was a kid, good triumphed over evil, ambition and the spirit of adventure was fostered and everyone left the cinema feeling good.

Feeling cold was the other feeling I remember. In the winter we'd return from the pictures to a freezing house. The fire had gone out so we'd stand in the kitchen with our coats on waiting while Mom boiled up the cocoa and the water for the hot water bottles. No wonder we were thin, we shivered all the fat off. If going to bed in the winter was a trial, it was nothing compared to getting up the next morning, by which time ice had formed on the inside of the window and the metal hot water bottle, now freezing cold, would destroy any bit of bare skin it touched. My thick pyjama coat was tucked into my thick pyjama bottoms but my feet were bare. No carpet awaited the soles of my feet, just lino which was at the same temperature as the surface of a frozen lake – it's a wonder I ever got out of bed.

Winter brought on the football season and from the age of eight I began to spend my Saturday afternoons at St Andrew's watching Birmingham City. We boys paid our shilling and sat on the wall behind Gil Merrick's goal. Gil was the England goalkeeper at the time. He had a café just round the corner and after the game we'd dash round to it, expecting to see our hero behind the counter serving cups of tea. We never did see him and I came to the conclusion that he was one of those people who were very slow at getting dressed after games, as I was myself if Mom wasn't there to dress me. We knew the names of all the players, many of whom were local chaps who really cared about the club they played for, not like the mercenaries in today's game. I went with a lad of my own age, Peter Box. There was never any worry about our safety. Several times while leaving the ground in a crush of bodies Peter and I would suddenly be lifted up by a couple of chaps behind us, riding on their shoulders until safely outside the ground, when we'd be returned to pavement level. Any similar assistance nowadays would be construed as child molestation. I no longer feel any allegiance to Birmingham City or to any other football club despite the fact that it's the done thing for celebrities to latch on to a team. The behaviour of football supporters, the obscene amounts of money paid to players and the glorification of yobbery both on and off the field means that I have little more than a passing interest in the game. Rugby, however, is a different matter.

Live theatre didn't figure large in my life except at Christmas time. Dad's factory took a block booking for the pantomime at the Alexandra where a great man of the theatre, Derek Salberg, produced a wonderful show each year. Dad made sure that we always got to sit in the front row and I always got to go on stage for the song sheet, it was the high spot of my year. I sat there with my bum in starting blocks and as soon as Idle Jack or Dame Trot began to ask for children to help them I was out of my seat and climbing the steps before any other kid in the house had moved. I desperately wanted to be up there participating in the show. Interesting to think that I've just completed my thirty-second panto, and that was at the beautiful, newly refurbished Birmingham Hippodrome.

During the first two weeks in August, Geo Ellison Ltd closed its gates and its skilled workers headed for the coast. It was a long way to the sea in any direction from Birmingham. Rhyl and Weston-super-Mare were the favourite destinations but the Macleans went further afield. When I was three and a half we went to the Isle of Man, the equivalent of nipping off to Florida these days. Dad carried a huge brown suitcase on his shoulder and Mom had me by the hand. When we got to Liverpool docks we were part of a mass of humanity. All I could see was skirts and trousers and all the trousers were exactly the same, grey flannels. Several times I reached for my Dad's hand only to find out that it was someone else's. When the gates opened, the crowd surged forward. In the rush my shoe came off and was never seen again. I spent each day in ecstasy on Douglas beach in a grey and red woolly cossie whose texture was a cross between a Brillo pad and Shredded Wheat, and each evening drinking Vimto while watching Mom and Dad slow foxtrot at the Villa Marina. One night we went into a hotel and Mom played the piano. I stood next to the piano and sang my full repertoire of songs and was given fresh orange juice, not the welfare stuff, all evening.

Not all annual holidays were that successful. When I was seven we went to Bournemouth for two weeks. The weather was terrible and we were in one of those boarding houses people joke about: 'use of cruet 4d extra'. As soon as breakfast was finished, the landlady stood over you, willing you to vacate her house. Having spent two weeks walking round Bournemouth in our Macs, Dad made a decision: 'Next year we're going to a holiday camp.'

That decision changed my life. Every August we'd spend two weeks at a different Warner's Holiday Camp. Mom and Dad would impress everyone with their ballroom dancing – he was king of the slow foxtrot was Dad – and I'd win the children's talent competition and be invited to take part in the adult concert on the Thursday evening. I had become a celebrity. The entertainment staff in their green blazers were my idols but I could never hope to be one of them – or could I? Returning home from holiday was traumatic, normal life was so dull by comparison and the return to school uninviting.

Things were starting to get serious at school, the eleven-plus exams loomed and Dad became more and more agitated. He'd had very little schooling himself and he believed education to be the most important thing in life. We were in the days of selective education. As ten-year-olds we would take an exam to determine our lives. The top twelve per cent academically would be elevated into the grammar school system whilst the unsuccessful were consigned to the dustbin of secondary modern education. A full year before I was to take the exam, my class was given an intelligence test, quite out of the blue, with no warning. I still do not know the results of that test but I know it changed the school's perception of me. Mom and Dad were asked to go to the school to see Mrs Phillips, my class teacher, and Miss Seal, the headmistress. They returned wreathed in smiles and began talking about 'when you get to St Philip's'. Two or three times a week, I'd be told to report to Miss Seal's office where we'd talk about literature and she'd hand me a book to read, Dickens, Mark Twain, Rider Haggard. Life had suddenly become easier.

I still attended St John's Convent each Saturday morning. I was the first child from there to be confirmed. This event was not nearly so inspiring as my first communion. St Chad's Cathedral was packed. It was the largest church I'd ever been in and I lined up with seemingly hundreds of other children, none of whom I knew. There was something very impersonal about the way I shuffled towards the altar where sat the Archbishop on a throne. I knelt on a cushion, my name and confirmation name, Franciscus, were proclaimed, a man placed his hand on my shoulder to indicate that he was my sponsor, but he was every other boy's sponsor too, and the Arch placed a gritty cross on my forehead with his thumb. I felt none of the elation I'd expected to feel upon becoming 'a soldier of Christ', I didn't feel special as I'd done when I made my first communion, in fact it was a real let down. I explained all to Sister Annuncia and Miss King the following Saturday. We regularly had discussion time when I aired my views.

'Faith, hope and love, and the greatest of these is love,' said Sr Annuncia.

'No,' I argued, 'the greatest is faith because without faith there is no God to love and without God there is no hope.' She indulged me. I never saw anything but real affection in her eyes, as when I told her that I could no longer offer up an act of humility after receiving Holy Communion.

'Why ever not?' she asked.

'I intend to offer up an act of pride. How can anyone feel humility when the supreme being of the universe has come to take possession of their soul? An act of pride is far more fitting.'

Sr Annuncia merely told me that 'Pride is one of the seven deadly sins,' and went off to ponder my ramblings.

I was also fascinated by evolution at that time and how this related to Adam and Eve. I was a difficult ten-year-old with an inquisitiveness that far exceeded my comprehension.

The eleven-plus examination took place over two days at whichever school your parents had selected as your first choice, in my case St Philip's Grammar School. The school was everything I expected a grammar school to be – cloisters, quadrangles, classrooms with individual desks. We were supervised by learned men in black, flowing gowns. Having taken the exam, I more or less forgot about it but Mom and Dad were rushing to the front door every time a letter arrived. Eventually the brown envelope came informing me that I'd passed and been given a place at my first choice school. We were in ecstasy. I dashed off to Clifton Road expecting to hear that several others in my class had also passed. No one else had in fact received notification; it was to be another nail-biting week before the others started trickling through. Mom and Dad were called to Clifton Road to see Miss Seal. As I'd done so well in my eleven-plus, the school had been asked to send me to sit the entrance exam for King Edward's High School in Edgbaston. Mom would have none of it, God had answered all her prayers and got her son into a Roman Catholic school, she wouldn't even consider KEHS as an alternative to SPGS.

SPGS was a culture shock. For a start, I was no longer the cleverest kid in the class – far from it – and secondly, having come from an area where everyone's dad worked in a factory, I was now mixing with the sons of professional men. I immediately palled up with a lad named Pat Barr whose parents were both teachers, his father being a headmaster. He lived quite close to me and we were virtually inseparable for the next five years.

* * *

The Christmas after I started at St Philip's there was a family trauma. Nanny was rushed into Selly Oak hospital. On Christmas Day I spent an hour at her bedside with my Uncle George who knelt saying the rosary. The only sound in the tiny side ward was the laboured breathing of the unconscious old lady and the clicking of rosary beads. Nanny died on Boxing Day. The aftermath was pretty awful. I'd never seen adults cry before, they were all at it. Tempers were vented and home truths told. While the grown-ups made funeral arrangements, my cousin Norma and I were surplus to requirements. Being on holiday from school we were given money to disappear and we spent every afternoon at the pictures watching Jerry Lewis, who was my hero.

On the day of the funeral, the cortège left from our house. Mom had insisted on having the coffin in our front room the night before the interment. She kept an all-night vigil, not going to bed at all. Mom and her brothers and sisters were in bits so Dad took charge, organising who was to travel in each car, etc. I remember being impressed and proud of him. That morning, Birmingham experienced a blizzard. We followed the coffin, walking through deep snow to the graveside. The snow squeezed inside my shoes and I tried desperately to keep the front of my Mac together so as not to expose my bare knees.

At the end of my first year at SPGS, I was 5ft 5ins tall and still wearing short trousers, I looked ridiculous. Mom sent a note to Larry Larkin, our much feared headmaster. He told me to stand up against the door in his office; I obviously exceeded the mark and permission for me to wear 'longs' was given. Oh joy! No more red knees, no more chaps at the top of my legs – if you'll pardon the expression. Progress was becoming the order of the day.

Dad bought a brand new car. WG 9440 was superseded by SOM 955. He used at least a tin of chrome cleaner on it each week. The house we lived in was rented from a private landlord. Some sort of legislation dictated that all those of us living in the eighteenth century should be dragged into the twentieth; every home must have a bathroom and an inside toilet. The long back bedroom in our house was divided by a plasterboard wall and a bath, toilet and sink positioned at the far end. Having been presented with these up-to-date facilities, we all wondered how we'd previously lived without them. Going to the outside loo in the dark had always been a terrifying experience for me. I would creep to the door, my footfalls making no sound. My thumb would depress the Suffolk latch and I would smash the door back against the wall to kill whoever was lying in wait for me. Once inside the loo it was necessary to scramble around for the bicycle lamp which would illuminate the interior with orange light. Now I felt safe, I could see the spiders, I knew where they were heading.

A family of spiders also lived in our tin bath which was suspended from a single nail on the wall of our outhouse. Every Friday they would be evicted but by the time we needed the bath again they'd resumed residence – you'd have thought they'd have taken the hint. Every Friday Dad would take the bath from its hanging place and bring it into the back kitchen. Water was boiled in a boiler which had a tap, allowing the bath to be filled from it. Cold water could be added from the sink, though this had to be ladled out by saucepan. I went in first, then Mom, with Dad getting the final go and all that remained of the hot water. There was a dreadful draught from beneath the ill-fitting back door and a bath was a most colourful affair. All down the right side you were red from the boiler, all down the left side you were blue from the draught, and on the backside you were orange from the rust. Once dried and in my pyjamas, Dad would drag the full bath to the back door and pour the water into the yard where it disappeared down two drains. The bath would be returned to its nail and shortly thereafter the spider family would move back in.

There was also progress of a more personal nature. Kids nowadays experience 'adolescence' and they're prepared, ready and waiting. In my day we had 'puberty' and no one would tell you what it was. I hated it, I wouldn't wish it on my worst enemy. Hair growing in the most inconvenient places, vocal cords which jumped the octave without warning and a presence in your trousers which seemed to have a mind in no way connected to yours. Yes, the equipment had arrived but I had no earthly idea of what to do with it; perhaps that was just as well!

School work was intense. The 'Z' stream were expected to take their 'O' levels in four years instead of five, enabling us to spend three years in the sixth form seeking Oxbridge entrance – well that was the theory. My social life was pretty full. Friday night, Pat

Barr and I were training with the school swimming team, followed by water polo with the bigger lads. Saturday morning we were both playing football for the school. Tuesday nights I went to the Co-op Youth Club where they had public-speaking lessons and entered us for competitions. It wasn't difficult, learn a lump of Shakespeare, stand on stage and spout. It did, though, give me my first introduction to the Bard, who after all was a local lad. Then on Thursday nights it was off to the English Martyrs Youth Club for a mean game of table tennis. Occasionally Fr Tolly would pop in for a game. He was the younger son of J. R. R. Tolkein, but we were more interested in pong pings than *Lord of the Rings* on a Thursday.

All this left insufficient time for homework – a bad mistake. Dad refused to have a TV in the house, which meant that radio was the home entertainment. *The Billy Cotton Band Show, Ray's a Laugh, Take it from Here*, all great stuff, but *The Goon Show* was the greatest thing I'd ever heard. Years later I had to make a short speech at a luncheon at which Sir Harry Secombe was guest of honour. In referring to him I said, 'Of course he'll always be Neddy Seagoon to me,' at which the great man leapt to his feet, put an arm round my shoulder and exclaimed, 'Ying tong iddle I po, folks!' – such wisdom from one so wise. I shared a stage with him on more than one occasion, and it was wonderful to feel the waves of love that came from the audience and headed in his direction. I suppose every generation has its 'cult', *The Goon Show* was ours; it shaped our sense of humour and put an entire generation on the same wavelength.

Humour was relevant in the classroom. Several of our esteemed masters used funny lines to get our attention, most notably Creamy Kiernan, a short, fat man who fostered in me a profound fascination for history. As he walked through the classroom door, he would announce the day's lesson with such phrases as 'Today we're going to talk about Elizabeth I, the Virgin Queen. Mind you, she was no virgin!' Immediately he had the undivided attention of twenty-eight fourteen-year-olds. 'Charles II invented birth control because he was distressed by the birth of too many illegitimate children to his mistresses' – we hung on his every word. Another classroom genius was Sarky Sutherland. That man gave me a love of the English language, of words and of the physical act of handwriting: 'If you write a beautiful hand, you will be judged to be a man of intellect.' I remember that and everything else Sarky ever said. Without his teaching it's unlikely that I'd be writing this book now.

The most charismatic teacher we had was James Patrick Augustus Mullholland, known throughout the school as the Masher. He was another short, fat man, far from pretty and God had never intended him to be an athlete, but when it came to football he was a tactical genius. He coached the Colts, the under-fifteens, the most competitive age group. Alf Ramsey was knighted in 1966 for using a 4–3–3 formation and winning the World Cup. The Masher had us playing 4–3–3 in 1958. With every team we met still playing the standard 2–3–5, we cut them to ribbons. The Masher turned me into a left winger, and his vision paid off. I really should have continued to play football after I left school but other pursuits claimed my interest. A few years ago, Pat Barr and I decided to see if we could get the old team together. The reunion takes place on the first Sunday of August each year. Last year there were fourteen out of the seventeen players who played for the Masher's Colts in 1958.

It was the Masher who cast me as Macduff in the Scottish Play. We were helped out in our yearly Shakespeare production by the girls from St Paul's, our sister school. This was the one chance we had to get near to our fantasy provokers or 'the virgins from Vernon Road' as they were known. It was seemingly impossible to get to know them otherwise. There was a rumour going around that their headmistress, Sr Veronica, had told her girls that if they swam backstroke in a lane where a boy had just done the butterfly, they were liable to get pregnant – no wonder they wouldn't have anything to do with any of us. Despite all the efforts of their teachers and ours to keep us apart we did manage to intermingle and it's amazing how many Philipians married Paulites over the years.

The Christmas before my sixteenth birthday, I met and was smitten by Paddy Jones. She was from St Paul's. She had short, dark hair and eyes the colour of polished mahogany. We were hopelessly unsuited. She was introverted and shy, I was outgoing and loud and I embarrassed her terribly. It was a wonderfully innocent relationship; we held hands and gazed at one another and when we were alone we'd kiss and kiss till lips became so raw that you couldn't stand vinegar on your chips for a week, but nothing more. I saw her again briefly a few years ago and I have to admit that the attraction was still there though, within a very short time, she'd reminded me three times of what a callow youth I'd been and I realised that, had we married, we'd probably have murdered one another.

At that age, I lived my life as though I was taking part in a film – I was performing and watching myself at the same time. Everything I did, I did for effect – sad really! Four years of Latin at school had given me what I considered to be perfect pronunciation. I'd respond at mass and sing loudly knowing that the people around me, filled with admiration, were saying, 'Listen to that, he must be a Roman,' when in actual fact they were saying, 'What is wrong with that boy?'

St Philip's was next to the Birmingham Oratory, the most beautiful of churches; if you can't feel holy in there you might as well give up. Once through its door you're in Rome. We attended mass *en masse* several times during the school year but I often popped in during my lunch break to commune with the Lord. Every old boy of the school retains a fondness for the Oratory, even those who no longer practise their faith. I knew every inch of the church but was always drawn back to the Holy Souls' altar where stood a life-size crucifix of Christ in Torment. It isn't your usual comfortable crucifix, this depicts agony. The muscles in the arms are stretched taut, pulling on the nails which secure the hands, blood runs from the nails and along the forearms, the eyes stare upwards to where the crown of thorns bites into the scalp. As an impressionable youth, I looked at this and I could hear the ripping of flesh and the crunching of bone. More than anything else it brought home to me how much my Saviour had suffered for me. Not that I needed any boost to my faith in those days, it was rock solid. Would it remain like that for life?

At the age of fourteen going on fifteen, a bloke needs money. Half-a-crown a week pocket money didn't go very far. I could save my bus fare if I cycled to school, which brought my income up to five bob, but there were youth clubs to frequent plus the Sunday night dance at the English Martyrs where, once the music started, you could legally press yourself up against young ladies. Together with Garth Aspinall, another lad from my form, I set off for central Birmingham determined not to return without employment. We left our names or filled out forms at all the large shops and had almost given up hope when we stumbled into a large Army and Navy type store. Yes, they would employ us and pay us the princely sum of one pound for a day's work. We were to report at 8.45 the following Saturday.

I worked there every Saturday from then until I left school. Garth was at the front of the shop selling overalls, socks and lumberjack shirts, I was at the back becoming an expert on rucksacks, sleeping bags, tents and all sorts of camping equipment including, much to Dad's delight, primus stoves. The store had it all: a storeman who knew where everything was but wouldn't tell anybody, a battleaxe of a cashier, an attractive thirty-something saleslady who three or four times a day slipped into the manager's office and emerged some time later somewhat dishevelled, and a Head of Sales who hated shop assistants in general and Saturday boys in particular. He'd made sneering an art form. He had a permanent smell under his nose, spoke in a flat dismissive tone and walked with a lisp. I've realised since that he was a homosexual but I was in my twenties before I knew such people existed – 'Puff' was just a magic dragon when I was a teenager. I worked on a counter with Gordon, a twenty-three-year-old slave to fashion. He was immaculate in his stiff collars, slim ties, Italian suits and winkle-pickers. He was quite short but every Saturday there'd be a stream of pretty girls popping into the shop to arrange an assignation with him. I really wanted to be like Gordon. I reasoned that I couldn't grow the slim moustache and small beard while I was still attending school but I bought the Brylcreem dispenser and turned my hair into patent leather and once I'd saved up eight pounds, I dashed next door to Hepworths to buy the suit.

Sport had always been a very important part of my school life. I was in the school swimming team and the football teams but athletics was my main sport. My mother had always moved at top speed and I did the same. When I was small I had to run to keep up with her and, as a lad, I literally ran everywhere. By the time I was in the second year at St Philip's, the teachers realised that I could run faster than anyone else of my age. At the school athletic sports each year, I won the 100, 220 and 880 yards.

During my final year at school, others too had noticed. The AAA had appointed a paid coach, unheard of in an amateur sport. His name was Lionel Pugh, he selected athletes with potential and took them off for weekends to various universities where they were put through their paces by current internationals. I was invited to a couple of these, sprinting with Peter Radford and middle-distance with Mike Rawson. I was also approached by Halesowen Athletic Club. They had an excellent middle-distance coach, Taffy Hier, but a trip to training from Sparkbrook would have involved three buses and taken two hours. The club, though, were so keen that one of the committee called for me twice a week and transported me to training. I don't think I ever showed any gratitude for this selfless act but I certainly rewarded the club by improving dramatically over 880 yards under the tutelage of Taffy Hier.

3

Earning a Crust

SPGS was a fine school but careers advice was nil. I had no idea what I wanted to do for a living. Performing was my great love, but surely no one would pay me to do that! I don't know why I decided to leave school at sixteen rather than carry on into the sixth form, as most of my mates were doing, but I have a couple of theories. Mom was not at all well. She had a gynaecological problem which needed immediate attention. I was in a state, fearing the worst. What would Dad and I do if my fears materialised? She went into Birmingham Women's Hospital and I went to mass and communion every morning. I concentrated on the Bible story of the woman troubled with an issue of blood who knew that she only had to touch the hem of Jesus' garment to be cured: 'Show me what to touch, Lord, so my Mom will be cured,' I prayed. Whether by divine help or not, the problem turned out to be ovarian cysts, not nearly so serious as suspected. After a period of hospitalisation and some discomfort, Mom was as right as rain and I gave considerable thanks to the Lord.

The other factor in my leaving school was Paddy Jones. She left St Paul's and started work immediately in the Civil Service. One week she was a schoolgirl in flat shoes and a straw boater, the next she was a woman in stilettos and she'd dyed her hair. Oh horror! She would certainly be lost to me if I remained a schoolboy with a pound a week pocket money. The double uncertainty over the two women in my life led me to bid farewell to St Philip's.

Full employment was the norm in 1959/60. There were jobs a-plenty and anyone with five 'O' levels could have their pick of the employment market. I had seven 'O' levels plus a life-saving certificate, I'd soon be snapped up – and so it proved. The Civil Service was the place to be – good pay and promotion prospects I was told. I decided to try my hand as a customs officer, it sounded exciting. Within a week, I'd been interviewed and accepted, not for Customs and Excise, whose applicants had to be eighteen, but for the Inland Revenue with a promise that, if I wanted to join Customs and Excise in two years' time, my chances would be enhanced by having worked in 'Taxes'.

I started at Birmingham XI tax district in Severn House, a building which housed four such tax districts. My starting salary worked out at just over £5 per week. I wasn't the only one starting work that day, to my surprise; the other new boy was Tony Donaldson who had been in my house at St Phil's. We'd been in the school athletics team together, Tony being a devastating hundred yards man. Two years my senior, he'd got his 'A' levels and opted for a career in Taxes. A wise choice for him as he ended up as a District Inspector.

Work was a tremendous shock for me. For a start, having been at a single-sex school, I now encountered women at close quarters. Well outnumbering the men, for the simple reason that the Civil Service was the first employer to bring in equal pay, they were aliens from another galaxy. One day they would be pleasant, the next they'd cut you dead. They cried in packs, joining in simply because another woman was crying, and they went shopping for pleasure, something I still fail to understand. Most were my mother's age but they had little in common with her, especially in their treatment of me. Everyone in the office spoke in initials. I was a TO (Tax Officer), not the lowest of the low – that right was claimed by the CA (Clerical Assistant). We aspired to become a TOHG (Tax Officer Higher Grade) and from there a TI (Technical Inspector) and eventually a DI (District Inspector). Every form had a letter and a number – P45, P50, P207 – and the senior people were referred to by their initials too.

Several factors saved me from early insanity. To begin with there were about half a dozen youngsters of my own age in the office. We were thrown together by the common struggle to maintain our youth and not become middle-aged in an attempt to fit in. We spent time together outside work, dancing and partying. We didn't frequent pubs; coffee bars were the thing those days, El

Toro, El Sombrero, establishments where the young met and drank frothy coffee from a glass cup. Drank is perhaps too expansive a word; you inhaled the froth then sipped the half-inch of dark liquid which remained. There was yet another coffee bar called La Bohème but all its customers wore duffel coats and sandals and called one another 'man' – not really our scene.

Each tax district had a table tennis team and I became a mean player, spending most lunch hours practising my control over the pimpled rubber, an art no doubt passed down through the genes from Dad. I was also introduced to rugby football, a game that gives me intense pleasure even today. I played for Birmingham Civil Service and wish I'd come to the game at a younger age when I could have excelled at it. As it was, I was a rather mediocre centre-threequarter. Until the age of eighteen, Civil Service employees were entitled to one day a week day release. This was spent at Bournville College, within smelling distance of Cadbury's, and was most enjoyable. It also gave me the chance to spend the whole day with Paddy who was also 'day released' but our relationship was waning rapidly despite, or maybe because of, all my efforts.

After a certain amount of training at the Inland Revenue Training Centre and, more effectively, by being attached to an experienced TO in the office, I was given an 'allocation'. This meant that I was in charge of the PAYE affairs of all the employees of a certain company. That company was Midland Motor Cylinder, a foundry in Smethwick. Ninety per cent of the firm's workforce was from the sub-continent of India, and the majority of these were Sikhs, tall impressive-looking men with large beards and coloured turbans. All Sikhs have the same surname, Singh, which wouldn't have been a problem had not the person who'd managed the allocation prior to me filed them in alphabetical order. It was a nightmare. An enquiry would come in by phone, letter or in person, and whether or not I got the right Singh was a matter of chance. I spoke to the senior wages clerk at MMC who told me that every employee was given an 'R' number. We formulated a plan. Every piece of paper relating to an employee would bear the 'R' number, which must also be quoted when turning up at the office. She further agreed not to re-issue the 'R' number of an employee who had left to a newly recruited employee – now I had a chance. It took me a while but I organised all my files into numerical order. Where Pritam Singh had been impossible to find alphabetically, R773, P. Singh could now be found instantly.

My mentor in Taxes was an old soldier, Jack Horwood. One of the most amusing men I ever met, he'd served throughout World War Two as an infantryman with the Worcestershire Regiment. Having finished his twenty-two years, he'd become the county's most disillusioned civil servant. He was a rebel and encouraged me to follow his lead. We both objected to the demands for money which accompanied our pay cheques at the end of each month. It was always somebody's birthday, then there'd be flowers for someone you'd never heard of who'd left years ago and had either given birth or popped their clogs, then there was money for the tea or coffee we consumed at 3.15 every afternoon, and then the contribution to the Inland Revenue Staff Association. It was endless. Jack and I decided to opt out of all of these, a move that made us extremely unpopular. It was my first experience of standing up for something and taking the consequences. It was good for me!

I realised after less than twelve months that Taxes was not for me. The general public think that civil servants spend all day drinking tea but the opposite is true. Many of us stayed after hours just to cope with the excessive work. I believe it's even worse these days. I survived the place because of Jack's irreverent attitude to life and because, away from the office, my time was occupied achieving minor greatness as an athlete. I was running in bigger and bigger meetings and winning most of the time. Tony Donaldson and I were selected to compete in the Civil Service Championships in London. We were given two days' leave and I returned with a large trophy having won the Junior 880 yards in 1 minute 58 seconds. I was regularly breaking the two-minute barrier in training and at meetings, but suddenly I started experiencing severe discomfort in my chest; it was as if someone was sitting on my ribcage. Often the pain would stop me dead, I'd be unable to breathe in or out for several seconds. It frightened me but nowhere near as much as it frightened Mom. She whisked me off to an alarmist doctor who had no idea what my problem was but told Mom it was exercise-induced and continuing with my athletic ambitions could be fatal.

That was it, all hope of an Olympic gold disappeared. I was devastated. Running was the most important thing in my life. Dad, not the most articulate of men, bless him, sat me down and carefully explained that if anything happened to me, their only child, both his and Mom's lives would be over, a sobering thought and one I never truly understood until I had children of my own. Dad said that he knew how important running was and how much it meant to me, but medical advice said it was dangerous and we must listen to that advice. We both shed a tear and there and then he drove me over to Halesowen to explain the situation to my coach, Taffy, who'd seen me pull up with chest pain on several occasions.

I never ran competitively again. For years afterwards the smell of new-mown grass or a crunching sound like spikes biting into a track would immediately transport me back and I'd be sprinting round the bottom bend and into the home straight with other runners coming back towards me. That's how it always felt to me – not that I was overtaking them but that they were coming back to me, until there was no one between me and the finishing line.

Now that my main diversionary activity was gone, I realised how unhappy I was with my work. Paddy Jones had outstripped me in the maturity stakes and decided to go her separate way. I'm not sure how upset I was about that but I quite enjoyed playing heartbroken. Having convinced myself that there was nothing to keep me in Birmingham and encouraged by Jack Horwood, I wrote to Warners Holiday Camps with an exaggerated list of my sporting abilities and achievements (the life-saving certificate was far more use than the 'O' levels) and within a few days, I'd been offered the job of Sports Organiser with the entertainment staff at Northney Camp on Hayling Island, Hampshire. Mom rehearsed several new songs with me to bring my repertoire up to date and I perfected my impressions act, adding an amazingly accurate Kathleen Ferrier (honest) to the already perfected Chick Murray, Ted Loon, Terry Scott and Jerry Lewis. Kathleen Ferrier, by the way, just in case you don't know, was an operatic contralto. Sadly she had died young but the few recordings she had made were often requested on radio and her voice was known to everyone. I suppose she was the Eva Cassidy of her day. I'd been working the local working men's clubs at weekends – sometimes I'd be paid, sometimes not, but the experience proved invaluable. I was more than prepared for the happy campers.

Having handed in my notice, one of the last things was an interview with the District Inspector. The only thing I remember of it was his saying, 'During your time at Birmingham XI you've never really conducted yourself in a true Civil Service like manner.' I took that as a compliment. I was surprised at how sorry I was to be leaving certain people in the office, particularly Jack. My leaving actually stirred him into action and shortly afterwards he and his wife, Alice, sold up and bought a post office in Helston, Cornwall, in the fresh air he longed for.

Mom and Dad delivered me to Northney in early May, a full week before the season was due to start. The camp was Warner's smallest, able to accommodate about five hundred campers. The place was a hive of activity with much to be done in the next seven days. The entertainment staff consisted of Nigel, the children's entertainer, two girls who were really nannies for the younger children, Reg, a wily old cove who'd worked for the company for years as a pianist, and me. But pretty soon Michael would be arriving. Michael was the entertainer. He'd been at Northney for the past two seasons and apart from entertaining he'd be in charge of Reg, Nigel and me, giving us our duties and keeping us in check. We spent our days checking the sporting equipment, erecting goal posts, filling the swimming pool (not personally) and getting the pianos tuned. During the evenings we had the option of painting chalet doors and window frames, which passed the time and earned us a few shillings.

The General Manager was a man named Mac Sced. He lived in a rather nice house adjoining the camp with his wife, Beryl, and four children. By Wednesday there was still no sign of Michael but on Thursday a telegram arrived informing Mac Sced that Michael had got a job singing with a band on the Isle of Wight and would not be coming. Mac lined the three of us up and said, 'We have no Entertainer, we open on Saturday. One of you will have to do it.'

'I'll do it,' I responded before the words had left his mouth.

'Come with me,' said Mac and I followed him back to his house. He'd started out with Warner's as an entertainments manager before being elevated to greater things. For the next two days he explained the entertainment programme and how to implement it. He taught me how to lead a sing-song, these were very popular at the time, and how to organise a ramble. My own holidays at various Warner camps stood me in good stead, when the campers arrived on Saturday I would be ready. I wasn't worried in the slightest, this was a chance I was determined to take. My promotion to entertainer left a vacancy for a sports organiser but by Saturday that had been filled. Portsmouth FC had a young centre-forward named Ron Saunders – yes, the same man who went on to manage Norwich, Manchester City, Birmingham and Aston Villa. He was available until the football season started in September – the entertainments team was complete.

A holiday camp was an amazing training ground. Showbiz is full of people, particularly comedians, who started life in Butlins, Pontins or Warner's as red, blue or green coats. In the 1960s there were very few professional entertainers on the holiday camp scene, they felt it was beneath them. This was great news for the red, blue or green coats, who were left to create the entertainment themselves. In my case, this took the form of some kind of show, competition or game show for an hour each night while the resident dance band took their break. On Thursday evening the Campers' Concert took place. There were any number of shaky sopranos and fractured tenors. Reg was the hard-working accompanist and the rest of the entertainment staff were well to the fore. I'd be involved in little comedy sketches, maybe sing a current pop song and finish the show with my comedy impressions act. I couldn't go wrong, it was like being everyone's favourite nephew. Although it lulled me into thinking that I was considerably better than I was, it also boosted my confidence tremendously. You often hear people say, 'It does a comic good to die.' Nonsense! It does a comic good to go well.

The campers had to like us really, there was little else on offer, they were trapped. In 1961 few people came on holiday by car, they arrived by train or coach. Once in the camp, there they stayed unless they took one of the trips to Portsmouth or ventured forth on one of our two rambles. There was plenty to occupy them; we organised athletics sports, swimming galas, football, rounders and cricket matches between the two houses, Cads and College. There were all the competitions: Knobbly Knees, Glamorous Granny, Young Tarzan, the Beauty Queen, which always pulled big crowds. Then there were the more bizarre ideas like Ladies v. Gents Rugby and Breakfast in the Pool. I worked for six and a half days per week from breakfast at nine till 'Goodnight Campers' at midnight. The half day was Sunday morning when I walked to church for eleven o'clock mass. By the end of the season I was thoroughly worn out but I probably learned more in those eighteen weeks than at any time of my life.

I was now convinced I was God's gift to the entertainment industry. The campers had loved me, it was time to give the unsuspecting British public the benefit of my comedy talent. How was this to be achieved? I had a couple of leads.

The Windmill Theatre was still going strong just off Piccadilly Circus in London. I'd written for an audition and one had been granted. Mom and Dad were pleased to have me home but I was confident it wouldn't be for long, I was about to take the professional stage by storm. I travelled up to London, arriving at the Windmill at noon to be greeted by a bored pianist with terminal dandruff. I handed him my 'dots' – 'Hello Dolly', 'What is life to me without thee' and 'Never smile at a crocodile'; he gave them a cursory glance.. There were two others auditioning. One was a magician and the other a comedian in an extremely large jacket. He practised shrugging it off his shoulders then dragging it back again. He then disappeared into it and re-emerged like a tortoise from a shell. Rather funny, I thought, but not my type, I was more your smart, fast-talking Jack-the-lad.

The magician went first. After about five minutes he returned. A woman with a clip-board said, 'Next!' and I heard the pianist launch into my music as I clambered up the steps from beneath the stage. I'd told him to play 'Dolly' very fast and by the time my feet touched the boards, he was halfway through. I recovered rather well I thought and launched into my Chick Murray: 'I was mowing my lawn – in my garden 'cos that's where I keep my lawn – when the man next door put his head over the fence which I thought was rather a macabre thing to do.' On then to Ted Lune: 'I wont take me coat off, I'm not stopping.' No laughs but the theatre was empty except for one person. Now for the Kathleen Ferrier – this'll get 'em, never fails. It was superb. As I hit the last note you could hear angels sigh.

'Yes, thank you,' said the man who was sprawled in the stalls, his legs over the seat in front so I could only see him from the eyebrows up. I smiled in his direction and carried on with my Terry Scott: 'We've got a new baby and my Dad knows nothing about it. I hope I'm not in when he gets home cos I gets blamed for everyfink in our house.'

'Yes, thank you very much,' said the man in a raised voice.

'No, I've not finished yet,' I responded. 'I sing again in a minute, that's when I've finished.'

'Will you leave the stage,' said the man. The pianist was holding my three pieces of music at arm's length. I took them and slunk off.

Now you're thinking, 'That must have been devastating, what a blow for the lad,' but no, I was resilient in those days. By the time I reached home, I'd convinced myself that my auditioner would live a lifetime of regret having missed me in my early days. I did, though, have to find employment, something temporary while I pondered my next move. I went to see Albert Weedall, the headmaster of the Day Continuation College in Bournville.

'I always thought you'd make a marvellous teacher,' said Albert.

'Why not,' I thought. 'That'll do nicely.' In those enlightened days, once one had applied for teachers' training college, it was possible to teach for an indefinite period whilst waiting to begin training. Primary schools, in particular, were full of ladies who were teaching extremely well without the benefit of accreditation. All that was to change within two years when the Ministry of Education declared an amnesty on all such unqualified teachers and packed them off to college to get a piece of paper. All that was required of me, though, was proof of my seven 'O' levels, attendance at a lax medical – 'Breathe in, breathe out, say "aahh", cough' – and I was given employment at Pitmaston Boys' School, Hall Green.

* * *

It took me just under a week to realise that I'd never make a teacher. I have absolutely no patience. I'll tell you something once but if you need to hear it again – tough! I taught English to 1A and 2A, Biology to the whole school and Maths to 3C. Every member of 3C had long since given up any desire for an education. My brief was to teach them vulgar fractions, 'vulgar' being never more apt. At the back of the class sat Fitzhenry, the most repulsive thirteen-year-old ever to draw breath. I was constantly pushing him back into his seat – you could do that in those days; nowadays I'd be in court for assault. Whenever I restrained or even spoke to Fitzhenry, his response was, 'I'll get me Dad.' At the mention of Fitzhenry senior, the entire class took a sharp intake of breath.

One morning, having endured his disruption for the first twenty minutes of a forty-minute period and having used both encouragement and threats, I resorted to the last resort. Taking him by the arm I propelled him to the door.

'Go to the headmaster's office,' I said.

'I'll get me Dad,' retorted Fitzhenry.

From the whole class came an audible 'Oooh!'

Things became quiet, and I was able to get on with teaching. It never occurred to me that Fitzhenry had gone anywhere other than to the Head's study. Suddenly the classroom door opened and a figure stooped to enter. He was huge and very red in the face. In truth it wasn't really a face, more a neck with eyes in. I don't think I dropped the textbook I was holding but I might have done. He spoke just one sentence in a surprisingly quiet Irish voice: 'You've been victimising me boy – don't.'

'I won't,' I assured him. He pulled Fitzhenry through the door, cuffed him loudly round the back of the head (the only bit of enjoyment I had all day) and exited the way he'd come. I'd like to tell you that things improved after that but I promised myself I'd be truthful with my readers.

Teaching was certainly not my vocation but an escape route beckoned. I'd written to the Robert Leyton Agency in Long Acre, Covent Garden. I received a letter inviting me to his office for an audition. If he considered me sufficiently able, he'd take me on as a client. I arranged a day off from Pitmaston and travelled to London.

A prim secretary sat in the small office and was clearly nonplussed by my arrival. Mr Leyton was ill, she'd cancelled all his appointments, except the one with me obviously, but she was resourceful. If I'd come for an audition, an audition I would have. We'd walk together to the Max Rivers rehearsal rooms in Little Newport Street. Pantomime auditions were being conducted there by Jerry Jerome. If he liked me, the secretary was sure that would be sufficient recommendation for Mr Leyton to take me on.

Jerry Jerome, flanked by his wife, Roberta Pett, and his principal comic, Marty Swift, sat at the far end of the room. I fidgeted while the four held a whispered conversation.

'OK, son, let's see what you can do,' said Jerry.

I launched into the act. It was very different from the Windmill – they laughed. Encouraged by the laughter, I worked extremely well. They even laughed at the Kathleen Ferrier, but I could live with that. I was allowed to complete the whole act and at the end of the Jerry Lewis number, the three of them stood up and applauded me.

'Tell you what son,' said Jerry Jerome, 'I'll write a part for you in pantomime with me this Christmas. Robinson Crusoe we're doing at Southend.'

I'd done it again, landed on my feet. I went back to the office, where the secretary asked me to sign a contract to appear in panto at the Palace Theatre, Westcliff at a salary of £10 per week less 10 per cent to the agency. I was about to become a star.

4

God's Gift to Showbiz?

I wasn't very good in the panto, even I had to admit that. I learned a tremendous amount about showbiz, though, the most important thing being that I wanted to be in it for life. But there was no one guiding me, showing me the ropes, which would have been very helpful. The day before the panto was due to finish, Jerry Jerome called me into his dressing room. He was a short, fat, jolly man, it was difficult for him to look stern but he sat me down and said, 'Listen, son, you're a nice lad but you're never gonna make it in this business. Comedy takes years and you're in far too much of a hurry. I know you were training to be a teacher, that's a worthwhile profession. Take my advice, go home and become a teacher.'

Such wise words from a respected professional would have been heeded by someone with less self-belief. In later years I encountered Jerry several times. He was always embarrassed about the advice he'd given me but I certainly didn't bear him a grudge, he'd merely tried to save a stage-struck kid from a life of disappointment. What I knew, and Jerry didn't at the time, was that I'd written off for a job I'd seen advertised in *The Stage* newspaper. My climb to fame would continue.

After a full week at home I was off again to continue my assault on the elusive peak of stardom. The Jesters had been a music and comedy quartet until two of their number defected. They were reforming. I'd replied to their advert and been accepted to join them. Rehearsals were at the Max Rivers studios.

I contacted a couple, Jim and Nell Warman, who'd been extremely lively campers at Northney and who'd foolishly said, 'If ever you get a job in London you can come and stay with us.'

They were real salt-of-the-earth cockneys who interspersed their conversation with a strange word 'bleetin', as in 'What's the bleetin time?' 'It's 'arf parst bleetin seven!' With their two daughters, they lived in a block of flats on the Newberry Down estate at Manor House. I was set up – I had a London address from which I could audition and rehearse.

Early rehearsals were OK, the two original members of the Jesters putting me and the other new boy through a series of movements, teaching us their repertoire of songs, getting us measured for suits, etc. We had a year's work booked on the US bases in Germany, according to our leader. The original Jesters were somewhat disappointed with me and the other recruit due to our lack of instrumental prowess. I had a guitar and could play three chords E, A and B7, norra lorra use really. My compatriot played the trumpet, or so he said, but either he'd pawned it or lost it because it never turned up at rehearsals. The other two played piano and double bass exceptionally well but didn't seem to be able to see eye to eye about anything.

Having been told that they couldn't pay me for rehearsals but they'd make it up to me once we arrived in the Rhineland, I took a job as an office cleaner, I needed money to pay my digs. Straight from rehearsals I'd hop on a tube to Moorgate, report to a sour-faced woman who'd assign me a vacuum, a tin of Brasso and a soft cloth and set me to work. After three hours, I'd return via the Piccadilly Line to Manor House. Nell Warman was one of the kindest people I'd ever known. She had the Blitz mentality in which everyone looked out for everyone else; she spent her life helping the young, the old, the infirm, I'm not sure which category she put me into. She'd share everything she had with you especially her wisdom and she was very wise.

After five weeks of intensive, unpaid rehearsals and badly paid office cleaning, things exploded. Yet another argument between pianist and bass player ended in fisticuffs. The bass player stormed out leaving the pianist with a rapidly closing eye. It transpired that the original Jesters had broken up because of this personality clash. 'There's no way we're going to get the act together in time to meet the US bases contract,' he said. 'Sorry, fellers, the party's over.'

Devastated is the word you seek. I'd flogged myself to death for five weeks with no financial reward, and for what? I arrived early at the Moorgate office block, the sour-faced supervisor asked me why and I blurted out my story before collecting vacuum, Brasso and soft cloth. As I prepared to leave that night, the sour supervisor was waiting. She slipped thirty bob into my hand and said, 'Go home to your mom, son.' I was on a coach the next morning. What an incredibly kind gesture and, do you know, I never even knew that woman's name. Do you reckon she was an angel in disguise?

Back home, with Dad to dote on me and Mom to spoil me, I had time to take stock. I wanted to be on stage, that was a certainty, but in what capacity – as a stand-up comic, a pop singer, a dramatic actor? I needed time to think and to further my craft. Drama school, that was the answer. Mom and Dad weren't keen on my leaving home again, they made that very clear, and having lived in London for a short while I'd got the capital out of my system and had no desire to return even if I could have got into RADA. Birmingham Theatre School was the obvious answer. I wrote for the prospectus.

Signing on the dole would be an embarrassing experience, I thought, but it had to be done.

'Previous employment,' it said on the form.

'Inland Revenue,' said I. Former civil servants have little chance of claiming benefit, they're far to valuable to the system.

'Come inside and work for us,' said the Department of Employment. I'd been bored stiff by Taxes but this was instant rigor mortis. After a very short period of training I was sent to Handsworth Labour Exchange.

'We'll start you on enquiries,' said the senior supervisor, opening a locked door and pointing me to a table on which stood a notice proclaiming 'All enquiries here'.

'But I won't know the answer to any enquiry,' I protested. He produced a list.

'Here are the reasons for which people come to a Labour Exchange,' he explained. 'Each reason has a number, and that number corresponds to a number on the counter there', he indicated the counter. 'Just direct them to the correct number.'

I took stock of the counter for the first time and was perturbed to note that there was a stout wire mesh from counter to ceiling, no doubt to protect the staff from attack but – hang on – I was *this* side of the counter, shortly to be sharing my large open space with the potential attackers and I was completely unprotected.

The supervisor blew a whistle, fearful faces appeared to take up station behind the mesh. He moved to the large double doors, undid the bolts then bolted himself, through the side door, to appear immediately behind the mesh. A mass of humanity poured in – I knew fear! All day I fielded bits of paper thrust at me, interpreted them where possible and directed the person to an area of the counter. The tedium was relieved mid-afternoon. The majority of clients at the Handsworth Exchange were West Indians. A well-dressed black man came in with a most attractive black woman on his arm. All heads turned. Suddenly another gentleman of West Indian appearance detached himself from one of the queues and threw himself on his knees in front of the woman. All interest in finding employment or providing employment ceased on both sides of the counter. I can't remember the exact conversation which took place but I do remember the woman's name, Magnolia, which I knew from a paint tin in our outhouse meant 'off white'.

'Why did you leave me for him, Magnolia?' wailed the man, at which her beau placed a hand on his head and pushed. He sprawled full length on the floor but was soon on his feet and laying into his rival. They grappled with each other, fell over and began to roll up and down the length of the concrete floor. I stood on the table to give them more room, those safe behind the wire dialled 999 and Magnolia waited patiently for the winner to claim her as his prize. What a first day!

Life there was never even slightly exciting again. I hated that job, short-lived though it was. I dreaded going every day, and if ever I've felt discontented since, I've thought back to the Labour Exchange and thanked God I've been able to earn a living doing something I love.

I auditioned for Miss Mary Richards, principal of Birmingham Theatre School, and was accepted – little did I realise that she accepted everyone. Next problem was to obtain a grant from Birmingham Education Department. The people who auditioned me for that grant were the same people who had adjudicated at the Shakespeare-speaking competitions when I'd been in the Co-op Youth Club.

'O pardon me, thou bleeding piece of earth, that I am meek and gentle with these butchers.' You can't beat Mark Antony for an audition piece, it brings out the ham in the best of us. I'd also learned a bit of Sean O'Casey and a bit of Jean Anouilh. They quizzed me about the plays and the playwrights, and my love of literature, fostered at St Phil's, stood me in good stead. I was given a grant because of my father's low income rather than my acting potential, if truth be told.

It was by now May 1962. Term started in September, not long you're thinking, but I knew I couldn't stick the Labour Exchange for another four months. The call of the holiday camp was strong in my ears. *The Stage* newspaper came to my aid again. Leysdown Holiday Camp on the Isle of Sheppey in Kent were looking for an Assistant Entertainments Manager. I wrote off, again exaggerating my qualifications – I knew I had something in common with Jeffery Archer – and was offered the job, to start as soon as I could get there.

Mom and Dad delivered me to Leysdown. Warners it was not! A privately owned camp, it lacked the finesse I'd been used to. That fact had obviously not passed Mom by either. I learned later that she'd cried all the way home in the car. The entertainments manager at Leysdown saw my energy as a real threat. He'd been having a cushy time there for several years, doing very little; the last thing he wanted was some kid, dashing around organising and entertaining. The campers would be enjoying themselves next and that would never do. He set about making my life hell and he was in a position to do it. I was extremely unhappy for two weeks but the cavalry were approaching rapidly.

'There was a phone call for you,' said the receptionist. 'Ring this number and ask for Mr Jones.'

'Are you the same Don Maclean who worked on entertainment at Northney last year?' I confirmed that I was. 'I'd like you to come and see me. I'm only down the road, I'll send a car for you.'

Only down the road was Minster, Warners newest and biggest holiday camp, accommodating over one thousand campers each week. Ross Jones, a former comedian, had been made manager there. He'd engaged a family from southern Ireland to run all the entertainment and it obviously wasn't working. 'I need an entertainer, someone who knows holiday camps, and according to the people at Northney, that's you.'

I returned to Leysdown and packed my bags.

The de Gabriels made a living travelling from place to place in Ireland, performing their family show. They comprised Alex, his wife, their two teenage children and an elderly drunk named Paddy who played piano very well unless he was sober. All of them sang, Alex played the violin superbly, his son was a capable guitarist and both his wife and daughter did the riverdance, though it wasn't called that then. Great for Ireland but not for Kent. Also on the staff was Hilary, a very talented singer and dancer of about my age, and a sports organiser, Kit Carson. He was the fourth sports organiser so far this season; none of them could cope with the abuse from Alex. Alex ruled his family completely, using his fists to maintain discipline and thought he could do the same with everyone else. Ross Jones introduced me to him. He took my arrival as a personal insult, an indication that he wasn't delivering, which just about summed it up. I'd read *Wuthering Heights* and Alex de Gabriel struck me as a middle-aged Heathcliff. He had a low forehead and heavy brows; he fixed me with an evil eye.

'Am I still in charge?' he asked Ross, though his eyes never left me for a moment.

'Yes,' said Ross, 'but Don will be taking his instructions from me.'

That week was one of the best weeks of my life. The de Gabriels, with the exception of Alex, were eager to help, Michael, the son, being particularly supportive and Paddy able to play anything on the piano provided we kept his whisky level up. I made sure there was something going on all day and all evening. Towards the end of the night, we'd get everyone on the dance floor for the Hokey Cokey, Bowling the Jack, Paul Jones, Cowboy Farewell. No one sat out, the floor was packed and the atmosphere electric. The campers' concert I produced on Thursday was a triumph. Hilary did a scene from *My Fair Lady*, which was currently the big thing in the West End, and Alex's rendition of 'Danny Boy' on the fiddle brought the roof in. He was beginning to warm to me, I could tell. On Friday night, one of the campers asked the band leader if he could use the microphone. He'd been at Minster for two weeks and stated that this week was the best week's holiday he'd ever had, and it was all down to me. He asked for a round of applause for me. Everyone in the room stood, they began to walk towards me. Suddenly I was lifted shoulder high and carried round the room while they sang 'Freeze a jolly good fellow'. I was ecstatic. Recognition at last! It was probably the worst thing that could have happened.

The arguments and general bad feelings continued for the rest of the season but I coped. The Warner Brothers came to Minster to see me for themselves and told me I could have whatever resources I needed for the entertainment. They said they'd put certain things which I'd devised into the programme at other camps for next year: Breakfast in the Pool, Ladies v Gents rugby, Pasa Doble competition, things like that. My wages were increased without my asking and Ross invited Mom and Dad down for two free holidays. Each Saturday morning, though officially I had no duties, I'd spend waving off the campers as they left by car or coach. One Saturday, my attention was drawn to a beautiful girl who was being quite noisy, laughing a lot as she waited with her parents and sister to board a coach. I began talking to her and her parents. They were Londoners and her mother told me that her daughter had worked in holiday camps. Warners? No, Butlins, she'd been a redcoat. That would explain the young lady's flamboyance but it didn't explain her big brown eyes, her wide mouth and perfect teeth – I do like teeth. I couldn't believe she'd been here a week without my seeing her. She boarded the coach and I felt quite depressed that such a beauty had slipped through my net.

The season at Minster ended well for me. Ross Jones invited Mom and Dad to spend the last weekend at the camp. Once the final week's campers had gone, he put on a wonderful dinner for the staff. Speeches were made and kind words said. Ross asked me to return the following summer. There would be no de Gabriel family, I'd be in charge of all entertainment. It was a tempting offer but I was committed to a drama course and I knew I couldn't just walk away from it next May. I explained all this and Ross agreed to keep a job for me which I could begin as soon as term finished.

Back home, I'd got it made. Mom was spoiling me, Dad gave me the use of his car and Birmingham Theatre School provided me with a demanding work load and a very sociable social life. I'm often asked by young people about the value of a drama school education for those wanting a career in theatre. All I can truthfully say is that you'll learn more in two weeks in a theatre than you will in two years at a drama school; but BTS gave me something I badly needed – time to think. I was also fortunate that my fellow students were dedicated, had acting ability and were, in the main, older than me. I believe I learned more from them than I did from my tutors. We lived and breathed drama, it was our sole topic of conversation, our only interest.

The tutors were a strange lot. They say that those who can do, and those who can't teach – not fair in drama as there are so many really good actors out of work at any given time. The principal, Miss Mary Richards, had been a protégée of Sir Barry Jackson, the man who founded the Birmingham Repertory Theatre. Mary was the oldest person I had ever encountered. Her lack of height was emphasised by the fact that she was rather bent. She wore a fur coat even in summer, was rarely seen without a hat, indoors or out and arrived each day carrying several shopping bags. We all thought that she was living in the 40s – the 1840s. I've always been mightily amused by Hinge and Bracket because Pat Fyffe as Dame Hilda was exactly like Mary Richards. She too called everyone 'Duckie' and me 'Don Duckie', which never failed to evoke laughter and she never worked out why.

We had lessons in speech, movement, dance, singing and fencing. At any given time we were rehearsing three productions which we would then perform to an invited audience. We also had lessons in 'variety' when we were encouraged to develop 'a turn'. An ex-musical and variety performer named Eileen Knight was in charge of this particular discipline, and she took an immediate shine to me. She produced a review each year when great fun was had by all. She also had a lot of influence with Mary and acted as a go-between for pupils and principal.

Most of the students were skint, but when you're all in the same boat, lack of money is pretty painless. We all had our own ways of earning extra cash. These ranged from working the night shift at Bird's Custard Factory to waitressing at a local café or ushering at the Alexandra Theatre. For my part I decided to extend my forays into clubland. I was a performer, I would earn money by performing. Working men's clubs were thick on the ground; they provided a large percentage of the population with their entertainment. They varied greatly. Some boasted dance floors and restaurants; others were real spit-and-sawdust affairs. A local agent, Dave Kenton, held court every Wednesday evening at the Birmingham Anglers' Club, Thorp Street, in the centre of Birmingham. 'Turns', as we were termed, would queue in the corridor outside his office door for hours awaiting the opportunity to prostrate ourselves before him to beg for a gig for the weekend. I'd worked for him occasionally in the past but I was now determined to try to work every weekend. Having queued for ages alongside far more experienced club turns than myself, I eventually got into the office.

Kenton gave me a dismissive look. 'No, I've got no work for male vocalists,' he said.

'I'm not a vocalist,' I said. 'I'm a comic. I've just finished a summer season as principal comic for Warners Holiday Camps.'

His attitude changed; the weasely features attempted a smile. 'Just a minute,' he said, consulting the sheets in front of him. 'Yes, Coseley Working Men's Club, Saturday. Two spots, £2.10s. Be there by seven. You have got two spots, haven't you?'

I didn't even grace the enquiry with a reply. Of course I'd got two spots, I could entertain all night if necessary. I left the office door open for the next 'turn'.

Coseley is not far from Dudley on the New Birmingham Road. I borrowed Dad's car and also Dad's flat cap. Bob Hatch was a local comic I much admired, he'll pop up again in this book later, and on stage he wore a smart suit and a flat cap. I decided that for my as yet untried second spot I'd do the same. I spent two days working out my second spot, but would I be able to remember it all? I had a plan, I'd write out the act in the form of a list and put the list inside Dad's flat cap. If, for any reason, I forgot where I was, I'd merely remove the cap from my head, hold it in front of me and read what came next – well that was the theory!

The Black Country audience weren't totally enamoured with my first spot, although Kathleen Ferrier and Jerry Lewis just about saved it. After innumerable games of bingo it was time for my second spot. Changed into smart suit, guitar over shoulder, flat cap with script secreted on head, I bounced on to the stage. Gags that had worked so well in my wardrobe mirror fell flatter than a filleted flounder. At first the audience just looked at me blankly, then they started talking. Several took off to the bar at the back. After about five minutes the inevitable happened, I panicked and forgot where I was. Plan B came into operation. Off came the cap, I looked at the script but couldn't read a word, the excess of Brylcreem on my hair had turned the paper into a piece of greaseproof, virtually transparent with just a few lines of blue that were barely recognisable as ink. I dropped the cap, picked up the guitar, sang 'Running Bear' and walked off to the sound of my own feet. The Concert Secretary paid me my £2.10s most grudgingly and, as I walked out through the audience, now happily playing bingo once more, he shouted for their benefit, 'I keep telling that Dave Kenton not to send me crap like you.'

That hurt. I got over it fifteen years later when I was starring in pantomime at the Grand Theatre, Wolverhampton and Coseley WMC sent no fewer than seven coach loads to see me. I bet they never realised that I was the same bloke!

Despite the lack of laughs, I continued to get work in the local clubs. I'd borrow Dad's car or climb on my bike – a dinner suit looks good with cycle clips. Mid-week gigs were rare so I was delighted to be offered a Thursday night at the Monte Carlo Club, Handsworth. I was shown into a private room where a stag party was in full swing.

'You the compère?' asked the chap at the door.

'Er, yes,' I replied.

'Dressing room's there, you won't have much to do, just find out how the girls want to be introduced.' I knocked on the door and went in. Two 'ladies' were trowelling on the make-up. I'd never met a stripper before, a Catholic education had in no way prepared me for this meeting.

'I'm the compère. How should I introduce you?' The younger one came out with some prepared spiel which I can't now remember but the other one, who reminded me of something from the Book of Revelation, fluttered her false eyelashes and purred, 'Just say "It's Tanya the Russian Spy".'

'Gentlemen; from St Petersburg, Moscow and Stalingrad, it's Tanya the Russian Spy.' I moved rapidly to one side as she swept on to the floor. The audience were unimpressed by this decaying nymphette but Tanya had been around a long time, she knew how to get their interest. The fur coat fell to the ground and she deftly undid her bra. Once unleashed, her thigh-length breasts pointed instinctively to her thigh-length boots. Taking one bosom in both hands, she proceeded to push it into the face of each member of her audience in turn. My attention was caught by a table of more mature gentlemen; I presumed them to be the dads and uncles of the younger chaps. As I watched, one of them, unseen by Tanya, removed his false teeth and held them out of sight. The Russian spy approached, but as she thrust the malevolent mammary at him, he raised his hand and bit it using the dentures. The audience collapsed in laughter and I must admit it's one of the funniest incidents I've ever witnessed, though I suppose you had to be there. I didn't often work with strippers, I'm pleased to say, but when I did they were all surprisingly nice people. More about disrobing ladies later in this chapter.

Despite several disasters, my appearances in various clubs had been noted by another local agent who was attempting to bring star names into Midlands clubland. Freddie Frinton was in a very successful TV sitcom called *Meet the Wife*, the wife in question being played by Thora Hird. He'd been a star of the variety theatre but that form of entertainment was a thing of the past so he'd been persuaded to do two weeks of one-nighters in the clubs. Naturally there'd be a show built around him, compèred by a young local comic, Don Maclean.

For two weeks I worked the really big clubs where I entertained people who'd come to see a show, not to play bingo, and I went from strength to strength. Freddie Frinton did a drunk act in top hat and tails. He had a broken, unlit cigarette which he never quite managed to get to his lips; it was all extremely funny. For his second spot he came on dressed as a pantomime fairy bemoaning the fact that age had caught up with her. He finished by singing 'Nobody loves a fairy when she's forty', the most memorable line of which was 'Your fairy days are ending when your wand has started bending.'

Also on the bill was a girl singer named Joan Walsh. She had a deep resonant voice and gave powerful renditions of 'Frankie and Johnnie' and 'You can't get a man with a gun'. She and her husband, Seamus – yes they were very Irish – lived in Coventry. Coventry in the sixties was a boom town due to the success of the motor car and motor cycle trades and consequently the club scene there was huge. They took me to two shop window shows; the audience was made up of concert secretaries from all the Coventry clubs. Each act went on and did a short spot in the hope of picking up bookings. Seamus marked my card. 'Do no more than ten minutes,' he said, 'and finish on the Jerry Lewis impression.' I did as I was told. The act went extremely well and, as I left the dressing room, there was a queue of chaps waiting to book me.

'Have you got your diary?' asked the first con sec.

'Yes,' I said.

'What's your fee?'

'Four pounds,' said Seamus, who'd appeared from nowhere. My mouth fell open, I'd never earned more than £2.10s and would have been happy with thirty bob.

'Four pounds,' repeated the con sec producing his large diary. 'Sign this.' I signed his diary on the suggested date and he signed mine; that's the way they did things in Coventry. Having set my fee, I picked up about two dozen dates. All my weekends were spoken for. I'd be picking up eight quid a week on top of my grant, I could live like a king.

The following week Joan and Seamus took me to Cox Street WMC right in the middle of Coventry. This was the headquarters of the Concert Artistes' Association Midlands Branch. In the bar, holding court, was a strange young man in a smart suit. Gales of laughter were coming from the group around him. He appeared to have something to say to or about everyone who passed:

'Thank your mother for the rabbit. Before I say any more, shut that door! Look at the muck on here. Have you seen my friend Everard?'

'That's Billy Breen,' confided Joan. 'He's a drag act.'

'A what?'

'He dresses up as a woman, tells gags and sings like Judy Garland.' Several years later Billy Breen was to dispense with the frock, do exactly the same gags as a man instead of a woman, and find fame as Larry Grayson.

Occasionally I'd get the chance to work Sunday lunchtime. I didn't really like doing this, particularly as the audience would be all male. I'm not too keen on working to all men even now. One of the first I ever did was at the Wyken WMC in Coventry. I was standing in the wings waiting to be introduced by the con sec from his little podium in the auditorium when the said gentleman pushed past me on to the stage,

'Gentlemen,' he said, addressing the large audience, 'you all know Tommy—' he mentioned a name which they obviously did all know. 'It's my sad duty to inform you that he passed away in his sleep last night.' I immediately went as cold as Tommy. 'I'd like us all now to stand and observe a minute's silence for Tom,' he continued, and they all complied. At the end of the silent minute, the organist, unbidden, launched into 'Abide with me' which the assembled sang with gusto. That completed, the con sec, with an instant change of mood, announced, 'Here he is, your comedian for the morning, Don Maclean.' He walked off stage as I walked on and, as he passed me, said, 'Get on there kid and make 'em laugh.'

Dad always made a point of coming with me to lunchtime shows. I enjoyed the time we spent together, just the two of us, as much as I had when I was small. Dad was a gentle, unopinionated man; the older I got, the more I appreciated and admired him. He'd fuss over me on these occasions, assuming the role of an unpaid valet. One Sunday we set off for Bewdley to a big pub in the country. Our navigation failed and we were very late.

'Get ready, you should be on by now,' said the chap who'd booked me. The room contained about four hundred men. As I've said, it was a pub not a club, and a platform rather than a stage stood at the far end of the room. There was a set of rickety steps, stage right, which Dad and I headed for. We then crossed the stage to a curtained area, upstage left, which served as a dressing room. Dad unpacked the case and I fumbled with cufflinks and bow tie, struggling to get into my stage wear; my street clothes I dropped in a pile on the floor.

'I'll sort this out while you're on stage,' said Dad.

'You'll be stuck in here,' I told him. 'You won't be able to get out of here while I'm on.' I was announced and launched into my act. All was going well when suddenly an attractive woman began to walk slowly up the room towards me. All eyes turned – well she was the only female in the place. She crossed the stage behind me and disappeared into the curtained-off dressing area. Shortly afterwards I heard a sound behind me and turned to see Dad's stricken face poking out from the curtain. It wasn't until after the show that I heard the full story. When the girl joined Dad in the confined space, he busied himself hanging up my clothes and averting his eyes as he assumed she'd be getting changed. He felt a tap on his shoulder and the girl said, 'Can you help me?' Dad turned to see her standing completely naked holding a G-string in her hand. 'Do they want a full strip here?' she asked sweetly, 'or can I keep my G-string on?' That was the point at which Dad panicked and attempted escape. We never told Mom!

5

A Sucker for Teeth

During my two years at drama school I probably spent more time with Mom than I'd done since pre-school days. My fellow students thought she was wonderful. If I turned up with a few of them in tow as I often did, Mom would disappear into the kitchen and return with a plate of sandwiches or egg and chips for all. I'd take her with me to Birmingham Rep where Derek Jacobi and Julie Christie were both members of the resident company, and to the Alexandra Theatre when touring shows came. She was a woman of great faith and great fire but her paranoia was becoming more apparent, or maybe I was at an age to notice it. She'd never been one to hold out the hand of friendship, presumably she feared rejection, but increasingly she would tell me that people didn't like her; these included neighbours whom she lived next to for years and even her brothers and sisters. It's a wonder I wasn't infected by it

'They don't like you, they're jealous of you, that's what it is,' was often her response to my telling her of a slight disagreement I'd had with someone. It actually had a positive effect on me. Instead of being like Mom, thinking everyone dislikes me until they prove otherwise, I assume everyone thinks I'm lovely until they prove otherwise – you have a far better life that way. Mom had never really recovered from the death of her father when she was only seventeen. She was obviously his favourite and his loss had meant a severe drop in living standards for the family. She often brought up the subject: 'They were all glad when our Dad died, they'd say, 'It'll do the Fields good to go without, serves 'em right.' Who 'they' were I never established.

* * *

At the end of my first year of drama school I'd played quite a few good parts, including making my operatic debut as Papageno. I'd improved my singing and speaking voice and my comedy act had developed considerably thanks to the Coventry clubs. Term over, I set off for Minster once more. I was reunited with Nigel, whom Ross had prised away from Northney, but my delight at seeing him was somewhat blunted by the news that Hilary, who was only twenty, had died of leukaemia a few weeks earlier. We'd not been romantically involved in any way but I'd so enjoyed working with her; she was really adventurous and keen to try anything new. She had a great talent, talent that sadly would never be seen on the professional stage. I was terribly upset by her death. She was the first person of my own age who had died, I suppose it made me aware of my own mortality.

Back at Minster, I was like an animal released from a cage. The restrictions of the 'straight' theatre had been lifted and I threw myself into my task of ensuring that the campers had a good time. There were so many people who'd been there last year and decided to return for a second holiday, I was forced to ring the changes, think up a few different things to include in the entertainment programme, but this year I had a much freer hand with which to do so.

Ross Jones talked to me about my future in Warner's Holiday Camps but I had no more desire to become a holiday camp star than I did to become a club star. Both clubs and camps were just a training ground, my future lay on stage and in television. Ross, though, was determined to nurture me. He insisted that I had a full day off every Tuesday as well as releasing me on Sunday mornings so that I could get into Sheerness for mass. Each Sunday I made sure I sat in the same pew, right next to a memorial in the shape of a Royal Flying Corps cap badge. The memorial was dedicated to three brothers, all of whom had died flying in the service of their country. They were William, James and Anthony McCudden. James had a host of decorations including a VC. I reasoned that it would be very easy to find out more about him, as indeed it proved, and so began a fascination with early aviation and with the First World War which is with me still. A few years ago I visited McCudden's grave, he's buried in Wavans Cemetery in Northern France.

Many of the staff – waiters, kitchen porters, maintenance workers – had been at Minster the previous year so I knew them. They were very keen to make the acquaintance of any pretty girl campers and I was in a position to assist. They spent Saturday afternoons helping the incoming campers with their luggage. The arrival of any attractive young ladies would be noted by them, I'd find out the names and a few personal details about such beauties and pass this on to the lads, making it easier for them, especially the shy ones, to strike up a conversation – oh all right then, to 'chat 'em up'.

It was the last week of August 1963, I remember it well. Two of my spies approached at the run: 'There's two sisters, they're from London we think. Dark hair, brown eyes, the one's a bit young but the other one's an absolute darling.' They didn't usually wax so lyrical; this could be worth my personal attention.

From nine till ten on the Saturday night we did a show in which the entertainment staff was introduced to the campers. It was quite a funny routine and got lots of laughs. At the end of it I handed back to the band leader and dancing recommenced. I had a little while before I'd be needed on the dance floor. I saw her almost immediately. She was sitting on a high stool, smoking exaggeratedly from a cigarette holder. She wore a blue and white check dress which showed just enough cleavage and failed to reach her knees, one of which was crossed over the other. With lowered eyelids and pouting lips she looked sophisticated, haughty and unobtainable but there was something about her. I knew I wasn't seeing this girl for the first time. I straightened my tie and walked over.

'You were here last year,' I opened.

'How clever of you to remember,' she said, smiling widely to show me the most exquisite set of teeth – I've always been a sucker for teeth.

I asked her to dance; I was pretty good at ballroom dancing thanks to tuition from Dad. I held her close during the last waltz and suggested that she might like to go for a walk a little later on. She gave me her chalet number and I said I'd call in about fifteen minutes. She shared the chalet with her sister, Jeannette, who was fourteen and very amused by my arrival. Toni looked different.

Gone was the revealing dress, in its place an extremely hairy, high-necked jumper and jeans. She made a point of showing me that the zip front of the jeans was anchored by a large nappy pin. 'I've worked in holiday camps, I know what entertainers are like,' she said by way of explanation.

We sat on a grassy bank overlooking the sea and talked non-stop for an hour; I'd never found any girl that interesting before. For the rest of the week I spent every spare moment with her. I was besotted. We were interested in the same things, had the same likes and dislikes, she was outgoing and not at all self-conscious. I'd been out with several girls who'd been moody and miserable but this one was permanently happy. Her parents too were lovely, open people, though I did almost fall foul of her mother very early on. The pastry cook who lived in the chalet next to mine had given me an apple tart which I'd decided to share with Toni and Jeannette, a sort of 'midnight feast' for those of you who read *Girls' Crystal*. Just as we three began attacking the pastry, Bet arrived to make sure her girls were all right. She was not amused to find me there at that hour.

'What do you think you're doing here?'

'I've just brought this apple tart.'

'You can take your apple tart and go!' instructed the mother hen, extending her wings to gather in her chicks. 'Take your apple tart and go' was to become a family catchphrase and can still be heard even now on occasion, but that night it spelled out a clear message of morals and values; I would have to keep my nose clean or the apple tart wouldn't be the only thing that went.

Saturday came all too soon. We stood on the same spot where I'd first seen her the year before, waiting for her to board the coach. I promised I'd see her on Tuesday, my day off. She told me afterwards that she didn't really believe that, she thought I might be shooting her a line. Not so, on Tuesday I set off for London courtesy of British Rail.

Toni worked in a fashion house as personal assistant to the managing director; the offices were in Dean Street, Soho. I found the place and waited outside to take her to lunch. I'd never had anyone so pleased to see me. I wandered around the West End all afternoon dreaming of appearing in one of the famous theatres, then met her again from work. She took me back to her home in

Pimlico. Knowing of my dietary peculiarities, her mom had made a vast amount of macaroni cheese which I devoured. The Rouxs were a lovely family, very affectionate, lots of hugging and kissing went on. I thought, 'I could get used to this.' Tom and Betty Roux had four daughters; Pat who was married and living in Sydney; Margaret who was married and living round the corner; Jeannette who was still at school; and Toni who lived at home.

After supper Toni and I went to the cinema to see Albert Finney in *Tom Jones* and, with promises of a similar meeting in a week – this time she believed me – I boarded the last train from Victoria to Sheerness. I remember it was a wonderful feeling. Suddenly stars were brighter, colours were cleaner, sounds were louder. Being away from Toni was actually painful but I welcomed the pain, I wanted to feel like this forever. I often think that when relationships go off the boil, you need only to think back to how badly you wanted to be with your loved one when first you met to rekindle it all. It was an original enhanced emotion, something very new for me. Was it love? 'It was like a lighted match had been tossed into my soul, it was like a dam had broken in my heart' – not my words sadly, words from a song, but never has the emotion been 'nutshelled' so well.

Toni wrote to me daily and I responded almost as regularly. This frequency of epistles was to continue for the next three years, and though they contained protestations of love, there was also opinion on current affairs, on plays and theatre, on books we were reading as well as day-to-day gossip. They would have made a valuable social history document but Toni, having kept them all, took the precaution of destroying them once the kids learned to read. I wonder if she's still got one or two tucked away.

The end of the season approached. It was to be my last season in a holiday camp. The three years had been invaluable but I knew it was time to move on. I was eager to get back to drama school to see all my fellow students and to introduce them to Toni who'd agreed to come to Brum by coach the following Friday. Whereas I'd met her mom and dad at the same time I'd met her, making life very easy for me, Toni would be meeting my parents cold and starting from scratch. She was undaunted by the prospect. She kissed both of them when I introduced her, which I think took them rather by surprise, and addressed them as Rose and Charlie – none of that Mr and Mrs stuff for her. She then set about making herself at home. Dad seemed quite impressed by my wide-mouthed beauty but I could see that Mom had some reservations, her character not allowing her to hold out the hand of friendship.

My relationship with my future father-in-law was a great one. This was in some part due to that fact that Tom believed he had chosen me for his daughter. Before Toni and I met at Minster in 1963, she'd been briefly engaged to a policeman – no don't laugh – named Wally – I did ask you not to laugh! The engagement had come to an end and Tom and Bet had opened a bottle of champagne to celebrate. They'd not wanted to tell Toni that she and Wally had nothing in common and that their relationship was doomed to failure, a mistake that Toni and I would repeat with our own son, but they were delighted when Toni worked it out for herself. Whilst quaffing the champers Tom apparently said, 'He wasn't for you. I'll tell you who you should have, someone like that Don who was at the holiday camp last year.' Spooky or what?

By the time of Toni's escape from betrothal, Tom, Bet and Jeannette had already booked their return to Minster, Tom persuaded Toni to join them and the plot was complete. There was no escape, I was a marked man. I wouldn't presume to claim that I was the son he never had because he had an equally good relationship with his other sons-in-law. It was more that he admired my spirit of adventure, the fact that I was in no way concerned about security.

Tom's upbringing had been hard. He really was the product of mixed parents, his mother being English and his father French. They had met while working for the Hennessy family in Scotland and, having married, Auguste had taken Alice back to France where they had bought a guest house in the seaside resort of Arcachon. Life seems to have been idyllic until the outbreak of war. Auguste was called up and on 22 July 1915, exactly one month before the birth of his son Thomas, Sgt Auguste Roux of 117th Régiment de Pieds died of wounds near Arras in northern France. As soon as Alice was well enough to travel following the birth, she packed up her small daughter, Louie, and the new baby and returned to live in her mother's house in central London. Auguste Roux has a place in our home; his medals, Médaille Militaire and Croix de Guerre with star, both bravery awards, are framed and hang in the lounge. A few years ago, Toni and I found his grave in a small cemetery at Aubigny sur Yon. We laid a poppy wreath and had a small service led by a priest who was part of the group we were with. It was a touching moment and I know that Toni feels a firm bond with the grandfather she never met.

Enough of the history lesson, back to 1963. Summer season over, it was back to MADA (Mary's Academy of Dramatic Art). I still hadn't made up my mind what direction to take. My success as Papageno meant that I'd be a valuable asset for the Royal Opera House; I was in demand in the Coventry clubs, working every Saturday and Sunday without fail and improving the comedy act all the time; and now I'd been cast to play Morgan Evans in Emlyn Williams' *The Corn is Green*. Toni travelled up from London to see me in the role and wept openly during the final scene, I'm not really sure why and even to this day have never dared ask. So – should I be a singer, a serious actor or a stand-up comic? My mind was in turmoil.

Miss Richards was very good about letting any of us off for professional work – well, it did give a certain kudos to her educational establishment. I determined to try to get something for the Christmas hols. Back to the *Stage* newspaper again – you're beginning to think I've got shares in it – but in my formative years it was invaluable. There was an open audition advertised: 'Male singers for pantomime, South of England'. It was at the Max Rivers Studios again, my happy hunting ground.

The auditioner was Ron Wayne, six feet three tall with blond hair and big blue eyes, all of which disguised the fact that he was one of the hardest men I've ever met. Ron was a fine tenor and he was looking for five other singers to join him to form the Ron Wayne Singers for a five-week panto run in Southampton. There were about fifty blokes there. We patiently waited our turn to go into the small room where Ron and a pianist awaited us. I edged towards the back of the queue. There were plenty of tenors, even more baritones, but not one really low voice. Eventually it was my turn. I introduced myself to Ron.

'What do you sing, Don, tenor, baritone?'

'No, I'm a bass,' I said.

His face lit up. 'Give the pianist your dots.' I selected 'Rose Marie' and gave it my best Howard Keel impression with plenty of volume on the low notes.

'Where do you live?' asked Ron.

'Birmingham.'

'Are you in a hurry to get home?'

'Not really.'

'Well perhaps you'd like to come back in about an hour, by which time I'll have seen all the rest.'

'Yes – thanks,' I said, collecting my music and slipping out the door. I wandered around Leicester Square feeling pretty pleased with myself and returned at the appointed time. All the remaining auditionees had gone.

'I'd like to offer you the panto,' said Ron. 'Just try singing the bass line of this for me.' The pianist launched into something called 'Marching through the heather' which I'd never heard before. He picked out the bass line for me and I looked carefully at the music in front of me as though I was reading it. 'Just sing the first sixteen bars,' said Ron. I did so and he joined in with the tenor part. It sounded so good I wanted to stop singing so I could hear it better. 'There'll be an Equity contract in the post tomorrow,' said Ron.

Southampton had a cinema seating two-and-a-half-thousand, The Gaumont, which 'became' a theatre each year at panto time. It has since been restyled and renamed The Mayflower and is permanently a well-patronised theatre serving the good folk of Southampton and its environs. The six Ron Wayne Singers were soldiers, courtiers, villagers, etc., but we also sang 'Marching through the heather' during the second half, to great acclaim from the audience.

The show, *Puss in Boots*, had three stars, each completely different. Richard Hearn or rather 'Mr Pastry' topped the bill. On stage he was a brilliant clown and tumbler and his Lancers routine brought the house in each night; but off stage he was another person, coming to the theatre wearing bowler hat and carrying a rolled umbrella, no one knew who he was. The floppy white moustache he wore on stage was false, which further added to the deception. He never once spoke to me nor, as far as I know, to any other member of the cast. Bill Maynard was Simple Simon. He would gladly talk to anyone so long as they were prepared to talk about him: yes, Bill had only one interest in life and that was Bill. I was chosen to understudy him which meant that I got to talk to him about himself more than most people did. I did get ten bob a week extra for that – understudying Bill, not suffering Bill. The final star in the show restored my faith in showbiz people. Joan Regan was then, and still is, one of the loveliest people you'll ever meet. I worked with her recently, she's singing as well as ever. She was always smiling, always ready to go out of her way for the lowliest on the bill. I made up my mind that I'd be like that when I was a 'star'.

Being on the south coast meant I was able to get to Toni's for Christmas Day, which was wonderful. The season went well and I felt I learned plenty, especially understudying Simple Simon, though I never went on. I got to know Ron Wayne very well. The previous summer he'd appeared in a show at Skegness and was signed to return for the coming summer season. 'I'll have a word, see if I can get you in there,' he said. I was excited but didn't hold out much hope.

At the end of February I received a formal letter from Ted Dwyer, the producer: 'We have been recommended to your work by Mr Ron Wayne. If you are appearing anywhere in the Lincolnshire area we would be pleased to see you work.'

I rang Ron Wayne and told him.

'Leave it to me,' he said. 'I'll get you a one-nighter at a club I know in Grimsby.'

Everything was set. It was a Saturday night, the club was full and Ted Dwyer was in the audience – I'd recognised him from Ron's description; very smart in fawn raincoat and matching corduroy trilby. I gave 'em everything as Ron had told me to: plenty of comedy, all my impressions and the Toreador Song from *Carmen* to finish. 'He wants an all round entertainer,' Ron had said.

Once I'd done my spot, I dashed out of the dressing room to see Ted Dwyer disappearing through the door at the back. I chased after him, not knowing what I was going to say when I caught him.

'Mr Dwyer,' I called. He turned. 'I er – I er.'

'You'll do nicely,' he said and was gone.

I spent an anxious couple of weeks before another formal letter arrived: 'We would be pleased to offer you SECOND COMIC in FOLLIES ON PARADE at THE PIER THEATRE, SKEGNESS. Salary £18 per week. Please advise by return if acceptable.' The only other possibility of work was ASM and Small Parts (that's a job description not a personal insult) at Sheffield Playhouse, salary £6 per week. It took me about two minutes to make up my mind.

I left MADA at Easter, which meant I was one term short of completing the course, but at least I had a job, a stage job, to go to. I'd like to tell you that all the fine young actors from my drama school made a living in their chosen profession, but alas no. Doran Godwin starred as Jane Austen's Emma on television and also had a lead role in *Shoestring*, and Peter Childs was a regular on *Minder*, but many of my contemporaries never even got a first acting job. There was David Fennel of course, I'll be telling you more about him in a minute or two.

'Skegness is So Bracing,' says the poster, which means that unless you're wearing lead boots, you'll find it difficult to keep your feet on the ground. I was having difficulty with that anyhow; I'd arrived in the professional theatre, my name and photo were on all the posters. This wasn't a holiday camp, this was the real thing, I was suffering from terminal ecstasy! The only cloud was the distance I now found myself from Toni but letters flying back and forth would, I hoped, keep our love on track.

Skegness Pier Theatre was three-quarters of a mile from the promenade. A magnificent wooden structure seating about six hundred on one level, it was to be my home for the next twenty-two weeks. At one time, every seaside town had such a theatre. Few are still in use but I'm sure you know North Pier, Blackpool; Wellington Pier, Great Yarmouth; and Cromer Pier, as well as the Westcliff Theatre, Clacton and the Sparrow's Nest, Lowestoft. All built in the 1920s and 30s, they continued to provide family entertainment until cheap foreign travel killed our domestic holiday trade. That was yet to come in 1964, and Skeggie was still the favourite holiday destination for the good folk of

Nottinghamshire, Derbyshire, in fact all of the east Midlands. Apart from the visitors, Ted Dwyer's show had an extremely loyal following of locals.

I don't suppose the format of the show had changed in years but Ted kept things up to date by featuring hit parade music and current West End musicals. Where the comedy sketches came from I'll never know but there'd be at least two in every show. We had a four-piece band with an MD waving the baton, six girl dancers and eight principals. Margaret Terry, a classically trained soprano, Audrey Mann, a very funny comedienne who went everywhere with a tapmat, and Dinkie Maurice, a pocket-sized blonde who played xylophone and sang, were the female side. Lined up opposite them were Ron Wayne whom I've told you about; Brian Grey, a delicate, almost sickly-looking chap who sang like Sinatra and wowed the ladies; then there was me, second comic and dogsbody. Add to that the principal comic and top of the bill, Stanley Waite, a lad from Lancashire with a voice like George Formby, eyes like two poached eggs and a manner of deportment which added twenty years to his age. Apart from the finale when, along with us other chaps, he wore white tie and tails, Stanley never appeared on stage without his pigeon-fanciers' flat cap. The other performer was Ted Dwyer himself. Not only producer and director, he was also the 'feed', the straight man to Stanley, and very good at it he was too, if a little pre-war.

The season was to last from early May until the end of September. During the peak weeks we did twice nightly, 6.15 and 8.45, plus one show on Sundays, no time off, seven days a week, but business was excellent. We changed our programme on a Thursday which meant that people holidaying could come twice and see two different shows, and they did. The locals, though, came every week; you could tell what day it was by who was sitting in the front row. Why didn't they get bored? I hear you ask. Well, probably because we did five – yes, five – changes of programme which, as you've already worked out, meant I needed five spots. Each cast member did a spot in each show. For the singers that meant two songs; for me, six minutes of patter and a short comedy number to finish. I was also involved in the opening, three scenas (potted versions of musicals or songs all on a single theme), two sketches and the finale. The sketches provided me with some great opportunities. I was always given a small part but vicars, village idiots and even a grandma enabled me to create characters and funny voices with which to score. I fell foul of Stan Waite occasionally but I could see that Ted Dwyer approved of my characterisations in his quiet way. The local paper warmed to me too: '*Then came the hilarious highspot of the evening when the whole audience were in hysterics for all of five minutes as Don Maclean modelled a vintage swimsuit. Just standing there without a move Don could have forced laughter from Scrooge.*'

I was accommodated in a bed and breakfast establishment at the end of the prom, just before the sand dunes started. The proprietor was a friend of Ted Dwyer's and would obviously keep a motherly eye on me. She was in fact a formidable woman in her seventies by the name of Mrs Croker. She ran the boarding house with her sister Minnie who was eighty-four. I paid £2.12s.6d for a very nice room on the second floor and a most substantial breakfast. Toni visited twice and Mrs Croker accommodated her, though she had to pay the holidaymakers' rate of £4 per week. I kept my nose clean for the whole season as I was rather intimidated by my harridan landlady. I was always on time for breakfast and when I got home at night, I let myself in and ascended to my room silently so as not to disturb the guests, most of whom were of a comparable age to the sisters.

The final week of the season, the town was very quiet; we were much nearer to Christmas than Pentecost. I was alone in the boarding house with no holidaymakers to be polite to. The show too was winding down, we were performing once nightly. Because we had an early finish, Brian Grey persuaded me to go over to Grimsby with him to see a friend who was working in a club there. Brian eventually dropped me back at my digs at 1.30 a.m. I got to the front door and, horror of horrors, I'd not got a key. The prospect of Mrs Croker's wrath stayed my finger before it reached the doorbell. I reasoned that a fit, athletic youth such as I could gain access to the house within minutes. The kitchen at the rear was a single-storey extension to the house; it had a nice, fat drainpipe which I scaled with ease. The first-floor toilet had a window which was always open – I knew that. I'd squeeze through and nip up the stairs to my bedroom. The window proved too small to get my head through, let alone my shoulders. Time to think again. A movement caught my eye, it was a curtain blowing. If the breeze was moving the curtain, the window must be not quite closed. Could I get my fingers under it? Indeed I could, what a stroke of luck! I knew there were no guests in residence, I was the only one in the house; this was going to be even easier than I thought. The window slid effortlessly upwards. I'd just slipped one leg and my upper body through the gap when a blood-curdling scream rent the air. I looked towards the bed where a shape was materialising, the screams were coming from it. Suddenly the bedside light flashed on and the shape became an elderly lady, clutching the bedclothes to her throat, eyes wide and mouth even wider. I said the first thing which came into my mind which I'm ashamed to say, was, 'Shut up you silly cow I live here.' She was unconvinced and the scream rose several decibels. I decided on retreat, caught my foot on the sill and sprawled backwards on to the flat kitchen roof. Lying prone and looking up I saw the upper floor lights go on. A window opened and Mrs Croker's head with curlers in the exocet position poked out.

'Who's there?' the imperious voice rang out. The screams continued unabated.

'It's me Mrs Croker,' I confessed, trying to sit up. 'I've forgotten my key.'

'Stupid boy, go to the front door.'

By now lights were going on all up the road – she could really scream, whoever she was – and in the distance I heard the approach of a police siren. Mrs Croker appeared at the front door wearing a full-length pink candlewick dressing gown. 'I'll speak with you in the morning,' she said as I hurried past her and scurried up to my room.

The screaming had stopped, there were just muffled sobs coming from the room I'd tried to invade. I considered popping in to apologise but thought better of it as I could still hear the police siren.

It wasn't until the next morning that I learned the facts. That morning, the lady in question had disturbed a burglar when she returned to her house. She was too frightened to stay there alone so her daughter had brought her to stay by the sea for a few days. She'd arrived after I'd left for the theatre, which is why I was unaware of her being there, and the first thing that happened was another burglar, namely me, breaking into her room. Dreadful really, but you have to laugh don't you?

Mrs Croker forgave me but I resolved that I would find alternative accommodation next summer. Oh, I forgot to tell you, only that day, Ted Dwyer had asked me to return for a second year.

6

Another Crossroads

So far I'd led a charmed life, straight out of drama school, straight into summer season. While in Skegness, I'd written a few dozen letters and had accumulated quite a bit of work for the autumn. The first job I'd managed to get after the summer show finished was a week at the City Varieties, Leeds. This wonderful Victorian theatre was featured on BBC Television in a programme called *The Good Old Days*, produced by a marvellous man named Barnie Colehan who'd started life as Wilfred Pickles's pianist: 'Give 'em the money Barnie'; there's probably no one still alive who remembers that!

I was to appear on *The Good Old Days* several times during the years ahead, but for now the good people of Leeds were to be given a whole week in which to assess my talent. I arrived in the city full of expectation. The theatre is right in the city centre. I scanned the shop windows for posters advertising this week's variety, keen to see my name on the bill. When I did eventually see a poster it stopped me in my tracks. My name was there all right, in very small letters. The title of the show dominated, *Prison without Bras*. You've guessed it; when weekly variety died, the brothers Joseph who owned the theatre attempted to revive it by putting on strip shows. Apart from me and one of the funniest double acts ever to step on a stage, Gordon and Bunny Jay, the bill comprised three strippers and a nude Chinese fire-eater. She wasn't easy for a lad from a good Catholic home to cope with. I've forgotten her name but not her aroma. Even to this day I can't smell Ronson lighter fuel without getting slightly excited.

On Monday night I died the death of a dog – no one laughed, not a single titter. I was distraught. Stanley Joseph came backstage afterwards, I was convinced he'd come to pay me off, 'You're not funny son, don't bother to come in tomorra!'; but no, he ignored me in my misery, he was there to take issue with one of the strippers who came on dressed as a Red Indian with interesting war paint and proceeded to do strange things with a tomahawk: 'You leave that bloody thing in the dressing room tomorra night, I'll get closed down else,' threatened Stanley.

Gordon and Bunny kept me sane. They were doing three spots while I was mercifully only doing two.

'All comics die here,' explained Gordon. 'They've just come to see the flesh. If you thought tonight was bad wait for tomorrow's matinee.' He was right. A couple of dozen men were scattered round the stalls. As I came on nearly every one of them opened up a newspaper and read until I'd left the stage to the sound of my own feet. This was a far cry from the tweeness of *Follies on Parade*. What a week! I stayed in pro digs called Novello House which were run by a permanently cravatted chap of dubious sexuality who kept telling me that in a certain light my profile resembled 'Dear Ivor', the Novello after whom the house had been named. I had only one good night in the theatre, and that was Thursday when the place was packed with students from Leeds University. They'd come to heckle and they were good at it. They heckled the strippers: 'Keep 'em on!' They heckled the nude Chinese fire-eater: 'There's a different slant on things!' But mostly they heckled the comics. I gave as good as I got and was rewarded with cheers and applause which enabled me to survive Friday and Saturday. I was pleased to leave that place. The week was an experience that I had no wish to repeat and yet, several years later, the *City Varieties* was to play its part in a surprising career change for me as you'll see.

There was hardly any theatre work for variety acts. Most theatres had closed and those that were still open struggled to get anyone through their doors. Clubland, though, was booming. I had my contract for next summer at Skegness and I needed work to keep me going between now and then. Sheffield seemed to be the centre of it all. I found some digs and trotted round to the south Yorkshire club agents. Work was easy to come by; laughs proved a little more difficult. Miners and steelworkers have an earthy sense of humour but I knew that a reputation as a blue comic would do me no good in my quest for TV stardom, nor in my need to develop new material for next summer season. Occasionally, I managed to get the audience on my wavelength and have a good night, but mostly I struggled. Entertainment secretaries, though, liked me because I had different gags and a different approach. I began to get a reputation. If I had a night off, or if I finished early, I'd dash off to another club to catch one of the comedy stars of clubland. There were acts that could fill any club: Norman Collier, Ron Delta, Ronnie Dukes and Rikki Lee, I saw all of those as often as I could. I was raw, they were polished, and there was much I could learn from them.

Any available time I had I tried to spend with Toni. Our relationship was passionate in every way and I'd like to think it still is. We feel passionately about one another and about the world around us. I still couldn't believe my luck, finding someone to whom I was so suited. I don't follow the belief that there's only one person in the world for each of us but I do think there are very few with whom you can achieve compatibility. I know many women of whom I'm extremely fond but none of them could I share my life with. During our courtship, as I've said, we kept the post office on overtime with our letters. I feel sorry for youngsters now; texting and e-mailing will never compare with the good old-fashioned love letter.

I also felt my knowledge of the contemporary novel was improving at Toni's instigation. She started me on books by Ian Fleming about a chap called Bond. We'd read the lot before Cubby had his first taste of broccoli. We also discussed religion; what we believed and why we believed. Toni wasn't Catholic but she always came to mass with me if we were together on a Sunday. She read a novel called *Judas My Brother* which she passed on to me without comment. It was written in the first person and followed the life of Jesus through the eyes of Judas and his brother. All the miracles of Jesus were explained away as little more than conjuring tricks. The entry into Jerusalem, the trial and the crucifixion were engineered by Jesus himself in an attempt to fulfil the prophecies of the Old Testament regarding the Messiah. Needless to say Judas didn't commit suicide but lived to a ripe old age. Fiction – yes, but I will admit that I was disturbed by it. I began to read extensively about the life of Jesus and particularly about the final week of that earthly life. I began to do something I'd never done before – question my faith. I needed to know what followers of other faiths, particularly the Jews, thought of Jesus. Was He my Lord and Saviour, or was He just a prophet, just a man whom religions had deified for their own reasons? I read St Paul. Were we all being manipulated by his great intellect into following a religion of his making? Had he set out to modernise Judaism using Jesus, whom he'd never met, as a figurehead? I'm very suspicious of St Paul to this day.

Far from broadening and opening my mind, this intense philosophical questioning made me more and more morose. Some days were filled with the Holy Spirit and surrounded by the knowledge of the love of God, while others were an emptiness of black despair. Maybe it's true, as has often been said, that inside each of us there's a God-shaped void which only God can fill. Eventually I came to a conclusion: I needed God. He was the backbone of my life, the thing that kept me upright. Should my investigations, misguided or otherwise, prove to me that God did not exist, that there was no afterlife, no retribution, no heavenly reward, I would be unable to cope with that knowledge. If what I did today had absolutely no relevance in the future, life would become meaningless. I stopped searching immediately. You'll brand me a cowardly Christian and you'll be right but belief is important to me. I pray each day, 'Lord give me faith, the faith I had as a small child to believe in You and in all Your wondrous works.' Yes, call it cowardice if you like, but I have never, since then, attempted to question.

I had other worries on my mind. We've all heard the cry of the out-of-work actor, 'Christmas Eve and still no offers of pantomime!' It wasn't quite that bad but it was nearly October and nothing had come up – perhaps my luck was running out. I wrote to Derek Salberg. He asked me to call at his office in the Alexandra Theatre where my love of panto had been nurtured. What a great man of the theatre he was, finding time to see a kid he didn't know from Adam. I was to get to know Derek quite well in later life, especially when I was invited on to the board of directors of the Alex. I never forgot his kindness. His pantos were fully cast but he gave me a letter which I was to take to Joe Collins, the father of novelist Jackie and film star Joan. He was a theatrical agent but this year he was producing a couple of pantos. The letter opened the door to his office in Charing Cross Road and I left with a contract to play Black Dog, a villainous seafarer, in *Mother Goose* – where? Back at the Gaumont, Southampton, that's where.

With panto in the bag there was just one more thing I had to do. I had decided to go and see Tommy Roux and ask for his daughter's hand in marriage. 'I'd be delighted to have you as part of my family,' said Tom. I made a note of that sentence and repeated it twenty-five years later when my son-in-law, Guy, asked for my daughter's hand. I went off to panto rehearsals with a sapphire and diamond engagement ring which cost me thirty quid in my pocket.

The cast Joe Collins had put together for *Mother Goose* was great. Clean-cut pop singer Mark Wynter topped the bill and unusually we had a female dame, Canadian comedienne Libby Morris. I was also to have the opportunity to learn a lot from comedy double act Edmundson and Eliot and from Ken Wilson who played Jimmy Goose. He was a brilliant business comic who did a hilarious sketch in which he put up a deckchair – yes, OK, I know that sounds boring but it had audiences in hysterics, believe me. Ken had also perfected the wallpapering slosh scene over many years. He couldn't do it alone so I became his straight man. It was great once you'd remembered when to keep your eyes and mouth closed, and yet another comedy string was added to my highly-strung bow. We opened just prior to Christmas and after the show on Christmas Eve I drove up to London to spend my only day off with Toni and her family. First thing Christmas morning I gave her the ring. Everyone there was delighted but I wondered how my Mom and Dad, sitting back home in Brum, were feeling about it.

Mark Wynter and I struck up a firm friendship. We were almost the same age but he'd had three top ten hits and was earning a three-figure salary whilst I was earning £22.10s. I could have had a problem trying to keep up with big earner Mark but he had a smooth way of picking up bills without embarrassing me in any way. Being very fond of young ladies himself, he berated me for getting engaged when there were 'so many women and so little time', but he was never sure whether those women wanted him for himself or for his wealth, a problem I certainly didn't have regarding Toni. We had some hilarious times together on and off stage, it's a period of my life that I look back upon very fondly.

At the end of the panto run, Mark and his current girlfriend took Toni and me to see the Palladium panto starring Cliff Richard and the Shadows, Arthur Askey and the wonderfully menacing Alan Curtis as Abanazar. This was the sort of pantomime I wanted to be in, I realised. I was to achieve that ambition but it was going to be a long, steep climb. After the theatre we had a wonderful meal, scampi which I'd never eaten before and Mateus Rosé, the chic thing to drink, at the outrageous price of 10s.11d a bottle. It was a superb night that still lives in the memory. Mark Wynter was to turn his back on the lucrative world of pop to become a fine dramatic actor, starring in plays and musicals at home and abroad. We're still in touch.

I'd made up my mind that my next step on the road from obscurity was to find an agent. I didn't rush into this because Mark Wynter's agent, an Australian by the name of Ian Bevan, gave some good advice: 'Don't get an agent that you want, get an agent that wants you.' OK, but did such a man exist? Actually, he was out there but I had yet to find him.

David Fennell – you remember he was at drama school with me – had really landed on his feet. A good-looking, broad-shouldered lad, he'd auditioned at ATV for a new soap opera and had been cast as Brian Jarvis, the juvenile lead. The show starred Noelle Gordon and was set in a Midlands motel called, yes you've guessed it, *Crossroads*. David was a real good mate and managed to get interviews with the casting director for most of his contemporaries, including me. Shortly after my panto ended I got a call to go to ATV for a reading, obviously at David's instigation, and was given two weeks in the epic playing Cy Townsend. The story line was that young Marilyn Gates, played by Sue Nicholls who now plays Audrey Roberts in *Coronation Street*, joined a pop group called Georgie Saint and the Dragons. Georgie was played by Deke Arlon who was later to become a top theatrical agent, managing Denis Waterman and discovering

Sheena Easton, and Cy Townsend was the bass player in the group. There were several scenes with some funny dialogue in which we planned Marilyn's assault on the pop charts, and at the end of two weeks, Sue had made a record and Deke and I went our separate ways.

When, a few weeks later, the episodes were transmitted, ATV was bombarded with requests for copies of the record. They quickly got Sue Nicholls into a studio and cut the single. Written by Tony Hatch, not by us as the story line would have you believe, 'Where will you be?' bounced straight into the charts. Writers hastily started adapting future scripts and I was called for as it was proposed to make Cy Townsend a running character, starting early August. All very well but I was due to open in Skegness. I contacted Ted Dwyer who informed me, in no uncertain terms, that I had a contract with him which could not be broken. Probably just as well, otherwise I'd still be doing the rounds, appearing briefly in *Emmerdale*, *Brookside* and *EastEnders*. Georgie Saint and the Dragons, minus their bass player, had quite a few weeks in *Crossroads* and Sue Nicholls had a hit record; I wonder if she includes that in her CV these days?

The Skegness season was to be slightly shorter, Easter being later that year. The cast was almost the same though Stanley Waite had given way to Colin Gaye (that word didn't have any connotation in 1965). I found myself a small bedsit a long way away from Mrs Croker and her hysterical guests, took the disappointment of not becoming a soap star on the chin and immersed myself in rehearsals. This year *Follies on Parade* needed to be stronger than ever as we would shortly have opposition. A show was being mounted at Skeggie's other theatre, the Arcadia. I was thrilled because the stars were Ronnie Hilton and one of my comedy heroes, Norman Collier. Norman was an original. He's remembered now as the man who did an impression of a cockerel, which I find rather sad. He was clean, very visual and the first comic who could truly be described as 'zany'. I made a point of getting to know both him and Ronnie well, though Ted Dwyer frowned on fraternisation between our company and theirs; they were the enemy. I've never felt like that, the more shows the merrier as far as I'm concerned, there were plenty of holidaymakers to go round. When Toni came to spend her holiday with me, Ronnie and Norman and their wives took us out for a meal at a posh hotel, we felt very honoured.

A management came to see me in the pier show and offered me panto at Kidderminster Playhouse. Yes, it was a small panto but the subject was *Cinderella* and I was to play every comic's dream part, Buttons. I told Ronnie Hilton about this. He'd played Buttons several times in the past and he gave me the Buttons suit he'd had specially made for himself. Bright red it was with four rows of gold buttons, and it fitted me perfectly. Norman Collier meantime put me in touch with an agency in south Wales and I wrote off hoping for work there once the season was finished. The season was over all too soon. Ted Dwyer invited me back for a third year but I declined. I'd learned all I could as a second comic. Next year I intended to be principal comic somewhere – but where?

Toni had also moved on from her job in the rag trade and gone to work for British Airways. For years she'd wanted to go to visit her elder sister, Pat, in Australia and the possibility of a cheap, affordable fare offered to employees was the main incentive. It was a good career move for another reason. Toni's supervisor, a delightful woman named Wyn, had lost her fiancé during the war and was very supportive of our relationship, letting Toni off early on Friday nights to enable her to travel up to Birmingham by coach from nearby Victoria Coach Station. Not every weekend of course, because often I was working in some far flung corner of the country.

South Wales was to become a happy hunting ground for me. I stayed in the tiny village of Bedlinog within reach of Newport, Llanelli and all points in between. The Welsh club scene had gone crazy, there were new places opening every week. I could work seven nights plus a Sunday noon. I needed the money. I'd bought a house or rather a plot – all right, let's be honest, a hole in the ground. An estate of new houses was being built in Selly Oak, near Birmingham University. There were three different designs available; we selected a three-bedroom semi with integral garage. Completion date was early 1967. I had the deposit of £395, now I needed to save like mad. Dad, who had shown little interest in my engagement, suddenly warmed to the idea once I'd signed for this house. I realised then that he had thought I'd be moving to London once I was married; comforted in the knowledge that I'd be staying close to him, his attitude changed.

The Welsh clubland was to be a great source of income and affirmation. Welsh audiences laughed more readily than their English counterparts, but some of the clubs, especially those in the valleys, were taken aback by the advent of professional entertainers; for years they'd been used to making their own entertainment. One such was deep in the Rhondda. I arrived there early for a Sunday noon show. Gradually, the place filled up with men. Once there were about thirty assembled, a single clear voice began to sing 'All Through the Night'. Immediately other voices joined in. I realised that they were seated according to their vocal range; tenors on the right, baritones on the left and basses behind. More men arrived and were careful to sit in their appointed place. By 12.30, the club was filled with people and music; the sound was truly inspiring. Apparently the village had a tradition dating back decades of entering choir competitions and considered their male voice choir second to none. The Ent Sec, a white-haired, cherubic-looking soul, confided to me that his voice had never broken so he was able to sing counter-tenor with the MVC and contralto with the ladies' choir. He gave me a burst of Kathleen Ferrier and I was glad that I no longer included that impression in the act. He suggested that I might finish with a bit of opera: 'We like proper music, yur see, none of that pop rubbish for us, isn't it? You'll be on first, we've got a famous recording star topping the bill, there's lovely.'

Despite the fact that I had to open, the act went OK. The recording star was a gravel-voiced singer who sounded rather like an Alsatian with bronchitis. He opened with 'Chantilly Lace'. The audience sat open-mouthed; they couldn't believe anyone with a voice like that would dare to enter their shrine to vocal excellence. He finished to a smattering of applause. Non-plussed by the total lack of reaction, he dispensed with the nicety of addressing the audience and launched straight into his next number, 'Ain't misbehavin' all by myself . . .'

'No wonder you're all by yourself, singing crap like that,' came a voice from the audience. The floodgates opened, everyone wanted to have their say.

'Call yourself a singer.'

'We don't have to listen to this.' The place was in uproar. The Ent Sec did what all ent secs do; sat there banging a gavel and shouting, 'Order! Order!' but no one heard, his contralto screech-ings fell on deaf ears.

The performer, understandably, started to panic. He stopped gyrating and looked into the hostile faces of two hundred Welsh miners. Now someone had put a heavy glass ashtray on the front of the stage. In a defiant gesture he kicked out at this ashtray which shot off the stage into the audience. The chap three tables back never knew what hit him but the edge of the ashtray split his forehead and a fountain of blood spurted out. As one man the crowd roared, stood and made for the stage. Gravel-voice ran into the dressing room which he locked from the inside then piled all available furniture against the door. It was a wise move, they'd have ripped him to bits. The Ent Sec, who had a penchant for uniforms, hurried to call the police, but even they were unable to clear a path to the dressing room door and eventually the singer was extricated via a window, put in a police car and driven off, never to appear in south Wales again. The Ent Sec paid me my money and suggested I leave too: 'No second spot for you, see then, is it?' As I left, the full concert room rang to the sound of 'We'll keep a welcome in the hillside' in three-part harmony. Obviously it wasn't intended for the gravel-voiced singer.

I also experienced physical danger, though not in Wales. It was on a Sunday night in north Derbyshire, and again the audience were miners and their wives. There was no other act, 'Just bingo and thee,' the Ent Sec informed me.

'How many spots?' I enquired, meaning, 'Do you want me to go on once or twice?'

'Six,' came the reply.

'Six?' I questioned.

'Thee, then bingo, then thee again, then more bingo, and so on.'

My mind was in turmoil, trying to work out how to spread two spots into six. The first spot was listened to but no one laughed. I finished with a song which was barely heard above the audience conversation and walked off to mild but unsustained applause.

The room then went silent for bingo, and I mean silent, not a sound anywhere. My turn again; even less reaction but much more noise. Then more bingo, played in silence. By my third spot I was a shivering wreck. The crowd, sensing fear, moved in for the kill.

'Why don't you gerroff?' shouted a voice. Agreement from all round.

'Open your mouth, I'll take a short cut,' I responded with my standard reply, which always got a good laugh but not this time; the entire audience took offence on behalf of the heckler.

I suffered twice more before the final game of bingo, after which half the audience left. Several of those who stayed did so only to make a point of leaving noisily as soon as I came on. Spot number six completed, I breathed the world's biggest sigh of relief, got changed and picked up my money. The concert room was empty; not so the car park. As I moved towards my car I was jostled and shoved.

'Call yourself a bloody comedian?'

'We've never had a turn as bad as thee.'

'You're about as funny as a fire in an orphanage, youth.'

I opened the door of my mini, scrambled in with case and suit bag and locked the door from the inside. The crowd surrounded me and, before I could start up, half a dozen burly miners flanked the car and began rocking it from side to side. The wheels were coming off the ground. I was hanging on for grim life, it was obvious they intended to turn the car over on to its roof with me in it. Suddenly they let go and I bumped back to earth. The steward had come out of the club to see what the commotion was.

'You barmy buggers,' he shouted at them. 'Leave the lad alone. Go on, get off home.' They began to disperse. The steward knocked on the window. 'Come on, son, out you get, I'll make you a cup of tea.'

'I'm staying here,' I said. 'I'm not getting out until you call the police.'

'No need for that,' he said. 'They're just being a bit boisterous, that's all.' He persuaded me out of the car and back into the club. I was in shock so he sat me down and made me drink a cup of tea with lots of sugar in it. After about half an hour, I felt well enough to drive back home.

I was grateful to that sensible man, it took guts to take on that mob. I experienced a lot of bad nights while learning my comedy craft in clubland but the nastiest were always the miners' clubs. At one such club on the south Yorkshire coalfield, I left the stage to no applause whatsoever, not a single clap. As I passed the Ent Sec in the wings he patted my shoulder.

'Very nice son,' he said.

'Very nice!' I retorted. 'Very nice! Nobody clapped.'

He fixed me with a wise eye. 'Nobody claps us when we come up pit,' he said sagely.

At Bolden, just outside Sunderland, an entire audience of miners flicked beer-mats at me as I tried to entertain them. By the end of the spot I was knee-deep in the things. About ten years later I was to upset the mining community greatly. Whilst being interviewed on a BBC local radio station, I was asked my opinion of the miners' strike which was paralysing the country. I replied, 'I think we should agree to the wage demands of the miners. Give them anything they want, provided they agree not to come up. Let them stay underground like pit ponies.' After the amount I'd suffered trying to entertain them, never were words more sincerely meant. All right, I know they worked hard in frightening conditions, but why did they have to take it out on me?

The Kidderminster panto was decidedly 'low budget'. The cast included a chunky Cinderella, a Prince Charming who was permanently in a daze, Ugly Sisters who hated one another, a Baron Hardup who looked young enough to be Cinderella's son, and one pony. The Playhouse was draughty, leaky and falling down. As soon as panto finished they pulled it down to make way for the proposed ring road. The cast of *Crossroads* came to see me *en bloc*, which was rather pleasing, and the other bonus was that I could live at home and spend Christmas with Mom and Dad – and Toni of course. I'd played Buttons with very little direction and got away with it. '*One of the highlights of the show is the performance of Don Maclean as a Buttons possessed of seemingly boundless energy and enthusiasm who never forces the pace beyond the children's*

ability to follow him,' said the *Birmingham Post*, but I vowed that
next time I played Buttons I'd be perfect.

I was beginning to get worried. February, and still no offer of
summer season. Something would surely turn up, or would it?
Toni was excited. She was about to fly off to Australia to see her
sister Pat, she was taking her younger sister, Jeannette, with her,
and together they would meet their brother-in-law and two small
nieces for the first time. She would be away for three weeks. I was
determined to have a summer season when she returned.

Jimmy O'Neill was a big man with a voice that rumbled up
from some great depth. He had a serious demeanour but his wife,
Mary Genn, was one of the few people I've met who could truly
be described as 'sweet'; she smiled at me throughout. Jimmy and
Mary were acquaintances of Ted Dwyer. For two years they'd put
on a show at Felixstowe on the Suffolk coast. The cast were of
their generation, that is the same age as my Mom and Dad.
They'd taken a decision to find a young comedian this year in the
hope of appealing to younger audiences and increasing business,
and that's how I came to be at the CAA, the Concert Artistes'
Association, in London's West End. That evening there was to be
a concert at the CAA; would I do a short spot? Certainly, much
better than a cold audition. The audience was good and I left that
night with a contract for twelve weeks at the Cavendish Theatre,
Felixstowe.

The night before Toni's return from Australia I spent with my
future in-laws. The following morning I picked up Jeannette's
boyfriend, John Robinson, and together we set off for Heathrow.
Even after a twenty-seven-hour flight, Toni looked radiant. I
couldn't wait to blurt out the news that my summer was secure at
a place within easy reach of London.

I got more than a shock when I arrived at Felixstowe in my
Hillman Imp. Having asked directions to the theatre, I was sent
to the Spa where a summer show starring Len Howe and Audrey
May was in rehearsal. I soon discovered that the Cavendish
Theatre wasn't a theatre at all, it was the back room of the
Cavendish Hotel. The posters outside said 'Music Hall' – another
shock – starring Don Maclean (got that bit right), celebrated
entertainers James O'Neill and Mary Genn, Ann Trevor, soprano,
and multi-instrumentalist Alan Beale. Music was to be provided

by Winifred on piano and Lionel on drums. There were no dancers, the stage had neither scenery nor tabs and the audience (capacity 230) would be seated at tables and served drinks by waiters whilst we performed. I must confess to being devastated. This was a far cry from *Follies on Parade* at Skeggy, but I was principal comic – OK, the only comic. I'd achieved my goal.

Jimmy had some good ideas, a couple involving my entering from the back of the audience and interrupting him while he tried vainly to get on with the show. In one such sketch, I was dressed in leotard and fishnets as a Playboy bunny complete with fluffy tail and large ears.

'Chocolates, Maltesers, get your nuts off me.'

'Madam, you're not supposed to display your wares until the interval.'

'You're running late and I've got a bus to catch. Cigarettes, ice cream, sucky things on a stick!'

You get the picture I'm sure. The cast, as I've explained, were all much older than me and I was indulged, to say the least. I had the lion's share of the comedy and managed to inject laughs into the musical numbers as well with never a single objection from the others. The press were extremely kind: '*A brilliant young comedian, Don Maclean, scored an instant and resounding personal triumph. His style is crisp and confident with a refreshingly original script. Once he has acquired a little more individual style, one might expect to hear a good deal more of this newcomer.*'

From my early beginnings, and certainly since my panto debut for Jerry Jerome, I'd been striving for a style. I knew I needed an approach which was different from any other comic – not just a gimmick, a complete style – but, like many acts who start out as impressionists, I absorbed the manner of anyone I admired. One week I'd be Ken Dodd, the next Forsyth, Tarbuck, Monkhouse. Try as I might I couldn't put my own individual stamp on my performance. Oh, it would come, but not just yet.

The press reports and word of mouth had an immediate effect. The show became the place for the young crowd from Ipswich to go. More and more came every week, business was considerably better than it had been last year. I saw plenty of Toni. One Sunday I would spend in London, the next she would come over to be with me. We were together on that marvellous Saturday when

England won the World Cup. What a day! We both had our first taste of champagne. We visited nearby Clacton several times. It had two summer shows and was packed with holidaymakers.

'Wouldn't it be great to do a show here,' I said to Toni, 'starring at a number one seaside resort.' Watch this space.

Several people came to see me work; some announced their presence, others sneaked in. However, it was not a theatrical agent but a banker who was to move my career forward. We did three changes of programme and one week a couple came to see all three – you couldn't miss them, they sat at the front and laughed like drains at everything. After the third visit they were waiting to see me.

'Do you have an agent?' asked the chap.

'No,' I replied.

'I'm a bank manager,' he confided. 'One of my clients is a large theatrical agent. I'll have a word with him when I get back home.' I was gobsmacked, so much so that I never asked his name nor the name of the theatrical agent.

The following week a letter arrived at the Cavendish from Aza Artists informing me that Morris Aza would be coming to see the show at the earliest opportunity. I'd heard of Aza Artists and knew that they represented Roy Hudd, who was doing very well for himself, and also the very funny Billy Dainty. Morris duly arrived, liked what he saw and offered me a sole agency agreement. This was just what I'd dreamed of, an agent who wanted me. Yes, 1966 had been a fantastic year so far. From what had seemed at first to be a twopenny-halfpenny show I'd achieved recognition, an agent and several friendships which have lasted to this day. Strange as it may seem, I felt at home in Ipswich and Felixstowe as though I'd lived there before, which of course I never had. If a magic genie turned up and offered to return me to any year in the past, 1966 is the year I'd choose. Don't tell Toni that, it was my last year as a single man.

7

A Wife, a House, a Mortgage

Bunny Baron had been to see me at Felixstowe more than once. I suppose you'd call him an impresario but on rather a small scale. He had several panto venues and was keen to produce summer shows. Before I knew it he'd contacted Morris Aza and booked me for panto at the Knightstone Theatre, Weston-super-Mare and also for next summer season at Clacton.

Before the Weston panto I tackled the north-east: Jarrow, Sunderland and South Shields. I'd struggled in a few clubs in my time but never like this; on Wearside, if they liked you, they let you live. It was soul-destroying stuff. The audiences were a miserable, unsmiling lot. They laughed at comedians but only ones that had been born there: Bobby Thompson, Bobby Knoxall, Bobby Pattinson – oh yes, they had to be named Bobby too. I was constantly told that I was 'too posh'. Posh! Me, posh! Anyone from south of the Tees was a southern softee and directly to blame for the Jarrow marches, an event as fresh in the memory then as it had been when it happened thirty years before. The saving grace of the north-east was the club agent who booked me, a man named Joe Mews. He thought I was hysterical. 'Most original comic that's ever been up here,' he'd say.

I was dying everywhere: miners' welfares, British Legions, Labour clubs, non-political clubs, you name it, I died there; but Joe kept booking me and his confidence boosted me. There was a very healthy night club scene in the north-east, known as the Bailey circuit. Their clubs were virtual palaces: La Dolce Vita and the Cavendish Club in Newcastle; Latino, South Shields; Weatheralls, Sunderland; Contessa, Middlesbrough; La Bamba,

Darlington. I'd slip into the nearest one after dying in a working men's club and lust after the opportunity of playing there. The booker was an attractive woman named Myrna Malinsky but I knew that asking her to come and see me work a north-east club would be the kiss of death. My time would come though, I was confident of that.

In panto I was to play Wishee Washee, with one of my childhood, radio heroes, Arthur English, as Widow Twanky. Lovely man though he was, I have to say that he wasn't a very good dame, and I realised then that being a great comic was no indication of an ability to play that most elusive of all roles. I decided it was something I didn't want to try, now or in the foreseeable future. I had other things on my mind.

My wedding day was fast approaching. Just prior to Christmas I'd had a bad attack of cold feet. Toni rang me from work because I'd been a bit distant with her. I'd blurted out that I wasn't at all sure about getting married; the Peter Pan in me had risen to the surface. She said, 'If that's the way you feel, that's fine by me,' and put the phone down.

Thirty minutes later I was on the way down the M1 in my car, deeply regretting the conversation but knowing that everything would be all right as long as I could see her face to face. I stopped at a classy florist in Pimlico to buy a large brown and gold chrysanthemum – I could only afford the one – and positioned myself outside her office; she'd be so pleased to see me when she came out. Only she didn't come out. Seeing me all forlorn with a rapidly wilting chrysanthemum, a girl who worked with Toni informed me that she'd been rather upset that afternoon and Wyn had sent her home. I dashed round to the flat – bad mistake. Jeannette opened the door. There I stood, sponge bag and pyjamas in one hand and big flower in the other.

'Who's been a naughty boy, then?' she said, pointing me towards the kitchen. Toni and her mom and dad were sat round the table planning my assassination. Bet just stood and turned her back but Tom rounded on me and gave me a severe dressing down for upsetting his daughter, finishing with, '. . . and if you think you're staying here the night, you've got another think coming.'

I was terrified; he looked capable of murder. I persuaded Toni out of the house and into my car. I drove round the corner and attempted to make my peace. I asked her to come back to Brum with me so we could sort everything out. She wanted me to stay in London but I was scared that her dad might try to kill me while I slept. After a weekend during which I curbed all my fears, many of which were financial if truth be told, the relationship was back on course. The incident was never mentioned in the Roux household again.

All right so I admit I had been worried. Marriage is a frightening prospect. Think how easy it is to make the wrong choice, then think of the consequences of that choice. I'll be ever so honest with you and tell you that I really didn't want to get married. I only married Toni because I was terrified that if I didn't somebody else would, and I couldn't bear the thought of that. In retrospect that's probably one of the best reasons for getting married that anyone's ever had. Toni, on the other hand, was very happy about the whole thing. They do say that someone who's completely happy doesn't understand the problem; for Toni there was no problem. I didn't have to make her happy, she brought her happiness with her. I always think that a happy wife is the most wonderful compliment a chap can have.

I've never been overly keen on weddings – even today I shudder when a wedding invitation comes through the door – but I did enjoy my own. On 11 February 1967, I was lead car in the convoy which travelled down the M1 to Pimlico. Various uncles, aunts and cousins filled the cars which followed. We all arrived at the flat of Ann and John Pearson, friends of the Rouxs, where we were plied with tea and biscuits and I was able to spend a considerable time shaving, changing into my wedding suit and combing my hair over and over again. Phil Pearson, Ann and John's son, was to be my best man, a role he'd assumed at short notice after Graham Weston who'd been my best mate at drama school landed a TV part. Phil was happy though a little nervous about his forthcoming fame.

The church of the Holy Apostles had been rebuilt in the 1950s. It was flattened during the blitz but daily mass continued to be said in the crypt until the reconstruction. The ceremony was joyous, Toni looked fantastic in a wedding dress she made herself at a cost of seven pounds. There were friends from the Skegness and Felixstowe shows in attendance. Everyone trooped back to the flat where Tom had removed every internal door so guests could pass easily from one room to another. Bet and her girls had done all the food, the drink flowed, Tom was always heavy-handed with a bottle, and everyone had a wonderful time. I suppose compared to today's weddings which cost thousands it was done on a shoestring, but when the time came for Toni and me to leave we did so very reluctantly, we were having such a good time. We were booked into the Skyline Hotel at Heathrow that night as we were setting off next day to Australia for our honeymoon. As an employee of BA, Toni got flights for herself and her husband – me – for £50 each; a bargain or what?

I'd had a love of aeroplanes since I was a small boy but this was the first time I'd ever been on one. What a thrill! The crew knew that Toni was 'staff' and that we were honeymooners, we were spoilt rotten. It took over twenty-seven hours in those days to reach Sydney. When our 707 touched down, Toni's big sister, Pat, and her husband, Ron, were on hand to meet us. They packed us and our luggage into their VW Beetle – I still don't know how they did that – and took us to the Charles Hotel on Bronte Beach where we were to stay for a few days at a most advantageous rate, due again to Toni's BA connections, after which we were to spend the remaining two weeks with Pat and Ron at their home. We had a beautiful, sea view room which we hardly left, not because of newly-wed pent-up passion but because we both experienced terrible tummy trouble and couldn't risk being more than a few paces from a loo. That took most of the romance out of the honeymoon, I can tell you.

On the fourth day, by which time pilgrimages to the porcelain had ceased but we still weren't eating, we received a call from someone called Percy King, a friend of Morris Aza's, who would be pleased to come and collect us for drinks. I was yet again impressed by my agent, he seemingly knew people in all parts of the world. An elderly, expensively dressed couple arrived, put us into the back of a large Jaguar and drove us the short distance to their magnificent home, right on Bondi Beach. Percy King and his wife, Jenny Howard, were great friends of Gracie Fields, probably Britain's biggest pre-war star, and Gracie was Morris's auntie – small world. Percy now had his finger on the Sydney club scene.

'I know you're on your honeymoon,' he opened, 'but Morris thinks you might be interested in doing a bit of work over here.' Toni and I nodded in unison. 'I've got a show going into a club on Friday, you'd be an extra act so I couldn't pay you more than $50.'

'I suppose that'll be OK,' I said without enthusiasm while my liver, spleen and kidneys were doing back flips. Fifty dollars, that was £25. The most I earned at home was a tenner a night.

The club was superb, better than a top English night club. It had a restaurant, separate dance floor and a beautifully appointed concert room. I only had to do one spot and the reaction was great. I was fresh meat, a fresh approach with fresh material. Jenny and Percy were delighted. 'I can get you as much work as you want over here,' he said, and so it proved.

The remainder of the honeymoon was spent battling the surf on a sun-drenched beach all day and working either a league (football supporters') or an RSL (like a British Legion) club at night. Toni and I thoroughly enjoyed our evenings in these splendid clubs, only wishing that the places we worked at home were comparable. We returned home with far more money than we'd gone with and a distinct feeling that we should have emigrated to the wonderful country of Australia on our wedding day.

The money came in handy as we'd spent every penny on buying the house. New houses in 1967 comprised four walls and a roof; there were no fittings, no tiles in the bathroom, not even a cooker in the kitchen, but I had two weeks to sort all this out. Toni had to return to London to work a fortnight's notice at BA, time enough surely for me to prepare our semi-detached palace. A handyman I've never been, all my attempts at home improvement have culminated in failure. I attached a cupboard to the kitchen wall. It was fine until I filled it with crockery, at which point it went into free fall. As we had no carpets whatsoever, I bought a goatskin rug which seemingly had a desire to return to the goat. Long hairs detached themselves from it and headed for the front door, there was more of it in the hall than in the lounge. I did a bit better externally, laying slabs, though I stupidly bought the biggest ones which I could neither lift nor manoeuvre, and turf which came looking like green-edged swiss roll. I unrolled the strips placing them side by side, having been assured that the gaps would close up as I watered the grass to encourage its growth. It never resembled the centre court at Wimbledon even from a distance. It was, however, a great way to get to know the neighbours; being all brand-new homes, people were outside all day doing what I was doing. They were a mixed bunch, a fire chief next door, two policemen and, due to the proximity of the Queen Elizabeth hospital, several doctors. There was also a midwife whom I christened Bertha Day. By the end of the fortnight when Toni arrived to take up residence I knew everyone in Pegasus Walk – yes, Pegasus, what an address for a lad needing a flying start to reach stardom!

I soon came to a conclusion following my failures as a handyman, one to which I still subscribe: 'If you want something done, get a man in!' If everyone did his own job without encroaching on anyone else's, the economy would work perfectly. OK, B&Q would go out of business, but we'd not be subjected to those terrible TV shows where people redecorate your house while you're out. *Ground Force* would never have seen the light of day, which means Charlie Dimmock's wayward bosoms would be controlled and Alan Titchmarsh would be a pauper. So I'd pop out, tell jokes, earn money, give money to carpenter, decorator, plumber, and slowly the house would transform.

Money was easier to come by than before, thanks to my new agent, and thanks to him I soon found myself back in the dreaded north-east but, this time, working the Bailey circuit I'd lusted after.

I had hoped to take Toni with me rather than spend weeks away from her. Did you ever see that TV ad where the feller from Birmingham looks into the camera and states, 'We wanna be together!' That could have been me. Toni, though, had found herself a temporary job in the admin department of Birmingham University which was just down the road from our house in Selly Oak. I suppose we needed the extra money but I'd married her so she'd be the last person I saw before I went to sleep and the first person I saw when I woke up; simple enough – none of that 'absence makes the heart grow fonder' rubbish for me.

I was busy working on my act. While in Australia, I'd been introduced to a new American comic called Bill Cosby. He'd made an LP, his first, called 'Why is there Air?' He talked about his childhood, going to nursery and primary school, just being a child. It was revolutionary. No one over here was doing it but was the British public ready for a comedian who didn't tell jokes? I would try it in small doses. The main thing in my favour was that no one except me had ever heard of Bill Cosby.

The venues I worked improved considerably; it was an age of plenty for entertainment. Gambling funded the cabaret clubs but the government were plotting legislation which was to put paid to all that. In retrospect that was the right thing to do if organised crime was to be denied a foothold on our shores.

In June we set off for Clacton. There were the bills: 'STARNITE SPECTACULAR starring DON MACLEAN'. I'd made it. The Westcliff Theatre was wonderful; it has a place in my heart even now. Bunny Baron had put together a great cast of really young performers, we had fun both on and off stage. The show was a marvellous showcase for me; there were two changes of programme and I was involved in each from start to finish. I worked hard on my solo spots, still striving for that elusive style. I also struggled to give a consistent performance; one night I'd work really well, the next I'd be mediocre.

We lived in a bed-sit very near to the theatre. The landlady was a lovely person named Brenda. As a new wife, Toni was keen to develop a reputation as a hostess, inviting the cast of our show and also the cast of the other show at the Ocean Theatre to supper. She'd have been hard-pressed to achieve this on the Baby Belling we had in our room, so Brenda gave her the use of her own kitchen and her dining room for these increasingly popular soirées.

The press again did me proud: '*The show has genuine star quality, Don Maclean is bound for the top. He has that outgoing warm quality which makes instant contact with the audience.*' I was extremely young to be topping a bill and rather like a teenager picked to play for the first team; it was inevitable that the premiership clubs would send scouts to check me out. One day there was a Rolls-Royce parked outside the theatre; not the usual mode of transport for Clacton's holidaymakers. Morris rang the next day to inform me that George Mitchell and Robert Luff, the men who ran the *Black and White Minstrel Show*, had been to see me.

'Why didn't you tell me they were in?' I asked.

'It would have only made you nervous and you'd have tried too hard,' he replied. I had to admit he was probably right. They were looking for a young comic to go into the existing show at the Victoria Palace. It would be a one-year contract and the money would be five times what I was presently being paid. Just think of that, me in a West End show! They would be coming to see me again, Morris told me. They in fact came twice more before booking not me but a young comedy impressionist named Peter Kaye whom they'd seen in another summer show. I had to accept the fact that I wasn't as good as I thought I was. The chance of being in the country's biggest light entertainment show was gone forever, or so it seemed. It made me more determined to improve.

The house, too, began to improve. We managed to afford a cooker so Toni no longer had to use the electric frying pan, we bought some carpet and a two-piece suite – we didn't have enough money for a three-piece. Toni resumed her job but I wanted her to come with me when I worked. The strain of working in an office all day, getting back from a club in the early hours then being up at eight to start again took its toll on her. Something had to go, it was Toni's job. Yes, we needed her money, but this was more important. We could live in one another's pockets as we'd planned. If I died at a club I had a shoulder to cry on.

Toni would stand in the wings listening closely to my act and afterwards make suggestions about the placing of a gag or a line, about where the act went well and where it struggled. We'd often spend some time working out the wording of a gag. I still believe that one wrong word can spoil a gag, but I would see it from a performer's point of view while Toni had a punter's feel, she was the voice of my audience. The act had become *our* act, which it is even to this day.

I worked at Club La Bamba in Darlington. Sharing the bill with me was a tall, good-looking lad who'd just released a record called 'Domage'. It was doing very well on the continent but nothing over here. His name was Jerry Dorsey; perhaps he needed to change it. When Toni first heard him sing she said, 'His voice makes me tingle, he's gonna be a big star,' but what did she know? Not long afterwards we were watching *Sunday Night at the London Palladium* and on he came singing 'Release me'. We didn't know it was him from the billing as he had changed his name – to Englebert. I took Toni's prophecies more seriously after that.

Working up north was all very well but Morris wanted me in London where people would see me. He was determined to get me television exposure. I made a few appearances on a BBC Radio programme called *Take a Bow* but it was TV that mattered. To that end I passed on a panto that Christmas and continued to work clubs with an occasional foray for a one-nighter in the London area. Morris watched me and tried to knock the rough edges off me. Several years in the clubs had made me aggressive. If anyone heckled I took them apart:

'Stand up, let's see if you're as big as your mouth.'

'This is where I work and you're interrupting me. If you don't stop, tomorrow I'll come to where you work and slam the lavatory seat down on your fingers.' I took no prisoners in those days.

'Don't you dare do any of those heckler stoppers on any of the London dates,' Morris warned me. He'd managed to persuade a young BBC television director to come and see me at Battersea Town Hall. It was Terry Hughes, who later went to work in America where he directed *The Golden Girls* and several other sit-coms. Terry said he had just the spot for me. It was even better than I could have hoped for. *Billy Cotton's Music Hall* was about to start an eight-week run on Saturday nights with Terry directing. It was *live* from the BBC Television Centre and I was to do a six-minute spot. Bill Cotton was a lovely old chap, another radio hero from my childhood. No one of my generation can hear 'Wakey, Wakey!' without smelling Sunday dinner and thinking of Bill and his band. He loved nothing better than to say, 'I gave this boy his first chance.' On 11 May 1968, I was that first-timer. The Seekers and Scott Walker were the singing stars but there was no comedy other than mine.

'You'll be all right as soon as you get your first laugh,' said Morris. Bill Cotton finished conducting his band and turned to face the camera. 'Now for the very first time on television, a young man with a great future who's really gonna make ya laugh – Don Maclean.' I walked into the light and the applause.

'I have to admit I'm nervous,' I began. 'I'm so nervous that before I came on, I threw myself on to the floor and missed.' For some reason this gag really appealed to the band, who were directly behind me; they roared with laughter. The audience, not wishing to be left out, joined in. I'd got my first laugh and from then on it was plain sailing. I finished with a chorus of 'Lonely is the man without love', Englebert's new single. The audience reaction was tremendous.

'Tom Jones, Russ Conway, Ted Rogers, stars who made their first TV appearance on my show, and here's another star I've discovered – Don Maclean. You'll be seeing him again later in the series,' said Bill.

I can't remember having ever been so euphoric. We stayed the night with Toni's parents; naturally they'd been in the audience. I sat up in bed refusing to go to sleep, not wanting the day to end. Six weeks later, true to his word, Bill Cotton had me on the show again. The stars that week were Professor Jimmy Edwards, Gene Pitney and Petula Clark. Afterwards Billy Cotton said, 'You've got a big future, lad. Next year I want you on every show, you'll be resident.' He'd done this with people before, Russ Conway and Mrs Mills, though they were pianists not comics. I was made; with that kind of exposure, star status was assured. Sadly it didn't happen. Later that year Bill Cotton died, and with him my direct route to fame.

Television opened every door in those days; well, there were only two channels. BBC2 was starting but very few sets could receive it. Offers for my services flooded in. I did a few local TV appearances, several radio shows, Butlins Holiday Camps. I even had an offer to make a record but Morris and I decided that would be detrimental to my comedy ambitions. I continued to work the clubs, including Greaseborough Miners' Welfare. I was there the week after the infamous (and oft-quoted) announcement by the concert secretary: 'Order, order ladies and gents! We've paid a lot of brass for this next lass and while we're on the subject of brass, we've had new gentlemen's urinals erected in the car park so from now on there'll be no more peeing up the car wheels . . . here she is –

Dusty Springfield!' I do wish I'd been there to hear that. Sadly I wasn't, but it is true.

Toni was travelling with me to every date. We stayed in 'pro digs', most of which were wonderful, though not all. In August, I had a double (that means working at one club then dashing over to repeat your spot at another). The venues in question were the Casino Club, Wigan and the Casino Club, Bolton. They were both awful; no one listened to a word I said. As I left the stage, the compère said, 'That was very nice son.'

I rounded on him. 'Very nice, what do you mean very nice? Nobody listened, nobody laughed.'

'Nay lad nay,' he said. 'Don't tek on, Frank Sinatra come here they wouldn't laff.'

I'd had enough. I rang Morris. 'If I stay here, I'll have no act left by the end of the week,' I whined.

'If it's that bad, just leave,' he said. 'I'll sort things out in the morning.'

'We'll have a week's holiday,' I said to Toni. 'We'll go to Blackpool.'

'I've always wanted to go to Newquay,' she said. Those of you with 'O' level Geography will know that Blackpool is about thirty miles from Wigan whilst Newquay is three hundred plus. Eager to please my bride, who had been acting a tad strangely of late, I set off in our VW Beetle for the south-west. The following night we went to Newquay's famous Cosy Nook theatre to see the summer show featuring Bobby Pattinson – I mentioned him earlier. We got the last two tickets.

Just as the curtain went up, Toni turned to me. 'I've got to get out,' she said. She was deathly white.

I pushed my way to the end of the row and managed to get her into the foyer where she promptly fainted. People gathered round, Toni opened her eyes and said, 'What are all these people doing in my room?' As realisation dawned, she became most distressed. She whispered to me, 'I've wet myself.'

'A glass of water,' I called. 'Can someone get a glass of water for my wife?' The water arrived, I tripped, spilling most of it on the floor next to Toni and averting any embarrassment.

I sold the tickets, there were several people in the foyer waiting for returns, and we set out to walk back to the guest house. Toni loved scampi. I stopped at a fish and chip shop and ordered scampi and chips.

'Ugh, I can't eat that,' she said. The next morning, the lady with whom we were staying put a nice breakfast down in front of us. 'Excuse me, I feel sick,' said Toni rising from the table.

'I think she might have something to tell you,' ventured the landlady, but I'd already guessed.

I wasn't at all sure how I felt about impending fatherhood. I'd expected five years of marriage before the patter of tiny feet, and besides, I didn't really like children. I had little time to contemplate this, however, because Morris had fixed a tour of South Africa for me, compèring a show starring French pop star Johnny Hallyday. The major news story at the time was that Rhodesia under Ian Smith had made a unilateral declaration of independence. Prime Minister Harold Wilson and Smith were meeting aboard a British warship to discuss this development. I finished my act on a topical gag: A woman went into a store in Salisbury and asked for a bra. She was a big girl and they didn't have anything to fit. After much searching through the old stock they managed to find her size – 52 DD. She was delighted until she caught sight of the label which said 'Made in England'.

'No, no,' she said. 'I can't have that.'

'Why not, madam?' said the assistant, 'It's the only one your size in the whole of Rhodesia.'

'I'd rather swing with Smith than rely on Wilson for support,' came the reply.

That even went down well in Pretoria where most of the audience were Afrikaans-speaking. Jo'burg, Durban, Cape Town, the theatres were packed everywhere but the audience was entirely white. I became quite disturbed when black men took off their hats in my presence and, if I spoke to them, addressed me as 'master'. I attended mass several times and was pleased to see that the congregation there at least was mixed. Not so, though, in the Dutch Reformed Church. A minister of the DRC found a black man kneeling in the church,

'What do you think you're doing, kaffir?' he asked.

'I was cleaning the floor, boss,' came the reply.

'That's all right then, but don't you dare let me catch you praying.'

I'm glad to have been back to that beautiful country since the downfall of apartheid and to have interviewed the joyful and charismatic Archbishop Desmond Tutu no less than four times.

But what of Rhodesia? The system there was very different from the apartheid-ridden Republic of South Africa. Their attitude to black Africans was more paternalistic. In those days Rhodesia was the breadbasket of the entire region, with cereal crops as far as the eye could see. They exported vast amounts of copper and tobacco, the economy boomed, they received neither aid nor subsidy from anyone, and every member of the population, no matter what their colour, were well fed. I bet they wish they could go back to those times now. No doubt somebody reading this paragraph will brand me a white supremacist – nothing could be further from the truth, but my heart bleeds for the people of Zimbabwe, terrorised from within and ignored from without.

8

White Heather – Rachel Heather

I'd been away from Toni for three unbearable weeks – I couldn't believe it was possible to miss anyone so much. I could have taken her with me to South Africa but the cost of air fares for her would have been more than I was earning. When I got home she'd bought her maternity wear although the lump was still little more than a gnat bite. She treated me to a fashion show which was fine until she got to the maternity tights. Room for the expected expansion meant that the tights came right up under her armpits.

'How do I look?' asked Toni.

'Like a kangaroo with all the kids on holiday,' I replied. That was the start of a comedy routine about tights which served me well for years.

I began using it the following week. It was the start of a short tour of the stage version of the popular TV show *The White Heather Club*. I was working theatres and those theatres were full. The stars of the show were Scottish folk singers Robin Hall and Jimmy Macgregor, two very different people. Jimmy was a lovable laid-back character while Robin was more of an acquired taste and one that I never got round to acquiring. Also on the bill was a lyric tenor by the name of Ted Darling with whom I would work for many years, though I didn't know that at the time. This was the chance I'd been waiting for. The act improved noticeably; at last the style I'd sought so long was taking shape.

I did mention that pro digs varied somewhat. Arriving for the week in Liverpool we found digs close to the Empire Theatre in Nelson Street, aptly named because no one in possession of both eyes would consider staying there. We approached a grimy guest house where we found a landlady noticeably short of the charm and sense of humour which we are led to believe flows through every Liverpudlian vein.

'Thirty bob a night,' she said with a wink. At first I thought she was being pleasant but quickly realised that the smoke from her half-inch of Woodbine was causing the involuntary flutter of the eyelid over one bloodshot eye.

'Seems OK,' I said, dropping our suitcase on the bed. With a clatter the suitcase slid to the floor and I judged the gradient on the bed to be about one in four. No time to worry about that, we were due at the theatre.

It was with leaden steps that we made our way up Nelson Street after the show that night but, as we got nearer, we could hear singing and the sound of a piano. Anticipating our approach, the landlady opened the door. What a transformation! Make up had been trowelled on, lip gloss, false eyelashes, the lot. The hair had been curled and topped with a tiara. The Woodbine was still in evidence, glowing redly from a long cigarette holder. The picture was completed by a strapless evening gown of white and silver sequins. Everything sparkled, including the teeth which had been conspicuous by their absence at our previous meeting.

'Come in, come in,' she slurred. 'My little boy has returned from the sea.' Her little boy was a short dumpy merchant seaman approximately the same size and shape as his kitbag which languished in the corner. A few of his shipmates were in evidence, so were one or two other guests. The room was filled with cigarette smoke and on top of the piano stood a brass urn with an inscription on the front. All the smokers, including the pianist herself, kept lifting the lid and flicking ash into the urn until eventually the son took it down, looked carefully inside and proclaimed, 'Lord bless us, Mother, Dad's purrin' on a birra weight, I reckon you're feedin' him berra now dan ya did when he was alive.' Gales of laughter greeted his observation and the landlady giggled so much she fell off the piano stool.

'She's absolutely pickled,' I whispered to Toni as the former pianist struggled to regain her seat.

'But she's only drinking tea,' said Toni nodding towards the delicate china cup atop the piano alongside the brimming urn. As we watched, the landlady drained the cup and poured another from the matching china teapot, topping it up from the milk jug.

'Hang on a minute,' I thought. 'Milk doesn't fizz.'

'No but Babycham does,' said the wife, 'especially when it's added to brandy.'

The 'tea' was going down a treat and so was the landlady. When she fell off the stool a second time, we left for bed. The landlady didn't notice our departure; she was too busy trying to fish her eyelash out of the milk jug.

We spent a particularly wretched night. Even after the festivities petered out we were denied sleep by the slope on the bed. It was so steep that I kept sliding towards Toni and nearly suffocating her. Inevitably we changed sides, which helped not at all as my extra weight increased the gradient. In order to stop herself rolling on top of me, Toni slept with one foot on the floor and her hand hanging on to the curtains.

'I can't stand another night here,' were the first words she spoke in the morning. We threw everything into the case and carried it into the small hallway. There she was. Tiara, eyelashes, teeth had gone, only the Woodbine remained, fighting for purchase on the lipless mouth.

'Wha's all dis den? Where d'ya tink you'se a goin'?'

'I'm afraid this place is not up to the standard we're used to,' I replied.

'Oh, not good enough for the borrom of de bill? Stars have bin 'ere; Frankie Vaughan, Jimmy Tarbuck, Cilla.'

'I'm not arguing,' I said. 'We're going, here's your three quid.'

'Tree quid! Tree quid, youse owe me six quid.'

'You said thirty bob a night and that's what you're getting.' I was angry now.

'It's thirty bob a night for people what stays de whole week.'

'I should imagine that's a rare occurrence,' I riposted and made for the door.

'I know youse,' she shouted after us. 'I'll get de po-lice onta youse, they'll be at the stage door tonight.' Needless to say the police never arrived. I should imagine our three pounds found its way into the china teapot that same evening. Mind, I'm not one to bear a grudge, I've recommended those digs to several people in showbusiness; the ones that have upset me.

* * *

After five glorious *White Heather* weeks, panto season was upon us. Bunny Baron's production at Lewisham was to be *Aladdin* again, the same as I'd done in Weston. Widow Twanky was to be another of my radio heroes, Derek Roy.

Lewisham was a terrible place to work; for a start it was a concert hall, not a theatre. The auditorium had a flat floor on to which lines of seats were bolted with a large butterfly nut securing each end. There was a small circle but this only accommodated about a hundred patrons. The audience, too, left much to be desired, groups of kids with no one to supervise them, running riot while we attempted to show them the delights of Old Peking.

One night we were visited by a large party from a notorious estate. Each year they had a Christmas outing. The previous one had been to the ice show and they'd melted the ice; the year before they'd been taken to the circus and the lions had refused to come out for the second half; this year we got 'em – innumerable unwashed children under the supervision of a mere eight adults, all of whom went over the road to the Black Horse as soon as the show started. And what a start! Standing behind the tabs we were surprised when after about sixty seconds the overture suddenly stopped. We learned afterwards that a well directed orange, launched from the stalls, had taken out the MD's music stand, scattering the score of the show all over the floor of the pit. This had to be collected up before the overture could recommence. The Genie of the Ring began her opening speech and was hit just above the eye by a bar of chocolate. She was quite badly cut but the St John Ambulance raced to her rescue. Every kid in the audience had been given a paper bag of goodies which they had no intention of eating; at the interval we swept up over three pounds of sweets from the stage.

The major incident, though, occurred just prior to the interval. You'll recall that Abanazar takes Aladdin to a cave wherein lies the magic lamp. He can't go and get it himself, if he does so he'll be struck dead; only an innocent boy can enter the cave. Abanazar was played by an elderly Shakespearean actor, Harry Orchid. Plagued by gout, Harry wore carpet slippers with the sides cut out to accommodate his throbbing toe joints, even on stage. Understandably he was never in pleasant mood. Looking towards the audience, his head and upper torso framed in the entrance to the cave, he demanded the lamp from the boy. Aladdin, Vikki Lane, was in the cave, lamp in hand, and the audience were actually listening to what was going on – obviously they'd used up all the ammo in their paper bags.

'Give me the lamp, boy.'

'Sharn't.'

'Then I shall close this cave and leave you to rot and die – heed my curse.' Harry's curse was the highspot of his night. Soliloquies as Henry V and Hamlet in his former career had equipped Harry to inspire awe with his vocal resonance, but the audience that night had other ideas. Before he could speak, a chorus of 'Off, off, off' came from the front stalls. This was immediately taken up by the entire audience. As they 'off, off, offed' they stamped in time to their chant.

Despite Harry's vocal projection there was no way he was going to get over that. Radio mikes had not yet been invented; there was only one mike on stage, that was the centre riser which went up and down when needed rather like an electric car aerial. Abanazar stepped through the hole in the cloth which formed the entrance to the cave. The audience stilled – well he'd told them that if he entered the cave he'd be struck dead and they didn't want to miss that bit. Aladdin stood transfixed; this wasn't in the script. When Abanazar didn't fall to the floor in mortal agony, the audience found their voice and their feet once more: 'Off, off, off,' but Harry had, by now, reached the front of the stage and the mike which rose to meet him. He began the famous curse again.

'You've wrecked my plans for this I'll make you pay. You never more shall see the light of day.'

'Off, off, off,' screamed the little terrorists.

'Don't you want to hear what I have to say?' asked Abanazar in desperation.

'No,' they chorused as one man.

'Oh, sod ya then!' said Harry, and, for the first time in a long and distinguished career, left the stage.

The cheers from the kids were deafening. Aladdin looked round despairingly but the quick-witted MD struck up the intro to a number she would be singing later in the show. The audience paused, in fact they fell silent but as Vikki opened her mouth a single clear voice rang out: 'Fer Christ's sake don't sing – rub the bleetin' ring.'

Vikki rubbed. The pyro went off and a surprised Genie appeared sporting a large plaster over a black eye. This was the cue for yet more missiles to be hurled towards the stage; the audience hadn't used up all their ammo after all. An alert stage hand brought the curtain down and the cast licked their wounds ready for the second half.

I was pleased when that panto run ended, for many reasons. Apart from the theatre and its clientele, the baby would be arriving within weeks and I was also eager to see my good friend David Charles again.

Dave and I had struck up a really firm friendship. He was the first real male friend I'd had since my days with Pat Barr at St Philip's. We'd met a couple of years earlier while working a club together. What a great singer he was! Born with a cleft palate, Dave had been encouraged to have singing lessons to improve his speech. They soon discovered that he possessed a voice that soared ever upwards. When you thought he'd hit the top of his range, he'd then go up another tone, he was amazing. He also accompanied himself on rhythm guitar. About a year earlier, the two of us had teamed up with 'The Three Jays' – as the name suggests, three girls, Jill, Joy and Jill who did a very professional, modern-day Beverley Sisters act. We went round as a self-contained show and were in great demand. We'd had some fabulous nights together. David and his wife, Maria, had two children, Sharon who was three and Andrew, our godson, who was eight months old. They arranged a babysitter so that the four of us could have a night out as soon as we returned from Lewisham. We wined and dined our ladies at La Reserve Theatre Restaurant, Sutton Coldfield, dancing the night away until two in the morning. What a fabulous night it was, we laughed until we cried which was the norm when we were together.

The next morning I was at 'Barry's', the trendy hairdressers which both Dave and I frequented. Afterwards I intended to drop in on Dave at the used car dealership where he worked part-time; it was virtually next door to the hairdressers. I was sat in the chair, listening to Barry's jokes, none of which were suitable for mixed audiences, when John from the dealership burst in. Despite the cold, he wore no coat and he was sweating profusely.

'Don! It's Dave, he's been killed in a car crash!' He buried his face in his hands and sank to the floor. I was dumbstruck but Barry began bombarding John with questions: 'When, where, how?'

Apparently David had set off for March in Cambridgeshire, where he'd appeared the previous week in a cabaret club. While on the A47, he'd overtaken a lorry and smashed head first into another lorry coming towards him.

I had to get home. I left immediately with my half-finished hair cut. I didn't in fact go straight home, I stopped at St Edward's, the nearest Catholic church. It may seem illogical to you but it wasn't to me at the time. I didn't genuflect as I would have normally done nor did I kneel. I marched up the centre aisle, stood in front of the altar and screamed at God.

'Why? Why has this happened? Why has this great talent been snuffed out? What about Maria and the kids?' I don't know if I expected answers but I got none. I left the church in more sober mood, glad that it had been empty and that no one had witnessed the confrontation I'd attempted with my Lord and Saviour.

I dashed home to my very pregnant wife, who was as distraught as me at the news. Together we went to Maria. A WPC was with her.

'She won't accept it,' she whispered to me before she left.

'It's not him,' Maria kept saying. 'Obviously somebody else was driving his car.'

David's mother and father arrived looking dreadful, then Maria's parents came. Everyone except Maria was crying. She stood in the middle of it all repeating, 'It's not him. I know it's not him.'

'What about Keith?' said David's dad. Keith was the younger brother; he idolised Dave. He had a day off from work which he was spending with his girlfriend. They knew her name and the road in which she lived but not the number. As no one else was capable of accepting the task, I set off to find Keith. I rang a few doorbells before I found the right one.

Telling Keith was one of the hardest things I've ever done. That afternoon I drove Keith, his dad and David's father-in-law to

Uppingham, Rutland, so that they could identify the body. They'd done their best but the injuries sustained were very apparent. Keith fell on to his brother, his body heaving with loud sobs; his dad stroked his hair. I stood aside, busy with my own thoughts. We drove home in complete silence, no one spoke a word; it was the longest journey I've ever made in a car. Back home with Toni my control finally went. Tears I had not shed over the body of my friend burst from me then. Toni tried to comfort me but I pushed her away. I needed to be alone to weep that day.

Keith and I attended the inquest the following week, where we learned that David had been thrown clear of his car with such force that he'd left his shoes inside. In 1969, seat belts weren't fitted in cars.

We buried David on a cold, cold February day. There were hundreds there. The overriding emotion I felt was anger, 'Why?' – a question I would ask my God many, many more times concerning many different happenings during my life.

Keith could not come to terms with the loss of his brother. Several weeks later he was neither eating nor sleeping. His girl-friend, who later became his wife, took him to see a spiritualist on the south coast. This lady, who had no prior knowledge of David, had many truly amazing things to say to Keith. She spoke of an aunt who had been very fond of David when he was a baby but had died before Keith was born. Disturbingly she also mentioned the framed photograph of David which she said was in the window surrounded by flowers. Keith knew this to be incorrect as the photo was kept on the mantelpiece. He returned home to find that, after he had left that morning, his mother had bought some flowers, put them in the window and moved David's photograph next to them. Keith found peace from that moment. During the 1914–18 war, many people who had lost their sons, including Sir Arthur Conan-Doyle, Rudyard Kipling and Mrs Asquith, the Prime Minister's wife, were comforted by Spiritualism but I must say that, as a Christian who has direct access to the living God, I would never be tempted in that direction myself.

I was wanted by the *White Heather Club* for another tour, starting in March. Toni was radiant and extremely well in the late stages of pregnancy. She was determined to keep travelling with me for as long as possible. My mother-in-law was furious: 'You should be at home, within reach of your hospital, not gallivanting round the country.' None the less we spent the first week of March at the Congress Theatre, Eastbourne, the second week at the Wimbledon Theatre, and Toni would have travelled with me to the New Theatre, Hull on 17 March but the baby was due that week.

Mobile phones are a great invention, especially in an emergency, but such things were far in the future. The arrangement was for me to ring Toni from the stage door phone as soon as I arrived at the theatre each evening. It was about six o'clock on the Tuesday.

'I'm glad you've rung,' she said calmly, 'I was just waiting to hear from you, now I'm off to the hospital.' She'd been in mild labour since early morning.

'I'll come home at once,' I said.

'No, come home after the show,' she advised. 'I don't suppose it'll be that quick.'

The whole performance that night was a blur. I dashed out from the stage door with the good wishes of the cast ringing in my ears. I arrived at Selly Oak Hospital in the early hours. Toni was in a ward and had been given something to make her sleep. She just about managed to acknowledge my presence then drifted off again.

'She won't have it till the morning,' said a nurse confidently.

I went home to bed. When I woke, I dressed quickly and dashed to the hospital. Toni was in the delivery room and in strong labour. She looked very distressed and I felt completely helpless. I kissed her and said, 'You'll have to have this baby soon, I've got to start back for Hull at half past eleven.' It would be Wednesday, matinée day, wouldn't it?

'You can't stay here,' said the large West Indian midwife. 'Wait outside.' The delivery room had two beds in it, there was another mother bearing down at the same time so I was not allowed to be there. Instead of retiring to the waiting room as instructed, I stood against the door. Every time it opened I slipped in, and every time the West Indian midwife pushed me out again.

Eventually, at almost exactly eleven o'clock, the door opened and the big black face split into a wide grin, 'In you come,' she said.

Toni was lying there with a small bundle in the crook of her arm. I hugged Toni, carefully I hasten to add, then turned my attention to my brand-new daughter. Her eyes were shut tight. I kissed her gently on the forehead, her eyes opened and she gave me a beautiful smile. I was instantly lost. That moment there began a love affair that persists to this day.

I set off for Hull in a daze. I really couldn't cope with the emotions which gripped me. I couldn't believe what Toni had done for me, given birth to my child, nor could I understand why I felt so strongly about this small creature who an hour before didn't even exist. I'll be honest with you, I didn't think that much about her before she was born, I definitely felt no affection towards her; but in a fraction of a second God had kitted me out with unconditional love. I knew instinctively that I would love her always, that no man would ever love her as much as I did and that nothing she would ever do could blight that love for an instant.

That night after the show we wet the baby's head; the Scots are experts at such things. Filled with a love for my fellow man and for those around me in particular, I informed them that my daughter would be named Rachel *Heather* in tribute to each and every one of them.

Tributes, in the form of press reviews, were heading my way too: '*A noteworthy newcomer is Don Maclean, from Birmingham despite his Scottish name. Fast-talking, energetic, very funny, he is quite the best laughter-maker I have seen for a very long time. The string of new jokes is unending and every one of them clean. This show is worth a visit for Don's performance alone.*' I was really sorry when that tour came to an end. The *WHC* had done so much for me. It had enabled me to be seen by people who would book me in the future, it had taught me to work a theatre audience and it had enabled me to continue developing an original style – it was nearly there!

More telly was on offer, including several appearances on a great comedy game show called *Jokers Wild.* Hosted by Barry Cryer, it pitted two teams of three comedians against one another in a gagathon. The format suited me down to the ground and, as an added bonus, I enjoyed the company of Ted Ray, probably the best patter comic of his generation. I was also befriended by Les

Dawson, a warm-hearted giant of comedy. That was for Yorkshire Television.

BBC North was based in Leeds too and they produced *The Good Old Days*. My second visit to the City Varieties was far less painful than the first. Barney Colehan, the producer, loved to find obscure music-hall songs for all the comics. On my first appearance I sang a song about a stage performer:

> He's a pro, he's a pro,
> and he'll make us all laugh in a minute or so,

went the chorus. For my second appearance, it was a fireman who got the attention:

> Running up the ladder with me squirter,
> they all shout fire, fire, fire.
> When the old alarm bell goes,
> I'm on the job with me little bit of hose.
> Everybody thinks that I'm a hero,
> my courage they admire.
> Once the nozzle got so hot
> that I nearly dropped the lot
> in the fire, fire, fire, fire, fire!

They were great shows and they gave me invaluable experience of working to the camera, but Morris was waiting for the big Saturday night show on BBC TV. He learned that the Billy Cotton slot would be filled by *The Castle Room*, a variety show hosted by Roy Castle, Mr Multi-talent himself. Yes they would have me for the show but instead of being resident as I would have been on Bill's show, I was booked for just one appearance. I was thrilled to meet Roy – we were later to become good friends – and also to meet Cilla Black. She too would be important in my life, though I didn't know that then. The show went OK but it didn't make any waves as I'd hoped. I felt rather disappointed.

Summer was to be spent at the Pier Theatre, Llandudno. The show was the *White Heather Club*. Yes, I know what you're thinking, kilts and bagpipes, just the thing for north Wales, especially during this important year in the history of the principality, with Prince

Charles being invested as Prince of Wales. The cast was drastically changed. Robin and Jimmy were replaced by Chick Murray whom I thought was wonderful though the locals must have collectively decided to duck because everything he said went over their heads:

'I went to the doctor's today, he gave me a recipe. I took the recipe to the chemist who took one look at it and said "Oh it's from Lance." He said, "You're due some pills, shall I put them in a box?" I said, "Please do, it'll save me rolling them all the way home." '

Chick's humour appealed to me but off stage he would tell the most outrageous lies, most of them relating to his future career; one day he'd have had a script accepted for a television drama series, the next he was off to Hollywood to make a film, or Stanley Baxter had asked him to tour in a play: 'It's a two-hander of course, just him and me.' I never worked out whether Chick believed all this, we certainly didn't.

I spent all my spare time developing the important father–daughter relationship. I now had two women to please; would I have enough love to go round? Surprisingly, yes! I would wake up when Rachel woke, dress her and take her out to buy a large punnet of strawberries which Toni and I would then have for breakfast. She travelled everywhere on my shoulders, holding on to my ears for support and steering. She was on my shoulders when Prince Charles, having landed by boat at the end of the pier, walked down past the theatre within touching distance of us.

Toni and I played a lot of tennis, which seemed to be the best way to mingle with the pros from the other shows at the Arcadia and Happy Valley theatres. I wasn't very good at tennis but I did like the feel of a racquet in my hand; could there be another racquet sport at which I might excel?

Regional television was the latest idea to come out of the BBC. In Birmingham, BBC output came from various old houses and converted churches in the Edgbaston area, but that was about to change. A wonderful complex was being built at Pebble Mill. Colour, too, was coming the way of the British viewer. What a difference that would make! You couldn't very well have a programme called *Rainbow* in black and white could you? And snooker would be a revelation; instead of all the balls being the same colour we'd be able to tell which was which. I was contacted at Llandudno by Edmund Marshall, a producer who just happened to be an old boy of SPGS. He was planning a documentary to be called *Stand Up Comic*. It was to feature Dick Lawler, a local comic in his seventies and therefore in the autumn of his career; Bob Hatch, really the top Birmingham comedian at the time, in his late forties; and me as the newcomer, just starting out. Jokes were told and comparisons made. I came out of the programme rather well and my name was noted by a young radio executive, Jock Gallagher. You'll see where he fits in a bit later.

No more offers of TV shows were forthcoming and there seemed to be nothing happening on the panto front. I knew that Bunny Baron would have a panto for me but Morris was holding out for a number one venue. At times like that you have to trust your agent's judgement but it's asking a lot. In October, that's leaving it late, someone from the Tom Arnold office came to see me work and immediately booked me to play Idle Jack in *Dick Whittington* at the Bradford Alhambra. Tom Arnold was the biggest name in panto, I'd cracked it!

We rented a house which was surprisingly cheap, we soon found out why. It was on the edge of the moor; at night you could hear Cathy calling Heathcliff and vice versa. The wind tore into the house; there was nothing between us and the Urals. We couldn't wait to go to the theatre for a warm. Soon after we opened, the cold got to Toni and she succumbed to a dreadful bout of flu. I left her tucked up in bed and took Rachel to the theatre with me, but what to do with a nine-month-old child while I went on stage was the question. Easy, really; before each entrance, I'd run up to the wardrobe where the wardrobe mistress had a large skip always full of costumes waiting to be washed. I'd drop Rachel into it and there she'd sit, quite happily, until I came to retrieve her. Toni soon recovered but for a week I'd proved that I could be both mother and father to my child!

Rachel took her first steps at the Alhambra Theatre, she also grew teeth. If she really liked something she'd bite it, and she really liked me. She bit my face so badly that I required hospital treatment. The story made the *Daily Mirror* under the headline 'Rachel's a right little nipper'. Top of the bill was Vince Hill. He and his wife Ann adored our rapidly growing baby, and after the biting incident, christened her 'Rachel Ratbag', a sobriquet that stuck for many a long year. Also on the bill playing Alderman Fitzwarren was Bobby Dennis. What a funny comic he was, and very original in approach. We spent quite some time discussing comedy style. He cleared away the fog from my mind, I now knew that I could put my own original mark on my comedy act. More on how to obtain an honours degree in comedy later!

A man from the Ministry of Defence had been to see me in panto. It was Derek Agutter, father of actress Jenny. He asked me to go on a tour for CSE (Combined Services Entertainment). I would be following in the footsteps of Vera Lynn and entertaining the boys in khaki. Together with several other acts and musicians, I boarded a VC10 at Brize Norton bound for Singapore. When we arrived there was no one to entertain. The Army, supported by the RAF, had that very day gone off to invade Burma. It was just an exercise, you understand, but everything was on a war footing so had they stopped us from coming that would have given the game away and 'the enemy' would have been alerted. We did a concert for the wives who'd been left behind and thoroughly enjoyed our ten days at liberty in Singapore.

On the way back we were to land at Gan Island in the Maldives and perform for the RAF castaways. What a place! Starved of entertainment, the airmen were a brilliant audience. We were then transported by Air Sea Rescue launch to various other tiny atolls where we entertained groups of radio experts; sometimes there were more of us than there were of them. I was taught how to scuba dive and often wonder why I've never been back to this jewel of God's creation.

9

Blackpool Beckons

The armed forces' tour of duty on Gan was one year – twelve whole months without seeing your family. I'd only been away a fortnight but I was pining for my girls. When I got home, thirteen-month-old Rachel refused to have anything to do with me; she turned her back and walked off. I'd opened my suitcase and dropped it in the lounge. When Toni and I returned to the lounge, Rachel had climbed into the suitcase and was covering herself with my dirty shirts, holding my socks to her chest. At first I thought it funny but then I realised that this small person was showing how she had missed me in the only way she could. I made a pact with myself that I would take her and Toni everywhere with me, regardless of expense; we were a family and families should be together.

Back to that degree in comedy: 'He who tries to analyse humour proves he has none,' said a wise man whose name escapes me, but that was exactly what I was doing. It wasn't so much the material but the approach to an audience that mattered, I concluded. I had to play to my natural strengths which were speed and attack. I worked hard on articulation; the more rapid the speech, the more articulate it has to be. I had natural aggression and a large mouth with plenty of teeth – perhaps the aggression could be sweetened by a boyish smile. A comedy spot in a theatre show would be no more than twelve minutes, not long in which to score. I had to be funny with everything at my disposal: voice, face, body and legs. Stance is important, it conveys your intention to the audience. With mike in hand I leaned towards them, knees bent, ready to pounce. The gag lines – and I emphasise 'lines', there were no 'jokes' in my act – came out fast. No need for the audience to laugh at every line – if they only laughed at every third line, I was still getting continuous laughter. Laughter is infectious, I knew that, so I'd find the ready laughers in an audience and home in on them, knowing that those around them would have to join in.

I now had the theory all worked out but where could I try it out? The Bradford panto had been directed by Maurice Fournier and Peter Roberts; Peter is now Sir Cameron Mackintosh's right-hand man. They recommended me for a summer show which had been devised by Maurice Fournier and which was to open at the North Pier Theatre, Blackpool on 5 June. I wouldn't believe it until I signed the contract at the end of April. Blackpool! The mecca of variety theatre and I was to be in a Bernard Delfont show there.

We rented a ground-floor flat with a landlady named Mary who fortunately loved children. The show had a fantastic cast: the Barron Knights, Peter Gordeno and his Dancers, teenage trumpeter Nigel Hopkins, sultry singer Sheila Southern, and one of the top comics of the day, Joe Church. I was to be in the opening, the finale and to play Lieutenant Pinkerton in the Madame Butterfly sketch. I also had an eleven-minute spot, very early in the first half. The opening night was an immense personal triumph. My comedy approach worked better than I could ever have hoped. I bombarded the audience, they reacted and by the end they were rocking with laughter. I felt a sense of power. I finished with 'Hava Negila' which further added to their mirth. The only black cloud was that I'd done thirteen minutes instead of eleven and had my wrist slapped by the stage manager.

The next night and the next were the same, I literally stopped the show. On the third night the people from the Delfont office came again.

'Don't dash off after the show,' said the stage manager, 'there'll be some people to see you.' They came to my dressing room, three men in expensive overcoats with velvet collars.

'We're altering the show round slightly,' said the spokesman. 'We'd like you to do your act in the second half, immediately before the Barron Knights.'

'But that's Joe Church's spot,' I said. 'What about Joe?'

'Joe will do your spot in the first half.'

'Does Joe know?' I asked, suddenly realising that this could mean the end of a friendship with a man I greatly admired.

'We've spoken to Joe, he understands the situation, he'll be OK about it. Now is there anything you're worried about?'

'Yes,' I said; they leaned forward. 'There's an illuminated sign for the show at the entrance to the pier, everyone else's name's on it but not mine.'

'We'll see to it,' said the man, and with that they left. I was thrilled that my success in the show had resulted in my being elevated up the bill but I was truly worried about the effect it would have on Joe. He was in fact a far bigger man than that. He'd worked every major theatre in the country including seven seasons at the London Palladium. He was very philosophical.

'Look,' he said. 'You're going so well at the beginning of the show that nothing can follow you; everything comedywise that comes after you is an anti-climax. Every year somebody takes the headlines in Blackpool, this is your year, you're the new sensation.'

A few days later, when I arrived at the pier, there was my name, 'Don Maclean', with lights behind it. I needed to look at it from a distance. I took a step back, then another. I heard a loud blast on a horn, there was a tram bearing down on me. I looked at my feet, I was right in the middle of the tram lines. I leaped for my life but believe me had I been struck by that tram I would have died a happy man. Joe Church became my mentor, giving me guidance and encouragement. I made a vow that when in the future I was usurped by a younger comic, as I inevitably would be, I'd be like Joe Church. He died not too long ago but the admiration I have for him lives on.

We were at the North Pier for eighteen weeks. I couldn't wait to get to work any night. They were wonderful days. The cast had several children between them, and we all used to meet on a patch of beach near to the South Pier and spend sunny, sandy days together. Being near the end of the show, my act went even better. I tried bits of new material but it was style and approach that I was concentrating on and that improved nightly. In August I received a further and completely unexpected boost. Ronald Bryden, the serious drama critic of the *Observer*, a man of great stature in journalism and theatre, visited as many piers as he could around the coast of Britain for a series of articles he was writing. Brighton, Bournemouth, Yarmouth, Morecambe, little impressed him until he got to Blackpool's North Pier:

> *On the North Pier, Peter Gordeno and his dancing girls grin and sweat through strenuous routines for a grudging hand-clap. Joe Church, a hard-working comedian, reminds you that the evening's fun depends on you too. 'Let's put a little life in it', but the hit of the evening is Don Maclean, a dark-haired, wicked young comic who works like a high-speed welder, showering acid, one-line gags over an audience almost too fast for laughs. The skill and pace are hard to resist and the material's all fresh. He's cheered like an outrageous licensed nephew at a family wedding, the one in the sharp suit.*

That appeared in the paper on Sunday 30 August; on the Monday, the men in the smart overcoats arrived again. Billy Marsh was the most important agent in the country. He was thin and bald and he smoked constantly, never removing the fag from his mouth. The ash would get longer and longer until it dropped off, of its own volition, usually landing on his expensive overcoat. He showed me the draft of a document which he and my agent Morris Aza would sign, the gist of which said, 'It is agreed that we shall jointly endeavour to further Don Maclean's career by all means at our disposal with special emphasis on live performances and television appearances.'

Things were moving faster than I believed possible. The following week a full-page article appeared in a national newspaper in which Billy Marsh announced to the nation who would be the comedy stars of the future, names such as Peter Hudson, Larry Grayson, Norman Collier and, top of the list, Don Maclean, '*I wouldn't be surprised if the Palladium grabs him shortly*' it said. Within a few days, I had a contract to appear in the Englebert Humperdink show for a season at the London Palladium. Now things were moving *too* fast.

It was November and bitterly cold, but I can't describe the warmth we felt as we stood at the front of the world's foremost variety theatre looking at my name and my photographs. There was a large picture of me almost at ground level; without hesitation,

Rachel walked over and kissed it. The Dallas Boys, me and Clodagh Rogers were the first half, leaving Englebert to do the whole of the second half. Louis Benjamin who ran the Palladium and Billy Marsh arranged a meeting with me and Morris – it was a 'good talking-to' really: 'You're in the West End of London now, the audiences are sophisticated, they're not northern holidaymakers. The stuff you did in Blackpool won't go down here.'

Now I was worried! I'd thought that I could repeat the act that had done so well all summer. Morris contacted Eric Davidson, who had written material for my first few TV spots. He wrote an opening and several lines. When he'd finished there was very little of the Blackpool material left. Opening night, I was a nervous wreck – unusual for me, I've always taken performing in my stride. Telegrams arrived, including one from Gracie Fields which I cherish.

The house was full to capacity. The Dallas Boys opened with a great twenty minutes, then it was my turn. There was no compère nor any off-stage announcement, the music played and on I strode. The audience burst into wild applause which then abruptly stopped. I heard a few disappointed 'Ohs!' In my immaculate midnight-blue mohair suit, and sporting black hair and sideburns, I'd been mistaken by the short-sighted and those at the back for Englebert himself. Needless to say the first few gags went for nothing. I was struggling and beginning to panic. I made the mistake of looking into the audience. In the front stalls I could see so many famous faces: Tom Jones and his manager, Gordon Mills, Racquel Welsh, Des O'Connor and Leslie Grade were just some I recognised; I went from bad to worse. The twelve minutes seemed a lifetime, I was so glad to leave the stage.

At the interval, Billy Marsh came backstage. 'Not what we'd expected son,' he said through a haze of smoke.

'It was the new material,' I countered. 'I haven't had time to judge the strength of it.'

'What was wrong with the stuff you did at Blackpool?'

'You told me not to do that,' I said.

'I certainly did not,' replied Billy.

'But you did, the audiences in the West End are sophisticated you said.'

'No certainly not,' repeated Billy. 'You must have misunder-stood me.'

I understood him well enough; I'd failed and he was determined not to take the blame. I lost all confidence in him then. He might be the top agent in the country but he'd told me that this London audience was different from the Blackpool audience, which was rubbish; they were exactly the same. Over the next few days I sneaked nearly all the summer season material back into the act and by the end of the first week I was getting good laughs again. Even so, I felt I'd missed my chance, as indeed I had. However, nothing could take away from me the fact that I'd appeared at the Palladium. I was to do so several more times but that first time is still the most thrilling – and not only for me; my father-in-law, Tom, would turn up at the theatre most nights and sit in the dressing room with me. He too couldn't believe my luck. 'If I was you, I'd sleep here as well,' he said.

By contrast, my Mom and Dad didn't bother to come. 'Too far,' they decided.

Straight from the Palladium, we went to Oxford for panto, *Sleeping Beauty*, in which I was to play Presto the Jester. Jimmy Edwards was the King and a man I'd seen often on telly played the boisterous, bumbling Queen – my first meeting with Peter Glaze. It was a bad panto and I was pretty bad in it but the three of us, Toni, Rachel and I, were happy enough. We'd learned our lesson at Bradford and had rented a lovely warm house at Cowley. Mom and Dad came to stay for a week and during the time they were with us, their house in Ombersley Road was burgled. The villains, with plenty of undisturbed time, took everything; only the furniture was left. Do burglars realise the trauma they leave behind? So often you hear people say, 'I feel violated, strangers have been through my things.' They could go through my things as often as they liked as long as they left them where they were, but I do understand what they mean. Mom felt exposed in that house, she became nervy and unable to sleep. Toni and I decided that we would buy a house near to us and that Mom and Dad would live in it. The house in Sparkbrook was rented so there would be no money from its sale to provide a deposit. We bit the bullet, took out a mortgage and they came to live just down the road; you could see their front door from our front drive.

Nothing seemed to be forthcoming from BBC Television. Had they lost interest? Regional television, though, decided to follow up on the success of *Stand Up Comic*. They got me to front a one-off show called *Seventy in the Shade*, a comedy look back at the year just gone. There I encountered John Clark, a director with a sharp feel for comedy. BBC Midlands then booked me as host and question master of a newly devised quiz called *Out for the Count*. The rules were based loosely on boxing, questions being rated 'haymaker', 'body blow' or 'upper cut'. Teams represented their county of origin. The show ran for seven weeks. It was a departure for regional television, being genuine entertainment. Its high ratings embarrassed certain people. Then, as now, there was an element at the BBC who thought the Corporation existed to dispense news and current affairs to the nation; anything else was irrelevant.

I was upset when they failed to commission a second series, and with good reason. I'd worked out that to succeed I needed to do something other than stand-up comedy on TV. I think I've always had the ability to evaluate myself. In the days before video recorders it wasn't possible to watch oneself, but I'd done three TV spots on *It's Tarbuck, Crowther's in Town* and *The Lena Martell Show*, all of which were pre-recorded, so I could watch them when they were transmitted. I wasn't pleased with what I saw. I had to be honest and admit that, on television, I had none of the impact that I achieved on stage. I found it difficult to work to the camera, trying instead to work to the studio audience. While the act went well with two hundred people in a studio, it was less successful with two people sitting at home in their living room. I imagined them pinned to the far wall by my aggression. What came over the footlights was very different from what came out of the tube.

Other comedians have suffered from the same thing, notably Ken Dodd who's considerably funnier on stage than he's ever been on TV. Bob Monkhouse is another, though he has cleverly built his reputation on a staircase of game shows, each a step better than the last. To truly appreciate the genius that is

Monkhouse, you have to experience him live. Think of the success Ronnie Corbett was to have a few years later, sitting in a chair. Dave Allen was achieving great acclaim perched on a stool but no one had thought of a way to calm down my manic stage approach for TV.

A producer named Johnny Hamp had gathered together a stable of mainly northern comics and was making a series called *The Comedians* for Granada Television. His technique was to fill a large studio with hysterical laughers then parade the comics in front of them one at a time. He'd record everything then spend hours in editing, chopping up each routine, inter-splicing one comic with another. It worked for television audiences. It made a few stars: Frank Carson, Mike Reid, Duggie Brown. It halted the career of Ken Goodwin, a very funny Manchester lad who was really going places before *The Comedians*, and it killed off stand-up comedy as we knew it on TV. An incinerator of material, by the end of the fourth series the general public had heard every joke that had ever been written over and over again. Yes, if you're wondering, I was asked by Johnny Hamp to be on his next series in 1972, but I turned it down.

Back to 1971, I got side-tracked a little there – sorry! Things were starting to go a bit pear-shaped. The Delfont summer show at Great Yarmouth starring Norman Wisdom, which I had been promised, fell through; ironically my place in it was taken by Joe Church. Feeling rather sorry for ourselves, Toni and I, with Rachel in tow, turned up for a Sunday night variety show at the Victoria Palace. I closed the first half with the act I'd worked on so hard for Yarmouth. I was delighted with the reception. I dashed back to the dressing room but someone was there before me.

'Bryan Feyon,' he said extending a hand. He followed me into the dressing room. 'You were fantastic.'

'Thanks,' I said.

'How'd ya like to go to Australia?' Toni and I were immediately interested.

'Love to,' I said. 'When do you have in mind?'

'I could get you on a plane Thursday,' came the reply.

This may strike you as slightly bizarre as indeed it did me; an explanation was forthcoming. St George's League Club was the biggest venue in Sydney at the time. They had booked a show called *Tokyo by Night*, plenty of dancing, plenty of spectacular circus-type acts but no one in the cast who either spoke or even sang in English. Yes, I know they could have got an Aussie comic to fill the gap but they had a reputation to maintain. Bryan Feyon was in London, scouting for acts, so the club had phoned him saying, 'Grab the nearest Pommie comic and throw him on a plane.' When one door closes another opens, I often wonder how much the good Lord has to do with that.

Morris Aza was none too pleased, he was trying to build my career and I was leaving the country. But what was on offer for me? A few Sunday concerts, odd nights at Butlins. For the first time I went against the wishes of my agent and by the end of that week we were in Sydney.

We rented a beautiful flat on Cronulla Beach. It was idyllic. Ron Wayne turned up almost immediately. A philosophical bloke was Ron, he realised that he wasn't going to break into television at home so he reasoned, 'If I've got to work clubs, I'll work clubs in the warmth and the sunshine.' He'd been in Sydney with his family for nearly a year. Ron took me off to the car auctions and I bought a Simca Aronda for $100. We were mobile and we were independent.

The show at St George's was a triumph. It was sold out anyway and, with very few adaptations, my comedy material appealed to the Sydney audience. Word got round and several local comics came to see me, notebooks at the ready. Toni was delighted to be able to spend time with her sister Pat, who helped out with babysitting so that we could attend a few social functions. Mind, many of those were far from convivial. Once there it was impossible for us to stay together. At any party, the men would be gathered down one end, talking sport and encouraging one another to down excessive amounts of the amber nectar: 'Get it down, it'll do ya good, mate,' or alternatively, 'Get it up, you'll feel better, mate.'

Bryan Feyon who took us to several parties had his own quaint philosophy: 'You've not had a good night unless you throw,' that is be violently sick. There were several dozen delightful descriptions of being sick: 'Calling for Hughie'; 'The technicolour yawn'. Chaps, if ever your wife or any woman for that matter accuses you of being a male chauvinist, just send her off to Australia for a week.

The ladies at such parties would be talking fashion, make-up, babies and moaning like hell about their men: 'He'd rather lie on a bloody surf board than lie on me.' 'The bastard thinks foreplay is what happens before the scrum-half gets it.' Yes, in those days, Australian women were very dissatisfied with their lot.

My brother-in-law, Ron, had been a typical hard-drinking Aussie but his life had recently changed. Pat, who according to Toni had always been a very religious person, had become a Jehovah's Witness and Ron had followed suit. The Kingdom Hall had become the centre of their social life as they embraced their new beliefs wholeheartedly. JWs receive a lot of criticism and some of their proclamations are indeed off the wall but, based on time spent with my Australian in-laws, I can find nothing bad to say about them. Ron is a holy man, strong in his faith. He and Pat have a sound marriage and have brought up five children who share and endorse their beliefs. I could never become a JW myself, I need something with a rock solid foundation and two thousand years of tradition behind it; but how many of us established Christians would be prepared to knock on doors risking insult, abuse and sometimes violence to share the Good News with others? I'll just leave that thought with you.

I was expecting to get the opportunity to appear on TV but I was only invited on to one live chat show and that was a disaster. Waiting in the green room, I watched the preceding guest, a young Sydney University student who had drilled a hole in his surfboard, passed a looped rope through it and attached that rope to his ankle. When he fell from his board, instead of having to follow it to the shore, he would merely reel in the rope and pull it back to him. He'd patented the idea and was set to make a fortune. He left the set and now it was my turn.

'I don't think that surfboard lariat was such an original idea,' I opened, 'especially when you think that a hundred years ago, every Australian had something attached to his ankle.' Bad mistake. Say what you like but don't call 'em convicts. The interview was scheduled for six minutes, I just about managed a minute and a half.

The four weeks at St George's passed quickly but Bryan Feyon had no intention of letting me return home. There was a week at another league club, Western Suburbs, plus a host of one-nighters. I was in demand. We were then sent up the coast to Newcastle. Things were very different there from the comparative sophistication of Sydney. I was booked to work a week at Wallsend RSL, supporting Julian Jorge, an operatic tenor who weighed in at twenty-five stone. They loved him because he could drink most of them under the table. They weren't too keen on me because I didn't drink lager and I had my wife with me, 'That's three times you've brought your wife to the club, what's wrong with you, are you some kind of poofta?' Yes that was the thinking; if you liked women and spent time with women you must be homosexual. A trip was arranged for Julian and me:

'We're off on a roo (kangaroo) hunt tomorrow, wanna come?'
'Why not?' I said. 'The wife'll like that.'

'Bloody hell, mate, we don't want our own wives, we certainly don't want yours,' came the reply and the invitation was withdrawn. Instead some kind soul took Toni, Rachel and me out in a motor launch on Lake Macquarie which was far more pleasant.

It could get tough on stage there, too. Given too much fluid, certain Aussies exercise their republican sympathies.

'The only good pommie is a dead pommie,' was a favourite one to which I'd reply,

'Ah New South Wales, land of culture where corrugated iron goes to die. Tell me, why do you live in cardboard dwellings and store your droppings under the floorboards?' – reference to houses made from plasterboard and the fact that there was little mains drainage there.

'Prince Philip is a paid stud,' was another shout one night.
'At least he's a real man,' I replied. 'Over here you have to have a land specially for queens' (Queensland).

The concert chairman was little help. I'd been on the one night without great success. Julian Jorge followed but the audience failed to pay attention to him. The chairman decided to threaten them: 'If you don't listen to the fat bloke, I'll put the poofta back on.' Who said political correctness started in Australia?

All in all I worked for eleven weeks in New South Wales and again came to the conclusion that I'd be happy to live and bring my children up in such a great country. We were sad to leave. As a thank you, Bryan Feyon arranged for us to fly back via the USA. We took Rachel to Disneyland and then flew on to Las Vegas. I went to every show I could; it was like being at a university of comedy.

But the man who had the most influence on me was Don Rickles, the king of the insult. He was outrageous. He paced the stage chanting his mantra: 'God damn, you sonovabitch, you give me a pain in the ass.' He would then stop and pick on someone in the audience. 'Lady, you're sixty-five if you're a day, what's with the blonde wig?' To the feller next to her: 'All the broads in Vegas and you end up with that!' The young didn't escape 'Oh, an adolescent, how long you had the pimples?' The more the insults flowed, the more the audience laughed. There was plenty of interplay between him and the crowd and much of it was obviously ad-libbed. I came to a decision then: if an ad-lib came to me, I'd just say it without considering the implications. I still do that now. It's occasionally got me into trouble but it's always worth the risk.

We arrived home in October pretty well skint and there was little in the book, though Morris had fixed panto for me at the Birmingham Hippodrome; we'd be at home for Christmas.

One more development, unplanned but delightful. We'd not taken Rory with us to Australia but we'd brought him back. He was due to make his entrance in June. Rachel, who by now was talking very well and had christened herself Rae Rae, a name that stuck with her until she was well into her teens, was in love with babies. She greeted any woman of any age whom she met with the question, 'Have you got a baby?' We explained to our small daughter that a baby was on the way but the wait for her was to prove interminable.

The new BBC building at Pebble Mill was to be opened by HRH Princess Anne in November. The Head of Network Centre, Pebble Mill's official title, had been taken seriously ill, a blow for him but a boon for me because the acting Head was Jock Gallagher. Out of the blue, he asked me to do the cabaret at the party following the opening. By so doing he had introduced me to everyone working for BBC Midlands. He decided to champion my cause. He put me in the hands of John Clark to see if we could come up with comedy inserts for a regional television series uninspiringly called *Scene in B.* There was a popular cookery programme on TV at the time called *The Galloping Gourmet.* John and I, armed with a film camera, decided to parody this and create *The Galloping Gardener.* With camera tricks and several strong visual gags, the finished product was very good and got a great reaction when it was shown. It was only a ten-minute piece, though. I forgot about it almost immediately, little realising that it would be the key to open a very big door.

Jack and the Beanstalk teamed me with Frank Carson.

'A week with him, you'll be screaming to get away,' everyone said. We not only worked together, we shared a dressing room and did nothing but laugh from the first day of rehearsal to the end of the run. A complex character is Frank. I don't know what makes him tick, neither, I suspect, do those closest to him, but he was great to work with. The Bachelors topped the bill, Frank and I played the Giant's henchmen: '*The high spot of the evening is the interlude between Don Maclean and Frank Carson. Maclean's political speech with heckling from Carson went down so well on opening night that I think they were genuinely surprised at their reception. One of the best bits of panto in the Midlands this year.*'

Also in the panto, playing Dame Trot, was Peter Glaze, my second year with him. Having done nine series of *Crackerjack* with Leslie Crowther and two with Rod McLennen, he'd been dropped from the show, which had deteriorated considerably since his departure. He'd now heard that the BBC were planning to drop it altogether. Coming up now, one of those really peculiar quirks of fate, are you sitting comfortably?

Jock Gallagher had sold the Controller of BBC 1, Paul Fox, the idea of a daily, lunchtime magazine programme, *Pebble Mill at One.* They'd made a forty-five minute pilot (for those of you who don't know, PILOT stands for Produced In Little 'Ope of Transmission), and Jock had included in it the *Galloping Gardener* film because he felt it needed an element of comedy. Paul Fox commissioned a series; he particularly liked the comedy piece and said it should be a regular feature. Flushed with his own and my success, Jock decided to push his luck. He offered to make

Mom and Dad's pride and joy!

The Masher's Colts. That's me on the extreme right next to the Masher.

Toni, complete with teeth.

Vintage swimsuit model.
Circa Skegness, 1964.

The night my son was born.
Chuffed or what!

'I've had my nose fixed; now it's your turn!' Cilla flanked by me and Johnny Hackett, as Rostal and Schaefer look on. (Photo: Jean E. Thomas)

Glazed!

Family tree.

'Squnkies All'. With Len Rossiter, James Hunt, Bill Franklin and Tommy Steele.

I always made Mandy Rice-Davies laugh. (Photo: Mel Figures)

What a mouth!

Grand jeté entrance with Jody Hall in *Chase Me Comrades*.

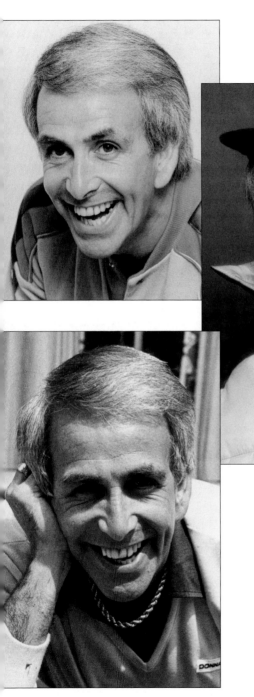

Have I improved with age?

Mom at 80.

Promoting Saab with
'bubbly' Eric Morcambe.

Birmingham's finest and funniest. With
Jasper Carrot, Malcolm Stent and Dave
Ismay.

With Colin Johnson, computer genius
and devisor of *First Letter First*.

Isn't that beautiful? No, not me;
the plane!

Last time I saw legs like that, they were
hanging over the edge of a nest.
My son 'Jack', Sue Pollard.

We've been down to London to
visit the Queen.

With Major Mollie at Ground Zero.

Rory's wedding. Me, Toni, Rory, Mel, Guy and Rae.

Dolly Parton and Mrs Foxtrot. Can you guess which is which?

We are the Cheeky Girls! Francesca and Gracie.

Available for Panto next year. Melinda Messinger, me and Bobby Davro.

another pilot, this time for a light-entertainment, children's series with me fronting it. Paul Fox not only gave him the go-ahead, he also gave him the director of the *Basil Brush Show*, Robin Nash. Robin was tall, loud and flamboyant. I liked him at once. We made the pilot, which was called *Boomerang*, in front of a live audience of kids, many of whom got lost on their way out afterwards; they were still finding kids in various parts of the building three days later. It was a bit of a farce, if truth be told, and I held out little hope for its future. I was however most grateful to Jock for having that amount of confidence in me.

I do believe that had Jock been retained as head of Pebble Mill, I'd have become a superstar; however 'twas not to be. A new man, Phil Sidey, was appointed and Jock reverted to being Head of Network Radio. His legacy, though, was *Pebble Mill at One* in which I was to appear every Friday for the first thirteen weeks. I had more immediate things on my mind: a wife who was nine months' pregnant plus opening in the Cilla Black show at Blackpool Opera House.

According to the contract, rehearsals were to start on Monday 26 June. Saturday 24 June began with my wife sitting bolt upright in bed, sucking air through clenched teeth.

'I'll get the car out,' I said, 'trying to free myself from an over-amorous sheet.

'No, wait a bit,' said Toni.

'I'll take Rae Rae down to Mom and Dad then,' I said. When I returned Toni was dressed and her small case was in the hall.

'To the hospital, then,' I prompted.

'No, let's go for a walk,' she said. It was bright but windy, we paced the local area for a short while then Toni said, 'It's stopped.'

'The baby's not coming, then?'

'Oh, it's coming, but not just yet,' she said.

The infant decided to make a second bid at tea time.

'This is the real thing,' Toni assured me. We set off for the Queen Elizabeth Hospital.

I had a problem; I'd not actually witnessed the birth of my first child and I was determined to see the second, but it was Saturday night, I had a job. I was to do cabaret at The Fisher and Ludlow Social Club.

Toni was placed in a side ward and there examined by a midwife.

'How long?' I asked.

'Two or three hours at a guess,' she said.

'I'll be straight back,' I said and dashed out the door.

The Con Sec at Fishers was surprised to see me. 'You're not on till about ten o'clock, Don,' he said.

'Look, I've just taken Toni into the QE,' I explained. 'I'm determined to see my baby born. I'm not coming back here until she's had it.'

I didn't register his reply, I was off back to the hospital. They dressed me all in green and told me to hold Toni's hand. I was fascinated by the whole process. Rory made his big entrance at ten exactly. I saw him appear, I saw I had a son and the midwife placed him in my arms.

'Well done, Toni,' I said, 'You're a genius.' At that precise moment, a nurse entered. 'Are you Don Maclean?' she asked.

'Er, yes.'

'There's a bloke on the phone, he says has she had it and are you coming?'

'Tell him yes and I'm on my way.' I arrived at the club and was almost immediately announced. I launched into my act, but as I did so, six very attractive young ladies appeared in the room each carrying a bottle of champagne and a tray of glasses. The Con Sec interrupted me: 'Don has just become the father of a baby boy, let's wet the baby's head.'

The crowd stood, champagne flowed. What a marvellous night, I'll always remember it and the kindness of the audience there. Toni meantime was trying to sleep with a very hungry young man beside her.

'I don't care what it is as long as it's healthy.' We all say that, don't we? But I had desperately wanted a son this time and God had granted me a son. Daughters are wonderful, every bloke should have one, but a son is a man's claim to immortality. I would be his hero, he would grow up to be a little carbon copy of his Dad. Everything was wonderful, I was suffering from 'theworldismyoysterosis'.

10

Its Friday, and its five to five ...

The euphoria didn't last long. The following day I set off for Blackpool. We had four days only in which to put the show on. Blackpool, as I've already said, was the number one seaside resort and the Opera House was its number one venue, 3000 seats making it the largest theatre in the country. Playing twice-nightly at 6.15 and 8.40, that's 6000 people a night, 36,000 a week – but Cilla Black could fill it, she was a star, added to which she had on the bill youthful piano duettists Rostal and Schaefer, Liverpudlian comedian Johnny Hackett, and me. The show was directed by Dickie Hurran, a commanding presence with a no-nonsense approach. The lighting, the staging, everything was lavish. Cilla, as the star of the show, would be featured throughout but all I had to do was one spot of twelve minutes and the finale walk down.

The dancers opened, Cilla appeared in a magnificent birthday-cake set, then it was me. A mere five minutes after curtain up and I was on, the audience were still coming in. The walk to the centre of the stage seemed to take an age. I looked out, and I'd never seen so many people in my life. I not only had to get their attention, I had to get them to laugh: 'Attack, attack, attack'. The first few lines went for nothing but then I got 'em. I played them like an angler plays a fish, I saw whole rows of people rocking back and forth. I reeled them in with 'Hava Negila' and left the stage exactly twelve minutes after I'd gone on.

Dickie Hurran stepped from the shadows of the wings. 'I have never in my life known a comic to get a reaction like that so early up in a show,' he said. At the finale, I thought the audience would have forgotten who I was, they'd last seen me an hour and forty minutes before, but as I walked down they cheered loudly.

123

I'd been really looking forward to working with Cilla but she kept herself very aloof; no dallying in the wings, straight back to her dressing room. Bobby, her husband, was very protective of her and after the show they left the theatre immediately. Very unlike the Cilla Black I knew from television, I thought. What none of us realised was that Cilla was experiencing ill health and travelling back to London for hospital visits. Johnny Hackett, on the other hand, seemed very friendly. I thought he was a good comic. He had a pleasantly ugly face and a loose-mouthed, easy smile. He didn't use a hand mike as I did, he stood at the microphone, thumb tucked in waistcoat pocket and addressed the audience in broad Liverpudlian tones. He did twenty minutes immediately prior to the interval, a good spot finishing with a comedy version of 'Granada' and accompanying himself on an out-of-tune guitar. It was very funny.

On the Sunday I dashed home to collect my recently expanded family and bring them back with me to Blackpool. Rachel was incredibly helpful with the baby, eager to bottle-feed him and dress him, but we couldn't leave her alone with him as we found out. He was sleeping when we arrived at the flat. We put him, still in the carry cot, on the table while we unpacked the car. When we came back, Rachel was on the table lifting him from the cot. As she saw us, she dropped him on to the table top. I can still hear the bang now as his head hit the wood; it probably explains some of the daft things he got up to in later life.

A week after we opened, Jimmy Tarbuck came to see the show. He said hello to me briefly, spent ages with Cilla – they were good mates – and then popped in to see Johnny Hackett. I never did find out what words passed between them, though Tarbuck has always been a wind-up merchant. All I do know is that from that moment Hackett's attitude to me changed. He was in the wings when I went on the next night. As I came off he waded into me: 'That gag routine you're doing, you can cut that, it clashes with something I'm doing in my act.'

'Hang on,' I said. 'You can't tell me what material to use.'

'I'm principal comic in this show,' he said. 'Cut that next house.'

I've never been one to surrender but I did in fact cut the gags, I really had no one to consult on the matter. Had I been on friendlier terms with Cilla I'd have asked her how I stood on this.

The following night I did a line about something topical that had been in the paper that day.

'If you're going to put something new in the act, you must call at my dressing room before the show and tell me,' Hackett said when I came off. He'd taken to watching my act at every performance. He was putting me off and getting me down. The crunch came the next night when he said, 'That "Hava Negila" you do at the end of your act, it's exactly the same as my "Granada", in fact you probably got the idea of doing it from watching me.' I was gobsmacked. 'You've got a week to change it, otherwise there'll be trouble.' What trouble? Who in their right mind was going to back up the rantings of this lunatic?

I rang Morris, who told me to write down everything that Hackett had said and send it to him: 'Stop worrying, don't argue with the man, I'll take care of it.' I did worry, I wasn't sleeping and the edge had gone off my performance. But the cavalry were about to arrive. The company manager popped his head round the dressing room door: 'Do a good one tonight, Dickie Hurran's out front.'

Johnny Hackett was watching me from the wings in the first house but was absent during the second. I finished the spot and went up to my dressing room. There came a sharp knock on the door and in walked Dickie Hurran, looking immaculate as always.

'Understand you've been having a bit of trouble.' Before I had chance to reply he continued, 'I've just left Mr Hackett. I offered him the opportunity of exchanging spots with you, he declined. I am perfectly happy with the content of your act which should be of no concern to anyone else.' He turned and left. I realised I hadn't said a word.

'Thanks,' I called to the closed door.

Hackett left me alone after that. He never spoke to me again but neither did he stand in the wings putting me off. I thought that was the end of it but it wasn't, there was a final chapter yet to come as you'll find out.

I got into the lift with Cilla and Bobby a few days later.

'I'm sorry you've been having a bit of trouble,' said Cilla.

'It was nothing much,' I said. 'It's sorted now.' I never pushed myself at all with our top of the bill, I got the impression that Cilla and Bobby were wary of anyone who wanted to hang on to their coat tails. I didn't, and I believe they appreciated that.

Next thing on the agenda was the baptism of my son and heir. This was to take place at the Church of the Sacred Heart right in the middle of Blackpool. It was a star-studded occasion, performers from all the shows were there. Father Paul Chamberlain, who had been at SPGS with me, had agreed to come up from Birmingham to officiate. He looked splendid. He had a fine beard and wore a cream, full-length vestment with a gold rope round his waist, prompting Caroline, the small daughter of our MD Paul Burnett, to ask in a loud voice, 'Is that Jesus?' Ruth and Frank Carson were the godparents, Frank being in *The Comedians* on the South Pier. We christened him Rory after Rory Maclean who had travelled to France in 1744 to see Bonnie Prince Charlie then returned to Scotland to alert the loyal clans of the advent of the Young Pretender; and Gregor after Gregory the Great, the Pope who sent St Augustine to bring Christianity to England. You can't just lumber a kid with any old name, you have to think seriously about such things. The christening was a truly joyous occasion.

It was an altogether joyous season, once early problems had been ironed out. The act was going well; though each night I had to fight for the first couple of minutes, it was all part of the learning curve. I was also learning more about being a father. A new baby demands time from his mother, which means that Rae Rae really became mine. In order to give Toni space, I'd take Rae on the beach or to the pool. She learned to swim that summer, and several evenings a week she would accompany me to the theatre. She'd sit in the prompt corner on the Company Manager's high stool watching me while I was on stage. I'd change into my street clothes, put on dark glasses to conceal the make-up and together we'd go to the children's indoor fair, roundabouts etc. for little ones, in the Winter Gardens. We'd get back in time for the finale. During the interval between shows we'd have a cake and a drink of pop then, after my spot in the second show, I'd take her home and put her to bed. Toni and I would have a bit of time together before I had to nip back to do the finale walkdown. Yes I know what you're thinking, it was only a part-time job but it wasn't my fault that I didn't have more to do.

A young man with a rich Northern Ireland accent stopped me one day. He worked in a furniture store but was obviously a real fan of my work. He talked like a professor of comedy and obviously studied the subject. He spoke knowledgeably about comedians from the past whom he was far too young to have seen. I told him he could come and talk to me any time he wanted to and he did – often. His name was Adrian Walsh and he's now one of the most sought-after cabaret and after-dinner comedians in the country. I'd like to think I had a small hand in his success.

I also acquired a devoted fan. Lottie was in her seventies and bore an uncanny resemblance to Old Mother Riley. She was registered partially sighted, but despite this she could spot me in a crowd of 4000 people. There were always autograph hunters at the stage door of the Opera House, we'd go out in between houses to sign their books. Lottie would be there at least three times a week. Her technique was to stand at the periphery until I had a crowd around me then make her dash, elbowing her way to my side and planting an unpleasant kiss as near to my mouth as her limited vision would allow. I was booked to appear on *The Golden Shot* twice during the season, which was great because it meant we got to go back home to Birmingham for the Sunday. I mentioned Lottie to Bob Monkhouse who always had a solution for every eventuality.

'Avoiding the unwanted kiss is easy,' said Bob. 'You're signing, you have a pen, put the pen in your mouth, there's no way she can kiss you.'

Why hadn't I thought of that? The next night, I was busy signing when I saw her coming. Just before she reached me, I put the pen in my mouth and turned towards her. Now you'll remember that Lottie couldn't see too well – she certainly couldn't see pens. The kiss came in regardless, the force of it ramming the metal pen backwards and ripping the roof of my mouth. I could taste blood throughout the second house. Bob Monkhouse gave me some extremely good pieces of advice but that wasn't one of them.

Towards the end of the summer, *Pebble Mill at One* started to go out five lunchtimes a week. Every Friday, presenter Bob Langley would say, 'Over now to our Raving Reporter, Don Maclean,' and I was on. Much of what I did was on film: *The Great Tram Robbery*, *The Maclean Olympics*. A very popular children's TV show at the time was *Ask Aspel*, in which children wrote in requesting clips from things they'd seen during the past week. Suddenly they began getting requests for my silly films. Michael Aspel, who'd been connected with *Crackerjack* for the past couple of years, brought the attention of the BBC to the fact that his programme was getting requests for me but the BBC were thinking of scrapping what was probably the most complete children's TV show ever because its viewing figures had dropped dramatically.

While in Blackpool, I'd signed a contract to appear at The Showboat Theatre Restaurant which was just off Trafalgar Square. Morris wanted me to be in London where I could be seen working and this was the ideal cabaret venue. I was to open in November for a six-month season, so after a very short spell at home, Toni and I set off for Twickenham. We rented a house in Clive Road; it was expensive but Toni's sister Margaret and her husband John lived close by, which was a bonus. Clive Road was a nice cul-de-sac which we thought would be even nicer once we got to know the neighbours. With that in mind, we wrote out little invitations and knocked on the dozen doors nearest to us, introducing ourselves and asking them to please come for drinks on Sunday. That Sunday, after mass, we prepared for our guests; crisps and nuts in abundance, wine uncorked, sausage rolls in oven, ready to be warmed up. Margaret and John arrived to help host the expected influx. Not a single person turned up – not one! Not a single person called to say they couldn't make it. So much for the warm-hearted, welcoming southerner. It was going to be a long, lonely six months for Toni with a babe in arms and a toddler for company.

To begin with she had me with her all day but that was about to change. Morris and I were called to see Robin Nash at Television Centre. I never fail to be impressed by that place even now. Then I was overawed. Robin told us that *Boomerang* had not been well received – there's a surprise – but the powers that be had liked what I had done and were proposing to reprieve *Crackerjack* with me in it. Furthermore, Michael Aspel, who'd stated that he didn't want to do another series, had said that he would reconsider if I agreed to do the show – not that we'd ever met, he only knew of me from *Ask Aspel*. I reckoned this put me in a pretty strong position as indeed it did. I was next asked who I wanted to work with.

'We thought we'd bring Peter Glaze back as the show was so successful when he and Crowther did it. Do you have any objection to that?'

'Fine by me,' I said.

'Previously we've had two girls in the show,' said Robin. 'We don't need two, what we want is one really funny lady.' The funniest lady on TV at that time was a dark, snipey-nosed girl who appeared regularly on *The Dave Allen Show*. Her name was Jacquie Clarke. I'd never met her but I knew I wanted to work with her. By coincidence, she was working for Robin that week on *The Basil Brush Show*. 'A good suggestion,' he said. The team was complete.

We were due to start the series in January. Would I be able to manage it as well as doing the Showboat? As the cabaret didn't start until ten o'clock, it was decided that I could. The Showboat was a joy to play. Parties of people came to celebrate anniversaries, birthdays and, at that time of year, office parties. Everyone was in a good mood. They were wined and dined then entertained by the floor show, after which they danced the night away. Think back to what I told you about Don Rickles and how he changed my attitude to ad-libbing. I would make a point of homing in on any large party; getting them involved in the act could only boost the laughs.

One night there was a table of twenty-four people immediately on my right; they should be good for a bit of banter, I thought. Sitting nearest to the stage was an extremely large lady wearing a black dress trimmed with a Greek-key design, rather like a gold battlement effect round the neck and sleeves.

'Hello, where are you lot from?' I asked and she, on her own, said, 'Elephant and Castle,' to which I replied, 'Which one are you?'

There was a stunned silence during which I had time to take stock of the others on her table. All the men had broken noses, cauliflower ears and tattoos on the backs of their hands. I reconciled myself to the fact that I was about to die, but the large lady saw the funny side and burst out laughing – I was reprieved.

Another memorable ad-lib at the same venue concerned a table of well-dressed young women who worked for a magazine, though I didn't know that at the time.

'Where are you from, ladies?' I ventured, and again a solo voice replied, 'I.P.C.' 'Do you?' I said, 'I bet that's salty.' Yes my ad-libbing owed much to devil-may-care. It still gets me into trouble as you'll know if you listen to Radio 2. The press though liked it:

The highspot is Don Maclean, the Birmingham comedian who is likely to be the toast of the nation by this time next year. Varied in attack and strong in material, he causes a laughter response the like of which has seldom been heard in a London nightspot.

There is only one entertainer in London for whom I would predict a star future and that is Don Maclean. I cannot understand why he has not yet made the big time and I implore agents, managers or impresarios to go to the Showboat in the Strand and see this young man who is the first comedian to make me laugh since I saw Larry Grayson at the Stork Room when he was unknown.

Everyone, it seemed, was tipping me for greatness; it was scary.

I'd become friendly with Leslie Crowther who lived in Twickenham too. I went to see him to ask his advice about *Crackerjack*.

'It'll make you a household name,' he said, 'but you'll no longer be a draw in clubs because you'll be thought of as a kiddies' entertainer. Don't stay with it too long,' he added. 'I did nine years and it took quite a while for me to be accepted for any other television.' Useful words from Leslie who was a truly exceptional bloke.

We began work on *Crackerjack* in January 1973. One of the main reasons for my getting the job had been the film insert on *Pebble Mill at One*. It was decided to make a five-minute silent movie for each episode; this would be known as 'The Don and Pete Film'. Charged with the task of making these was Alan Bell, and if you think you know the name of course you do, he directs and produces *Last of the Summer Wine* and has done so for a very long time. These speeded-up films took shape almost immediately, the two of us appearing as road sweepers, zoo keepers, window cleaners, firemen. We filmed each one in one day and what Alan Bell managed to achieve was truly amazing. We worked a very full week on *Crackerjack*. Wednesday we were up early and off to some location to make a film; I took Toni and the kids with me on every one. Thursday, Friday and Saturday we were in the rehearsal room by ten o'clock. Sunday we had off but Monday morning we did our 'tech run'. Sound, lighting, wardrobe, make-up watched a run through of the entire show. In the afternoon we polished it because next day we were to record the show, which would be transmitted the following Friday.

From early morning each Tuesday we rehearsed on set at the BBC Theatre, Shepherd's Bush Green. The audience of about five hundred schoolchildren arrived at five. After a warm-up in which Peter and I were heavily involved, the audience were hushed, the cameras began to roll,

'It's Friday–'

'It's five to five–'

'And it's–'

'*Crackerjack*,' screamed five hundred throats, and we were off.

Michael Aspel handled all the games, often coming out with little gems that missed the kids completely but you knew they'd bring a smile to moms and dads watching. The comedy was my domain. First thing was 'The Double'. Pompous Pete would begin to lecture the audience, interrupted within seconds by me:

'The other day I paid a visit to a zoo, the head keeper came up to me and said . . .'

'What are you doing out of your cage?'

'Maclean!'

'Yes I had a bath this morning.'

The double was written each week by Bob Hedley. Bob combined with Tony Hare to write the sketch and the musical finale. Tony was a complete original, he thought differently from anyone I've ever known, while Bob was a gag mechanic. It was a strong writing partnership. The finale would be woven around current chart hits, often parodied to fit in with our theme. The three of us managed to sing 'Bohemian Rhapsody' in harmony in a finale entitled 'The Fat Tum of the Opera'. We'd try anything.

My birthday being 11 March and Robin Nash's 10 March, we arranged a combined party at the house in Clive Road. We didn't invite the neighbours this time but the place was full with cast and production crew. Robin made a speech telling us how we'd saved *Crackerjack.* Viewing figures had increased considerably every week; there would certainly be another series next year and we would all be in it. This was great news and I vowed that next year I'd do the programme and nothing else. Working cabaret as well had taken its toll on both Toni and me. Every morning except Sunday I left the house at nine to get to rehearsals. I'd get back by six, have a snack then fall asleep. I had to get ready to go out again at nine for the Showboat, returning home at about one a.m., by which time Toni would be asleep. It was a strain I was not prepared to endure again.

At the Showboat I became very friendly with a young theatrical agent who happened to be going out with one of the show dancers; his name was Laurie Mansfield. Working for International Artistes, he had a small stable of acts, all of whom were doing well.

'I've not got a comic on my books because there's only one comic I want,' he said. 'I could make you the biggest comedy name in the country.' Laurie and I were the same age, we'd both grown up in Birmingham at the same time, we thought alike and both had burning ambition. It would have been some coalition. I was tempted.

'I'll think about it.'

'You've got until the season here ends,' he said.

How could I possibly leave Morris Aza who'd worked so hard to get me into television? It would have been treason. Before the end of the run I gave Laurie my decision. He was quite philosophical, 'If that's definite I'll go and find myself another comic.' He did. That comic was Jim Davidson.

Laurie went on to shape the careers of several major names. He also produced several stage shows including *Jolson* and the long-running *Buddy*, and he's the man you see greeting and hosting Her Majesty the Queen when she arrives for the Royal Variety Performance each year.

* * *

There was to be no seaside season for us this summer, something much better was on offer. The *Black and White Minstrel Show* was to return to the West End, bigger and better than ever. Instead of the Victoria Palace Theatre they were going into the New Victoria. Recently converted from a cinema, it had nearly 3000 seats. They needed a comedian who would be guaranteed to score in such a large auditorium. Someone told them that there was a comedian doing just that in the Cilla Black Show at Blackpool Opera House. Five years after they'd seen me at Clacton, George Mitchell and Robert Luff came for another look. This time they decided that I was ready and, unbeknown to me, pencilled me in for the new show. And so it came to pass. We finished at the Showboat and headed home to Selly Oak, but not for long. We rented another house in London and started rehearsals for the B&Ws.

The new show was to be directed by Ernest Maxim, who will figure quite a bit in this book. Ernest was a genius and I don't use the word lightly. He could sing and dance so well that he could have made a living as a performer, but that would never have suited him. He needed to be in charge, telling others what to do and giving full rein to his creative side. He had plenty to work with, twenty lovely girls, sixteen minstrels plus the four principal minstrels: veterans Les Want and Les Rawlings, young Canadian baritone Karl Scott and the tenor Ted Darling whom I knew so well from our days with the *White Heather Club*. There were a couple of speciality acts plus comedy duo Hope and Keen. They were to do three spots. My single spot was in the first half just prior to the interval. We opened at the very beginning of July. Again the national press were very good to me:

One man scores what must be the biggest ever personal success in what is essentially a team effort. Don Maclean collected the only encore of the evening and had he been allowed a solo entrance in the finale, the odds are he would have raised a louder response than the Minstrels themselves.

A splendid ape-man from Birmingham called Don Maclean won roars of approval for his naughty patter about women's tights and the problems of living in Golders Green.

I can't give you the whole tights routine here but you're dying to know what I said about Golders Green aren't you?

'My agent lives in Golders Green (he did as well)! "It's the most convenient place in the world to live", he says. "Over the road I've got the synagogue, next door I've got a branch of weight-watchers and on the other side of me there's a strip joint so I can pray a bit, weigh a bit, hooray a bit and still stay kosher." ' No one complained about that, though I did do a routine in which I parodied songs from current TV commercials one of which went, 'A million Hebrews every day pick up a tin of beans and say "There's one missing." ' A Jewish association who came to the show complained to the management that I was being anti-Semitic and the management asked me to take the gag out. You see, long before *Good Morning Sunday* I was upsetting people.

In August I received a disturbing phone call at the stage door from one of the newspaper critics who had given me such a great write-up on opening night.

'I went to review the show that opened at the Palladium last night,' he began. 'There's a chap there doing most of your act.'

'What show is this?' I asked.

'The *Cilla Black Show*.'

'And did you get the name of the comic?'

'Johnny Hackett, he's even wearing a suit the same as yours.' So Hackett intended to have the last laugh after all.

'Thanks,' I said. 'I'll try to get over to see him.'

'Look, this would make a great story,' said the critic, changing into his investigative reporter's hat.

'It probably would,' I said, 'but I think I can handle it myself.' The following day I ordered a taxi to pick me up at the stage door when I came off from my spot. I arrived at the Palladium and slipped into the rear of the circle. On he came, mike in hand, leaning forward in what had been described by one reviewer as 'the Maclean pounce'. He wore a biscuit-coloured suit like mine and he did all of the act I'd done last summer, including gags about Blackpool trams:

'A little Scotsman, in his kilt, was terrified to cross the tram lines. He said to a policeman, "If I put my foot on that rail will I get an electric shock?" "No sir," said the policeman, "not unless you can cock your other leg over that wire up there." So he did and we all got a shock.' Little relevance in London, one would have thought.

I popped backstage to see Cilla and Bobby.

'We wanted you to be with us here,' they told me, 'but you were already contracted for the *B&Ws*.'

'No matter,' I replied. 'You've got my act in the show.' They both looked rather sheepish. There was little I or they could do. You can't copyright a gag. I could have got back in touch with the press and become the Ulrika of my day but I reasoned that my material was changing all the while; given a few months I'd have replaced all of it. I did, though, send Hackett a telegram:

'Delighted to watch my act going so well at the Palladium, loved the suit. Granada's doing a bomb here at the New Vic.' While I had worked hard to develop an original style, Hackett, after all his years in the business, was still 'borrowing' from other people. No basis for longevity – before much longer he had faded from the scene, bless him.

11

Becoming a Squnkie

The incident didn't bother me for long; family life was very pleasant that summer. I had my days free to enjoy the kids. We'd get babysitters when we could, Toni would come with me to the theatre and we'd go out afterwards. Rae Rae and I would nip off on our own sometimes. I promised to take her out one Sunday afternoon,

'Where would you like to go, the lido, the park?'

'I want to see *Jesus Christ Superstar*,' she replied. The film had opened in London the previous day, a fact she'd picked up from TV, though we'd had the sound-track LP for a little while and we played it a lot. I tried a few more suggestions but nothing would deflect her.

'She'll probably get fed up half way through,' said Toni.

'If she does, I'll leave and bring her home,' I said. I paid full price for her at a cinema in the Haymarket, no reduction for children, and she sat on my lap, sucking her thumb throughout. She knew all the music and was completely enthralled. As we left the theatre she said, 'Daddy, what did Jesus mean when he said "to conquer death we only have to die"?' She'd remembered that single line from the dialogue. I was impressed by her intellect but mine didn't stretch to being able to explain that to a four-year-old. Even today, that's one of Rachel's favourite films.

Alan Bell asked Peter Glaze and me if we'd be prepared to do some of the films for the next series during September. We'd start early in the morning and make sure I was back in time for first house at the New Vic. I did all my own stunts and Alan was determined to extend my derring-do. We were to make three films in a week. In the first he had me sliding down the roof of a circus big top. Not only did I singe my botty, I also hit the ground with a bump and sprained my ankle. The next script called for me to whisper in an Alsatian's ear, which I did.

'No, no,' said Alan Bell. 'Do it properly, lift up the dog's ear and then whisper in it – Action!' The dog was quite happy being whispered at – being German he probably didn't understand what I was saying anyway – but was none too keen on having his ear fondled. He turned and sank a canine into the bridge of my nose – blood everywhere.

This, however, was nothing compared to film number three. Peter and I were removal men, clearing everything out of a house, down the front path and into the waiting van. The action was for me to scoot a set of library steps, jump on top of them, steer them down the path where I would collide with a cycling policeman, end up on his handlebars, he'd lose control and drive up the ramp into the back of the removal van – are you following this OK?

'Action!' I got quite a speed up but then the front wheels of the steps caught the gatepost. I catapulted, literally, through the air to land in the road. My eyebrow split open like a ripe melon. Both my hands, one arm and both knees were devoid of skin, having come into contact with the gravel road. Off to the hospital we went but were back two hours later and managed to complete the film. When I arrived at the New Victoria that night, cast and audience were standing outside in Wilton Road. A bomb warning had been phoned to the theatre. After a short while we were called back in, and so were the audience.

'Mr Maclean to the stage at once,' said the tannoy as I got inside. The stage manager thrust a mike into my hand,

'Go on stage and talk to the audience as they're coming back in,' he ordered.

'What shall I say?'

'You'll think of something,' came the harassed reply. I want you to recall the filming injuries – got them? There was a large scab in the middle of my nose, five stitches over an eye that was mauving towards purple, my left hand was bandaged and the short-sleeved shirt I wore exposed my right arm which was bandaged up to and including the elbow. The incoming audience looked in amazement as I headed for centre stage with a pronounced limp.

'I've found the bomb,' was all I said. It was the only time during the entire run that we had a standing ovation before the show started.

I got loads of letters at the theatre from *Crackerjack* fans which I always made a point of answering. One day there was a most complimentary letter from a lady named Marion Guenigault. The address, I noted, was not far from the theatre, just over the river in fact. In my reply I suggested that she came to see the show.

It was several weeks later that she wrote to me again. 'On Wednesday night, look for the powder-blue whale in the front row,' said the note. I looked out and sure enough there was a little, dumpy woman in blue. She came round afterwards with her daughter, Jayne, and I got the full story. Marion was agoraphobic; she hadn't been out for quite some time. Her daughter had intercepted my letter, bought two tickets for the show then presented Marion with the letter and the words 'You're going.'

Marion continues to come and see me now, nearly thirty years on, and credits me with curing her phobia.

On another evening there was a lovely little blonde in the front row. Throughout my act and in the finale she kept waving to me. After the show, her mother brought her round and explained that six-year-old Francesca was deaf. She'd started lip-reading and as yet I was the only person on television that she could understand, something to do with my big mouth no doubt. I can tell you that those two incidents are ones of which I'm extremely proud. For entertainers it's easy to reach people but to help people, even without knowing it, is a real bonus.

The second series of *Crackerjack* was even better than the first; we knew one another and worked well together. The doubles were really sharp:

'If music be the food of love . . .'

'Get your fish fingers off the piano.'

'Maclean!'

'Yes, I had a bath this morning.'

'I'm talking about music, do you like Handel's *Largo?*'

'I never drink anything else.'

'Handel was a composer.'

'He was a lawyer.'

'He wasn't a lawyer.'

'He was, he got Rachmaninoff.'

'Rachmaninov was Russian.'

'That's right, he was up for speeding. Ask me anything about music, I know it all.'

'All right, what's a semibreve?'

'One nostril bunged up. Ask me another.'

'What is the value of a crochet?'

'It keeps Long John Silver from falling over.'

That double also included the oft-quoted line:

'Why are you playing that old violin?'

'Because I gave Yehudi me new 'un.'

Crackerjack was produced not by the Children's Department but by BBC Light Entertainment; that was the secret of its success. The press thought so too: '*Programmes like Crackerjack should be shown at peak viewing time. The comedy partnership of Don Maclean and Peter Glaze has almost reached the standard of Morecambe and Wise at their brilliant best.*'

We often bumped into Eric and Ernie at Television Centre. Eric was always delighted to see me.

'What are you doing this week?' he'd ask.

'A sketch with me as Wellington and Pete as Napoleon.'

'We'll be doing that in a couple of weeks then. How do you fancy being Napoleon, Ern?' He always claimed that their writers got their ideas from watching *Crackerjack*.

The audience figure continued to rise. Eight million people now tuned in on a Friday. We even left *Blue Peter* in our wake – 'Get down, Shep!' At the end of our thirteen-week stint, Jacquie Clarke told us she wouldn't be coming back next series. I was upset. Jacquie had wonderful natural comedy flair. I saw her in a play recently; her character had to collapse and die on stage, it was one of the funniest things I've ever seen. She taught me a lot. She'd help me every week with my characterisation for the sketch or the finale. Next year I'd have to work things out for myself. Mike Aspel, too, was on the move; he had many other projects to pursue. The two of them were to be replaced by blonde, bubbly Jan Hunt and Ed 'Stewpot' Stewart. It was good casting.

* * *

The *Minstrel* show, having finished in the New Victoria, moved to the Festival Theatre in Paignton. Toni and I rented a flat overlooking Paignton harbour. It was just lovely. Rachel went to the local school, where she immediately fitted in, and the four of us had a splendid summer.

In the autumn, Glaze and I did a few prestigious things like presenting *Disney Time* and we were also cast in the BBC pantomime. Peter was Widow Twanky, I was Wishee Washee, and Aladdin was played by our incoming *Crackerjack* girl, Jan Hunt. Dana, one of my very favourite people, was the Princess, and the girl dancers were Pan's People – you're impressed, I can tell. My memories of that panto are marred by the fact that, during rehearsals, the IRA bombed Birmingham city centre. I took it personally. I remember being so angry and somehow ashamed that I was in London not in Birmingham when it happened – does that make sense? A lad I'd known from Ombersley Road was in one of the pubs; they never found enough of him to bury. As with all bombings nothing was achieved. What an evil, indiscriminate thing is a bomb; how many lives are destroyed, apart from the lives of those killed?

Toni and I started house-hunting; yes, I know we already had a house in Selly Oak, two if you count Mom and Dad's, but the cost of renting in London was so great that paying a mortgage would actually save us money. As luck would have it, the adjoining semi to Toni's sister Margaret came up for sale. We bought it, fully furnished, for £13,000. We'd be spending plenty of time in it because immediately after *Crackerjack* I was to start rehearsing for the *Black and White Minstrels* TV show.

The top names in pop were queuing up to appear on *Crackerjack*. The Osmonds and the Carpenters from America, Showaddywaddy, Slade, The Bay City Rollers and, one of my all-time favourites, the Wombles, were scheduled for this series. Jan Hunt fitted in really well. Peter Glaze had many endearing qualities – he was one of the most generous men I've ever known, always first to the bar, always wanting to pay the bill in a restaurant – but he did have a 'Mr Hyde' side. I thought the writers Tony Hare and Bob Hedley were getting better all the time but Peter would rub them up the wrong way, constantly complaining that he didn't have enough to do. At the start of each week, he'd get the script and, before he did anything else, he'd count how many lines he had. If in his opinion there weren't enough, he'd throw the script on the floor and walk out. It was becoming increasingly wearing. One week, Tony and Bob had written a super sketch in which I was a British spy parachuted into Nazi-occupied France with a radio as big as me, Jan was a French resistance girl and Pete a German Officer.

Peter read the script. 'How can I get laughs being the villain in every sketch? I'm sick of the parts you write for me.' With that, he threw the script on the floor and left the rehearsal room. We had a cup of coffee, knowing that he'd soon be back.

'I've got an idea, Pete,' I said when he returned. 'Let's swap parts. You be the spy, I'll be the German.' He liked that and so did I. I got far more laughs as the German than I'd ever have got as the spy.

He had a lot to commend him, did Glaze. I was delighted when recently he was the subject of one of Danny Baker's *TV Heroes* programmes. He died in 1983 while he was appearing in the musical *Underneath the Arches* in the West End. Shortly after his death, his wife, April, sent me a set of four stainless steel cups in a leather case which Pete always took with him when we went filming. We'd imbibed every drinkable liquid imaginable from those cups.

'Something to remember your little pal by,' April had said when she gave them to me. They're with me whenever I'm in a theatre dressing room; if you ever come to visit me after a show, you'll get a drink in one of them and you can raise a toast to him too.

The *Black and Whites* was the big Saturday night show; up to twenty million people watched it. Ernest Maxim was to direct, straight from his triumph winning the BAFTA for the *Morecambe and Wise* television show. He was a great ideas man. Like many television light entertainment directors of that time he was a product of the theatre. Nowadays programmes are made by young men with business studies degrees whose knowledge of things theatrical would fit on the back of a postage stamp.

'I want you to do two spots in each show, Don,' said Ernest. This was even better than I'd hoped. 'You need a gimmick, I've decided that you'll make your entrance in a dustbin.'

'He's lost it,' I thought. 'Like all geniuses, he's finally gone over the edge.'

'I'm talking about a very large dustbin which will be your dressing room. We'll cut a door in the front and, on the door, will be your name and a star.' I began to like the idea, and I was right to. The dustbin was on wheels, the Minstrels would pull it into the spotlight, the door would open and out I'd pop. It was a brilliant entrance. In my second spot, Ernest wanted me each week to be an important figure behind the *Minstrel* show. These were wonderful. I was Blodwyn Leeks, the BBC tea lady; Cyril Cutback, Head of Finance; Dr Tom Katz, Medical Officer; Gideon Goodbody, costume designer, you get the idea.

I suppose that year, 1975, I was at my peak. I was never to get any higher. Eight million viewers on *Crackerjack*, sixteen million plus for the *B&Ws*; every kid in Great Britain already knew who I was and now so did all the adults. It meant a change of lifestyle. I couldn't go out and do normal things like shopping (mind, I hate shopping). If ever I got mobbed, Rachel would stand in front of me facing the crowd, determined to protect me. To give some idea of how things were, I was asked to open a toy shop in Newport, Isle of Wight. This gridlocked the town and caused traffic problems all the way back to the ferry at Ryde. During the summer there'd be a constant stream of kids knocking on the door; some had cycled miles. We kept a pile of signed photos just inside the front door ready to give out. Ah, the fame! I loved it though, having experienced it, I appreciate even more the anonymity that radio gives. Nowadays people don't recognise me until they hear me speak.

At about this time two things happened; Billy Marsh who'd been pretty quiet since my Palladium debut suddenly remembered me. As he'd recommended me for the *Cilla Black Show* in which I'd been seen by the *B&W's* management, he was demanding 5 per cent commission on everything I'd done for them since. I know what you're thinking, 'cheek', which is exactly what I thought and why I refused to pay – a big mistake, you can't afford to make enemies in showbiz.

The second thing was a chance meeting. I was yet again invited on to the *Golden Shot.* Bob Monkhouse always had a few writers hanging around, he'd give anyone a chance would Bob. He introduced me to a chap called Howard Imber who said he was a fan of my work. I thought perhaps he was just being pleasant but, as we talked, it was obvious he'd seen nearly everything I'd done. 'Why don't you jot down some stuff and let me have a look at it?' I said. The material was good and, what's more, Howard wrote the way I spoke, there was very little adjustment needed. At last, what I'd always wanted, a writer of my own. I decided to employ him for my forthcoming summer season in Bournemouth. There began a great partnership. For the next few years there wasn't much I said on stage that didn't flow from Howard's pen – well his typewriter actually; neither of us could read his writing.

At Bournemouth I discovered squash. Showbiz is famous for its golfers but I never saw the point of golf. You put a ball down, hit it and walk after it. If you want it badly enough to walk after it, why hit it in the first place? But squash was different, I became obsessed with it. I was what's known as a 'squnkie', that's a squash junkie; if you don't play for twelve hours you get withdrawal symptoms. I played at every opportunity. I was leaner and fitter than I'd ever been. Toni started playing too. The kids hated it. It was to become my major passion for the next ten years.

For the fourth series of *Crackerjack* we had a new director, Brian Penders. He was fantastic. Like Ernest he'd come from the theatre, he really knew comedy and certainly brought out the best in me. It was during the so-called 'winter of discontent' when the miners took on the government and vice versa.

'*The one good thing about the four-day week is that we're all home on Friday to watch Maclean and Glaze on* Crackerjack,' wrote the *Daily Mail* TV critic. Alan Bell made another great set of Don and Pete movies, including three at Windsor Safari Park. I always took the family when we went filming. Rachel and Rory were in ecstasy; they rode on elephants, cuddled lion cubs and baby zebras and, most exciting of all, swam with the dolphins. When they appeared on *Whose Baby?* aged six and three respectively, host Roy Castle asked them if they were planning to go into show business like Dad. 'No,' they replied. 'We're going to train dolphins.'

I also managed to fit in my second Palladium season – two weeks with Eddie Fisher and Judy Garland's younger daughter, Lorna Luff. Also on the bill was ventriloquist Roger de Courcey and a very funny comedy band, Fiddlygig. There was no one giving me advice on material as had happened in 1970 and I was certainly not overawed by the theatre as I had been before, I felt very much at home. I was altogether better than I'd been the first time. '*Don Maclean glides and lopes about the stage, India-rubber walk, gleaming grin. It's a routine about tights and suspenders, fish and chips, car workers and snogging in the cinema. The laughter ripples and the ripples become waves.*'

As soon as *Crackerjack* finished we were into rehearsals for the next *Minstrel* series. The dustbin was still featured but the characters for the second spot would be people promoting exotic holidays. I insisted on having Howard on the writing team. Ernest Maxim as always was full of ideas which included using Pam Ayers as resident poetess. We were rehearsing the last of the series, the dancers had been there all morning, but principals, and that included me, weren't called until the afternoon. Karl Scott was the bass with the show. Trained as an opera singer in his native Canada, he'd arrived in England only to be snapped up by George Mitchell before the Royal Opera House got their hands on him. He had a voice like melted chocolate and was featured heavily throughout the show. That afternoon Karl didn't arrive. They rang his home in Dunstable, to be assured that he'd left in plenty of time. We carried on rehearsing without him. It was several hours before Karl was located. He'd obviously felt ill and pulled into a motorway service station. His car was found there and Karl was dead inside it. He was just twenty-eight.

En masse the company attended Karl's funeral. As often happens when someone departs this life too early, those around him are shaken and forced to acknowledge their own mortality. I found that there were those who envied me my faith and confidence in the afterlife. Those with no spiritual platform in their life were floundering. Over the next few weeks, several brought their concerns to me; I hope they were encouraged by my answers to investigate their own spirituality.

* * *

Morris was eager to further my career and so was I. Bill Cotton Junior was Head of Light Entertainment; he had said he wanted to bring on new comics. He charged his top producers with finding a comic each and building a forty-five minute show around him. Such names as Mike Reid, Charlie Williams, Lennie Bennett got a show – why not me? Peter Whitmore, famous for the *Terry and June* sitcoms, had suggested me for my own show but Bill Cotton had said, 'Don's all right in *Crackerjack*, let's leave him where he is.'

'It took him years to replace Crowther when he left *Crackerjack*,' Peter said by way of explanation, 'there's no way he'll let you leave.' I began to see *Crackerjack*, which had launched me, as an obstacle to my advancement. I told Morris, who arranged for us both to see Bill Cotton.

'I really feel it's time for me to move on from *Crackerjack*, Bill.'

'Nonsense, it's never been so good; in fact we'll do twenty-six instead of thirteen next year, if you're game.'

'What I really want is an adult show.'

'You've got the *Minstrels*, that's for adults.'

'I was thinking of a show of my own, Bill.'

He looked thoughtful then said, 'Be honest, Don, what can you give me that Dick Emery can't?'

I realised then that, in his eyes, I was a kid's entertainer and would always be so. 'You've got *Crackerjack*, you've got the *Black and Whites*; come back next week and let me have your decision.'

Morris should have been firmer with me. The following week I made the biggest mistake of my life. 'I've decided, Bill, I won't do another series of *Crackerjack* but I'll do the *Black and Whites*.'

The man I looked at was very different from the man who'd been so pleasant a week ago. His eyes narrowed. 'You don't do *Crackerjack*, you don't work for the BBC again,' came his reply.

Could he do that? Surely not! Not only could he, he did. I'm sure I'm not the only performer to feel the wrath of Cotton, not a man to be crossed. As I've already said, you can't afford to make enemies in showbiz. A couple of years ago I interviewed Bill

Cotton for *Good Morning Sunday.* He'd written a book, *Double Bill,* about himself and his famous dad. Surprisingly, I felt no animosity towards him. I don't suppose he even remembers turning me into a television leper. At the time, though, I was pretty distraught.

I went to see Leslie Crowther. He was comforting: 'Look, Don, as soon as ITV realise you're no longer a BBC man, they'll snap you up.'

I rang Bob Monkhouse. 'You're more than welcome on *Celebrity Squares,*' said Bob, 'I'll arrange it.' And he did, but sitting in a little box with eight other celebs is a far cry from being resident comic on the *B&Ws.*

After two most successful seasons at Paignton and Bournemouth, the *B&Ws* got what the management really wanted: Blackpool Opera House. I was to have a sort of compère's role, doing a warm-up, two small spots then my main twenty minutes immediately before the finale. There were other acts: Nino Frediani, the world's fastest juggler; Fiddlygig, who'd been with me at the Palladium; Don Dunfield, a trampoline act from Las Vegas; and a young comedy impressionist who'd just won *New Faces.* Lenworth George Henry was his name. He was tall and gangly with seemingly little control over his limbs; he walked into things, he knocked things over.

What a start for a teenager, his first job the country's number one summer show! But it could easily backfire, he had little experience of working an audience and he was being thrown to 3000 people each performance. I decided to take him under my wing. I watched him each house, making notes as I did. We'd then get together in the dressing room, reformulate, add gags, subtract gags and try again. He was a very willing student, doing everything I suggested without question. By the time the season was halfway through he was more than holding his own and I felt a sense of pride every time I watched him. I still do, if truth be told.

The company was held together that year by the Karl Scott Memorial Fund. We opened fêtes, held raffles, had cricket and football matches; all proceeds went into a bank account. Robert Luff was most impressed by the efforts we'd made. At the end of the season he asked how much we'd accumulated; it was a substantial amount.

'I'll double it,' he said. What a gent! We sent the money to Karl's widow who had two very small sons to bring up on her own.

One September evening while in the theatre I was called to the phone. It was Toni in a terrible state. Her dad had just died.

'I'm going to be with Toni,' I said to Lenny. 'Can you fill in for me if I don't get back?' I couldn't leave Toni; she was in shock, I thought she'd never stop crying. Lenny went on and did my act word for word, the actions, the voice everything. People listening on the tannoy didn't realise it wasn't me. What a mimic!

Toni went off to London, leaving me with the kids. Two doors away from the house we were renting lived Pat and Brian Parker; they had three girls and our kids and their kids played together. Pat took charge. Before I set off for the theatre in the evening, I'd give Rachel and Rory their tea then take them to Pat. They'd stay the night there, Rachel sleeping with the two older girls and Rory sleeping with the youngest, Alison. She's a high-flying lawyer now, I must remind her of this next time I see her. Without Pat and Brian we'd never have got through this difficult period; you'll be pleased to know that we're still in contact with them. It was a really sad time for all of us. Tom had been ill with leukaemia for a couple of years but no one had expected his death at the age of sixty-one. Toni was very worried for her mom's state of mind, living in a flat in Pimlico.

'Why don't we move your mom into the house in Twickenham?' I said to Toni. 'She could be our housekeeper.' After consulting Margaret and John, who said they'd be delighted to have Bet next door to them, we put the proposal to her.

'We'd like you to move into our house in Twickenham, Mom,' Toni said to Bet. She wasn't even slightly surprised, but we were by what she had to say: 'Your Dad knew you'd do that.'

'Pardon.'

'Your Dad said, "When I'm gone, Don will ask you to move into the Twickenham house." ' Not only that, he'd left a specific amount of money for her to have the whole house rewired before she moved in because he was worried about the electrics. I still find that all rather uncanny.

* * *

We took the *Minstrel* show into the clubs – revolutionary or what? Places like the Wakefield Theatre Club, the Double Diamond, Caerphilly, we packed them all. Lenny Henry had learned a lot and audiences loved him. He had a rare quality which meant that everyone, pros and punters alike, would forgive him anything, even big mistakes. He was truly delighted to be part of what was the top variety show of its generation. His mother, Winnie, and all his brothers and sisters came to see him and were equally pleased. It saddened me years later when in an interview Lenny spoke of the shame of being associated with a show which so demeaned black people; he certainly didn't think like that at the time. In my opinion, the *Minstrels* in no way ridiculed black people any more than panto dames ridicule women or Frank Spencer and Mr Bean ridicule people with learning difficulties. I was saddened even more when George Mitchell died recently and no mention of his passing was made by the BBC for whom he had fronted the top-rating show of the seventies. I mentioned him on *Good Morning Sunday* you'll be pleased to know, but was not allowed to play a *B&W* record in case the politically correct Gestapo were listening.

12

Solihull, Here We Come

That Christmas I went into *Goldilocks and the Three Bears* at the Grand Theatre, Wolverhampton and my place in *Crackerjack* was taken by Bernie Clifton, an excellent choice I thought. Humphrey Standbury who ran the Grand was a great man of the theatre, he really knew what the panto audience wanted. He booked Paul and Barry Harman who later found fame as the Chuckle Brothers, and a young, bizarre-looking girl named Su Pollard whom he cast as the dame – strange, I thought, but it worked.

Paul, Barry and I re-created a visual comedy routine which had been done on the halls by an act called the Three Pirates during the 1930s. Dressed in white tights with leopard-skin tunics, we performed an unbelievable balancing act with Paul lifting me with ease and throwing me across the stage for Barry to catch. The tricks became more and more outrageous until Barry jumped on to the end of a see-saw, catapulting me into the air where I performed a perfect somersault before landing in a chair on a pole held by Paul. Throughout we communicated and argued with one another in cod Japanese. Although what we said was total rubbish, the audience understood every word. The routine became funnier every performance.

Apart from the two BBC pantos, I'd not done panto since just before Rory was born. Very soon he would be starting school, so I took him with me two or three times each week. He'd sit on a high stool in the wings, watching every minute of the matinée, he knew it by heart. I'd take him for tea then bed him down in the dressing room. He never woke up when after the evening show I carried him back to the car and drove home. I do feel that the children of performers should be encouraged to watch their parents from the side of the stage; it's their entitlement, their heritage.

Humphrey Standbury had been so keen to get me to Wolverhampton that he'd offered me a percentage of the profits on top of my salary, provided we exceeded the box office total from last year. As I've already said, I was known to every child in Great Britain, and the theatre was packed at every performance. By the end of the fourth week we'd already passed last year's take. Humphrey put on extra performances to accommodate the demand. At the end of the ten-week run, I was given a £9000 bonus.

'What shall we do with this windfall?' I asked Toni.

'Simple, buy a house,' she said. Funny how things work out isn't it? If I'd heeded Bill Cotton's threat, I'd never have come to live in Solihull.

We found a house that was being built by a private builder, Ernie Greer. He and his wife, Peggy, were to become very dear friends. We bought this '4 bed, dble gge, det' home for £40,000 and we're still in it now. Before we left Selly Oak, we threw a party for all the neighbours, who were a delightful lot. My Dad, a man of austere sobriety, got very drunk. Toni and I helped him back to his own house, which you'll recall was a short step away.

'You've disappointed me you know,' he said in slurred tones.

'How's that, Dad?'

'If you'd worked harder at St Philip's you could have gone to Birmingham University, you could have been a sports master in a school now instead of this comedian lark.' Education was so important in his mind. Interesting, isn't it, that eighteen years later his grandson would graduate from Birmingham University with a degree in Physical Education and is now an extremely fulfilled teacher – spooky or what!

Rory started school that year at St Augustine's RC Primary in Solihull. He was unimpressed, he never wanted to go. Getting him there was a trial, he much preferred to stay with me and Toni. The teachers had words with us.

'Rory arrives at school and from the moment he gets here all he wants to do is go home. When the bell goes he's first out of the classroom.'

I decided to question him about it: 'You don't like school much do you, son?'

'No, Dad.'

'Why not?'

'They've not found anything to interest me yet.' Small wonder. Rory was interested in things that flew, preferably in outer space, and things that swam under the water. As a five-year-old he could identify every different type of whale and dolphin, telling you what they ate and where they could be found, and he could identify every type of shark from its tail or dorsal fin. His problem, it seemed, was not uncommon in small boys. They fear that some harm will befall their mother while they're away. They believe that if they are with her they will be able to protect her – sweet, but educationally counter-productive. You'll be pleased to know that he grew out of this last year.

For a year at least, I couldn't get arrested at the BBC. Morris kept hitting brick walls. I was frustrated; my career was no longer in drive, it was in neutral and would soon be in reverse. The ambition that had made me strive to be the best was replaced by a television obsession. I was just desperate to get back on the box. I went to see people I'd worked for, like Brian Penders and Ernest Maxim. They seemed off-hand and dismissive but perhaps it was me expecting too much. I turned to squash. I spent every weekday morning either playing or training for it. I was even turning down gigs to play in squash matches. There were things to do in our brand-new home, but after only two months in residence we were off for Scarborough, jewel of the east coast, famous for sea frets, the only seaside resort where the donkeys are fitted with fog lamps.

My Mom went a bit funny on us that year when she and Dad visited. She was quite unpleasant to Toni, which hurt more than angered me. She told us she disliked the house we'd bought for her in Selly Oak. Obviously, now we'd moved to Solihull, she wanted to move there too. I made up my mind to sell that house and buy another which would again be near to us.

Robert Luff and George Mitchell were really spoiling me, I've never been treated so well, but I knew that this was to be my last year with the *Minstrels*. After five years with the same show, I needed to move on. I was confident that I'd have little difficulty getting a good season next year, and as I was no longer featured in the *B&W's* TV series, I felt my value to them and theirs to me had diminished. Bob Luff was upset and annoyed that I didn't want to stay with the show and, as I keep saying, you can't afford to make enemies in showbiz.

Lenny Henry did his very first panto playing the Genie of the Lamp with me in Bournemouth. He and I spent a lot of time together. When we talked to one another people laughed, we'd somehow got on to the same wavelength and at the same time tapped into a seam of humour that had the potential for wider appeal. I mentioned it to Howard, who made notes of some of the conversations between Maclean and Henry for future reference.

Howard was writing really well for me. We were in contact on a daily basis, changing the act bit by bit. He was brilliant with topicals:

'Two car workers walking through Canon Hill Park, the one said, "I see the tulips are out"; the other said, "Will it affect us?" ' Yes, we were in the grip of trade union power. I am the son of a trade unionist and I have to say that I respect the right of a worker to withhold his labour, but in the mid-seventies unions held our country to ransom. There was to be yet another strike at British Leyland, the media were outside the gates waiting to *vox pop* the workers as they came off shift. A worker by the name of Ron Hill achieved momentary fame by looking into a camera and saying in impassioned tones, 'We wanna work, we just wanna work.'

Ron Hill inspired Howard and me to write 'The Carworkers' Anthem' as a tribute to the beleaguered lads on the track. The chorus went:

> Come to Birmingham where the car workers am,
> We mek nineteen Minis a day.
> Come to Birmingham where the car workers am
> And we'll drive your worries away.

I'd only performed it three times in public when a local record company approached me. They booked Fisher and Ludlow's Social Club (you remember that?) and filled it with the chaps who pressed the bodies for British Leyland and their wives. We made a live recording; the audience reaction sounded great. It sold like hot cakes particularly to people in the car trade. However, the management were upset because they felt it ridiculed the company. They objected to lines like:

> We launched a new model the other day
> With a do at the local Locarno.
> It goes like a Rolls but it's so full of holes
> That we've called it the Morris Meccarno.

I'd done it again; you can't afford to make enemies when you're in showbiz. If you do have a copy of that record by the way, hang on to it; they change hands today at several times their face value.

The appearances on *Celebrity Squares* continued, keeping me in contact with Bob Monkhouse. Francis Essex, the Head of Comedy at ATV, wanted a sketch show. Bob had come up with a most original format, the idea of which was to have four sketches running at the same time. Needless to say, performers from one sketch ended up in another, people who were in more than one sketch appeared wearing the wrong costume; despite this the whole thing was logical. Bob put together a group of comics who were relatively unknown: Bobby Knutt, Pete Price, Bobby Pattinson, Pat Mills, Linda Cunningham, and Dave Ismay who is now my agent. The show was to be called *Comedy Connection* and in overall control would be the Connector in Chief, which Bob described as a master chef in the kitchen trying to bring everything to the boil at once. Francis Essex had Kenneth Connor or Kenneth Williams in mind for that role, but Monkhouse wanted me and he got his way. Both Bob and I were great fans of Bilko, Bob saw something in my performance that reminded him of Bilko. 'That's what I want from you,' he said. 'Take command of all the elements and bring them under control, but do it like a maniac.'

I knew what he meant. It took two days to film the show at Elstree. Bob directed but not from the gallery, from the studio floor. I have to tell you that *Comedy Connection* was the best thing I ever did on TV and Francis Essex said it was the best thing he'd ever commissioned. The show was transmitted as a one-off. The reaction was amazing and the show got into the top ten in that week's ratings.

'I must have a series of six,' said Francis. Bob dashed to his typewriter. The cast were contracted to start the series on 13 March 1978. The American who had taken the Muppets to the States, thus earning ATV a fortune, turned up at Elstree. Francis couldn't wait to show him *Comedy Connection*. He sat stony-faced throughout.

'Well?' asked Francis.

'I didn't understand it,' came the reply. 'No one else will understand it, there's no way you'd sell it in the US.'

Francis, having been besotted with it, now decided it was rubbish. Yes I know what you're thinking, 'If the man is Head of Comedy and he is incapable of making his own judgements, he shouldn't have had the job in the first place.' 'Pillock' is the word you seek.

He sent for Bob. 'I've changed my mind, the show stinks.'

'Then what are you going to do?' asked Bob.

'Kill it,' came the reply.

He did just that. He paid all the cast their full money for the series and told us not to bother to come. I was devastated. That American, whose name I do not know, denied several comics, including me, the opportunity to become household names because there's no doubt that *Comedy Connection* would have been a huge hit. I don't bear the man a grudge; I just hope that a rottweiler on heat falls in love with his shin.

Although another bid to get back into TV had failed, summer would be wonderful. We were to work with Cilla in Torquay. We rented the same flat overlooking Paignton harbour. I was second on the bill and Cilla had the idea of us doing a double at the top of the show. Howard set to work, and the result was a comical discussion between Cilla and me of the merits of Liverpool compared with Birmingham:

'What have you got in Birmingham to rival John, Paul, George and Ringo?'

'Ansells Bitter, sex and bingo,' I'd reply.

Cilla was the best feed I've ever worked with; her comedy talent has never been utilised on TV. She also managed to laugh like a drain at lines I said every night as though it was the first time she'd heard them. We would repeat this success the following year at Bournemouth. The company included The Second Generation and Rachel, aged nine, fell in love with the head boy, Jeff Thacker, who's now one of Britain's top choreographers.

Rae fitted in at the local school extremely well but not Rory. Again we had terrible trouble with him; he wasn't happy until school holidays began.

Cilla organised parties, the most memorable of which was a Hollywood extravaganza at which we were all to turn up as either a star or a character from a film. No one was more determined to keep secret his intended disguise than Bobby, Cilla's husband. Toni and I arrived as Gina Lollobrigida and Elvis, but where were Cilla and Bobby? Cilla's Rolls-Royce had been stopped by the police because of the strange appearance of the driver. The policeman told the Invisible Man that unless he removed the bandages from his face he could not continue driving. He changed places with Cilla, and Jean Harlow drove to the party. The Invisible Man was the toast of the night. However, he couldn't join in with the toast as holding a glass with hands swathed in bandages proved difficult, besides which he'd forgotten to leave a hole in the bandages for his mouth. Bobby Willis was one of the most amusing dinner guests you could ever have. An endless repertoire of Liverpudlian stories flowed from him while Cilla sat at his side giggling at them all. I was extremely sad when this lovely man succumbed to cancer.

Cilla's mom and auntie Nellie would come to visit and it would be my job to get these devout Catholic ladies to mass on the Sunday morning.

'She likes you, does our Cilla, can't you get her to go to mass with you on a Sunday?' said her mom. Bringing Cilla back to the faith was something I hesitated to attempt.

Francis Essex reared his head again. He was visiting veteran comedian Cyril Fletcher, who lived in Torquay, and together they came to see the show. I had an exceptional night. Afterwards Francis came round.

'I want you and your wife to come to lunch at Cyril Fletcher's place tomorrow,' he said. Toni and I were dubious but we found someone to look after the kids and turned up at Cyril's magnificent apartment.

'You are the best comedian of your generation,' Francis began. 'You will be the new Des O'Connor.' They haven't worn out the old one even now so I couldn't really follow the logic of that. 'We'll build a new variety series around you, top names but you'll be the host and the star.'

This was what I'd dreamed of, I was going to get back into television after all. We started rehearsing on 6 November. What a bill – Frankie Vaughan, Danny la Rue, Mary O'Hara! Howard's script and links were a masterpiece, I was so confident. On the day of the first recording, 19 November, the electricians went on strike. Nothing could be done. It took a while to settle the dispute, by which time Fickle Francis had gone off the idea. Instead of six one-hour shows, I did one which was well received but led to nothing.

I was becoming increasingly frustrated, this quest for stardom was eating me up. Perhaps God was showing me that there are other things in life, as indeed there were. While we were resident in Twickenham we were members of the Hounslow Swimming Club. Both kids were good swimmers and, at the age of six, Rachel was swimming breast-stroke leg in the under-eleven medley relay team. She was much smaller than all the others but extremely fast through the water. Both Rae and Rory were very happy in the water; at one point we feared they'd developed gills.

Rachel was also an excellent gymnast. From an early age she'd decided that the world looked better upside down and that she looked better with the bottom of her dress tucked into the legs of her knickers. She walked around on her hands and returned to the upright on request via a hand spring, a neck spring or a cartwheel.

'What is wrong with that girl?' I heard myself saying. She was extrovert and carefree. Rory on the other hand was painfully shy; he just wanted to be at home with the three of us. He was anti-social. He'd come out of school clutching a party invitation and saying, 'I'm not going.'

'He'll grow out of it,' everyone said, but by the age of seven there was no improvement. 'Get him to join something.' Good idea! Cubs – he flatly refused. Gym club with Rachel – no chance.

'You've got to do something,' I said, 'but you're not interested in anything.'

'Yes I am,' he said. 'I want to play rugby.' Where had that come from? The following Sunday morning we turned up at Solihull Rugby Club; the ground was just at the back of our house.

'Under-eights,' said one of the coaches. 'There they are, over there.' He pointed to a long line of small boys running one behind the other, passing a ball as they ran. Rory squeezed my hand tighter, he wasn't going to loose it. 'Here we go again,' I thought. I looked at him, his eyes were full of frightened tears.

'I've changed my mind, Dad, I don't want to play rugby after all. Shall we go home now Dad?'

I'm a real softy where he's concerned, it would have been so easy to walk away, but I held my nerve. The line was getting nearer, any minute now they'd be passing right by us. As they did, a gap appeared in the line, I pushed my son into the gap. The boy in front threw the ball to him, he caught it, passed it backwards and ran on. I stayed close by but he never looked for me, he was too engrossed. They split into teams and played a game. He came back to me an hour later smelling of earth and grass and sweat.

'See you next week, Rory,' said the coach.

'Are you coming next week?' I asked.

'Oh, yes please, Dad.' He was jumping up and down with excitement. I bought him a club jersey and socks and his rugby career, which would be a source of pride and pain of ecstasy and disappointment, had begun.

My own sporting exploits were getting me far more publicity than my comedy. I insured my teeth for £10,000 against damage during a squash game. I turned out regularly in matches for my club, Solihull Arden, and was invited to play for the showbiz squash team. This was organised by actor Bill Franklyn and included Leonard Rossiter, Tommy Steele and racing driver James Hunt. We would go to a squash club and take on their first team, all proceeds going to the Malcolm Sergeant Children's Cancer Fund. While the others played the game properly, I was determined to give the audience a night of entertainment. I worked out loads of visual gags and I also regularly left the court to involve the audience and berate the umpire. This went down so well that Peter Verow, captain of the England squash team and recently qualified as a medical doctor, suggested that we combine to put on exhibitions at squash clubs up and down the country. The *Squash Road Show* was born and proved very lucrative for many a year. BBC Sport were to televise the British Open. They suggested that the showbiz squash team might like to compete against one another for the title of British Celebrity Champion; an edited version of the final would be televised on *Grandstand*. I got to the final where I was to meet Tommy Steele. I was fit, I was quick but he was more determined and easily beat me three–love.

For the next twelve months I trained twice a week with 'Bomber' Harris, the man who coached Jonah Barrington. The following year, I again met Tommy in the final. Tommy, despite his public image, could be quite obnoxious on court. He was uncompromising, unsporting even; it gave me enormous pleasure to beat him. He was appearing in *Singing in the Rain* at the time so his tears of frustration didn't show. The following year, I retained my title, beating the very skilful Len Rossiter in the final. The competition never took place again so I suppose that means that I'm still the reigning celebrity champion.

Summer season 1979 was to be with Cilla again, followed by panto at Wimbledon, which was important because I encountered Frankie Desmond. Cilla and I played Aladdin and Wishee Washee, while Frankie was our mother, Widow Twanky. He was the loveliest dame I ever worked with, and although at the time I had no intention of ever playing dame myself, he was to be my template when the dreaded time came.

Still television eluded me. I saw a lot of Lenny Henry socially. He was living at home with his mom in Dudley and would often pop over to us. He'd pester Toni in the kitchen, he was so interested in cooking. Is that where the series *Chef* started, in our kitchen? He'd done quite a lot on telly but felt he'd never been used properly. I'd had an idea brewing for some time and I took it to John Clarke at Pebble Mill. It was very simple; a comedy show with the very minimum of scenery and no costume. Characters would be recognised by their headgear; if we put on policemen's helmets we were police, stetsons, we were cowboys.

John had a group of writers who kept sending gags to him for which he had no use. He decided to contact them all and get them to submit material. Howard Imber would be script editor. John found a young local actress who would play any female parts we needed. Lenny and I would wear black and white, indicating that we couldn't afford colour, and the show would be called *The Cheapest Show on the Telly*. It ran on BBC Midlands for six weeks and was an immediate hit.

The Head of Light Entertainment in London asked to see a tape of the show.

'Ah,' I hear you cry, 'that's that Bill Cotton chap and he doesn't like Don any more.' But hold hard, B.C. had been promoted to Managing Director Television and his place had been taken by Robin Nash, whom you will recall had been the producer of *Crackerjack*. Was this it? Would I be allowed back into the fold? Robin sent for me.

'I like this show,' he said. 'We'd like to do something with you and Lenny but on a bigger scale.'

'The whole point, Robin, was that it was cheap, that was the idea.'

'This show would have sketches, quickies, musical numbers . . .'

'But would we get to do the doubles where Lenny and I just talk to one another?' I asked. They'd been the mainstay of the show.

'Probably not,' replied Robin. 'You see, we have some other people who we need to find a vehicle for and we'd be putting them into the show with you.'

'How many people?' I asked.

'Four,' came the reply. 'We intend to call the show *Six of a Kind*.'

I went back home and called Lenny, who was waiting by the phone for news.

'I think we should hang out,' I said. 'They like *The Cheapest Show*, they'll do something with the two of us and maybe a comedienne. We know the format works, we have control of it, I don't think *Six of a Kind* is what we want.'

It was what Lenny wanted. 'Tell them we'll do it,' he said. 'It sounds great.

Great it indeed was. Ernest Maxim was to direct, which calmed most of my fears. Making up the six with Lenny and me were: Leah Bell, a petite, dynamic singer; Karen Kaye, who impersonated every known female vocalist and a few male ones; Pearly Gates, a beautiful black American who'd recently split from an all-girl trio; and David Copperfield, a very funny but totally uncontrolled comedy impressionist. Rehearsals were intense, no expense was spared and the shows looked spectacular. The middle of each show found the six of us in a flat which we all shared – was this the forerunner of *Friends*? During the recording of the series we were hit with another technicians' strike which disrupted things to such an extent that we ended up with only four programmes instead of six. None the less, Ernest had great hopes for the shows and we all returned home to await their transmission.

Several months went by. Lenny disappeared; we didn't hear from him but read nothing into that. I rang Ernest, he in turn rang Robin, but no date had yet been scheduled for *Six of a Kind*. Suddenly, it all fell into place. A marvellous new show appeared on our screens called *Three of a Kind*. Of the original *Six of a Kind* team, only Lenny and David Copperfield remained. They were joined by a very clever young lady, Tracy Ullman. The show gave Lenny the opportunity to prove he could be a star. I certainly don't begrudge him that but it would have been nice if I'd known about it before it hit the screen. I presume he was sworn to secrecy by several people, including his agent Bob Luff, but *Three of a Kind*, which was hailed as such an original concept, was in every facet *The Cheapest Show on the Telly*.

So, it had happened again, my third attempt to re-establish myself on TV had floundered or been sabotaged – perhaps it was time to read the writing on the wall.

Another Brummie comic, Jasper Carrott, was making a name for himself. Jasper is a friend, someone I admire and actually envy to some extent. While I was waiting for others to offer me TV opportunities, Jasper had control of his own destiny, manoeuvring himself into a position where he could tell TV companies what he wanted to do. Now of course he makes programmes himself through his own company, Celador. The present generation of comedy performers all make their own TV shows. I believe they have Jasper to thank for this. He was the first.

13

Fun in the Falklands

Ambition went on the back burner for a while. I'd sold Mom and Dad's house in Selly Oak and bought another in Shirley, approximately four minutes from us by car. They were very content there and we saw plenty of them. Dad, like most men, had never been health conscious and had ignored symptoms which should have alerted him to the fact that he had a serious problem. He was diagnosed with cancer of the lower bowel. I was devastated. He spent three weeks in Solihull Hospital undergoing tests and being prepared for a major operation. The surgeon was frank with me, telling me that provided the tumour was contained within the colon, the prognosis was good; if, however, it had broken through the intestinal wall to stomach and liver, Dad would have a short time to live.

The day of the operation came. I was at the hospital by 6.30 a.m. Dad was scared of operations but my presence always seemed to calm him. He was first on the surgeon's list. I sat by the bed talking quietly to him. Dad didn't share my Catholic faith, he'd never been a churchgoer, but he certainly believed.

'I'll be praying for you, Dad,' I told him.

'I'd rather you prayed for the surgeon,' he said with a twinkle.

They let me go right to the door of the theatre with him. I squeezed his hand and he disappeared through the rubber doors. I went back to the ward and sat in an easy chair next to the space where his bed had been. I told God how important my Dad was to me and I asked God to make sure Dad knew how much I loved him. I was still there three hours later when they brought him back from the theatre.

'Charlie, come on Charlie, wake up.' There were two nurses trying to get a response but Dad was having none of it. I leaned over the bed.

'Dad,' I said quietly. He opened his eyes,

'Hello, mate,' he said and slid back to sleep with a smile on his face.

I left the ward with a light step. I'm not sure that it was God who told me but I knew Dad was going to be all right. That evening the surgeon confirmed it; the growth had been contained, he'd removed all of it. The recovery period would be long and Dad would have to get used to his colostomy which was not reversible. He approached his physical readjustment philosophically saying, 'People lose arms and legs, I've just lost me bum.'

I couldn't blame the trauma of Dad's illness for my increasing dissatisfaction. Although being recognised, stopped and pointed at in public did have its drawbacks, I'd enjoyed the fame. People's memories are short. Now I could walk around unmolested and I missed the adulation. Radio 2, though, kept faith with me. Tony Hare had written a bizarre radio sitcom, *Maclean up Britain* with me as the mad Professor Pontius Maclean. Producer Martin Fisher brought in Jan Hunt, Bob Todd and Chris Emmett to play the other parts. *Maclean up Britain* was followed by three series of *Keep it Maclean.* Jan and Chris remained while Bob Todd made way for announcer, Gordon Clyde.

'Here's the latest news in the case of the old lady who went into the Tate Gallery and broke off a certain part of the anatomy of a male statue. She's extremely pleased after the magistrate ordered her to keep the peace.'

'Oh come on now – keep it Maclean!'

Tony Hare and Howard Imber wrote the scripts. They were joined for one series by two young men straight from university, Jimmy Mulville and Rory McGrath. They weren't very reliable as writers but it was obvious that they would both find fame soon, as indeed they did. I now acknowledge that radio was and is my forte. If that fool Logie Baird hadn't invented television, my stardom would have been assured.

* * *

I was approaching forty and I began to realise at last that it wasn't going to happen, I wasn't going to become an international or even a national name; time was against that. Fortunately my home life was great. Toni was my backbone, my rock. Every morning when I wake up, I look at her and say to myself, 'I'm gonna be as nice as I can to this woman all day.' A day spent without her, even now, is a day wasted. The only important thing was to know that she and the kids loved me just as much as ever. It didn't matter to them that I hadn't achieved stardom. Bob Monkhouse, upon whose words I'd always hung, had said to me one afternoon while we were sat in his garden watching Rachel and Rory swimming in his pool, 'Never let other people have the benefit of your kids' growing up.' Bob had been very busy building his career when his children were young and I always feel he regretted that.

I spent as much time as I could with mine. I'd get up to take them to school in the morning no matter how late I'd got in from a job the night before. They were my main source of entertainment. Rory and I spent hours kicking a rugby ball to one another. He was becoming very skilled and of course, every Sunday after early mass, we were off to mini rugby together. I went to gymnastic competitions where I'd watch a hundred leotarded little girls doing the same floor exercise to the same piece of music. I went to innumerable swimming galas. I was at the end of the pool when my ten-year-old daughter won the girls' breast-stroke in the district sports. She sprang from the water and launched herself at me, one of my happiest and wettest memories.

My Dad's obsession with education was starting to rub off on me. The schools in Solihull were of a very high standard but the grammar school was a thing of the past. We put Rachel in for the entrance exam for St Martin's, a girls-only private school with an excellent reputation for sport, music and drama as well as academia. She passed with ease. In her class was a pretty dark-eyed girl, Melanie Westley – do remember the name. Melanie was a very accomplished diver. Rachel added diving to swimming and gymnastics but her biggest out-of-school pastime was rabbit breeding. When we asked her, 'What would you like for Christmas?' she replied, 'A shed.' The shed was fitted out with various breeding hutches, all of which she kept spotlessly clean, and most Saturday mornings were spent at rabbit shows. We'd set off early in the morning and return just after lunch, usually covered in rosettes. We rarely had fewer than thirty bunnies in residence. Rachel's reputation spread and kids would turn up with rabbits in boxes or just stuffed up their overcoat, seeking advice from the expert.

I would have loved Rory to have gone to SPGS but my old school was no longer in existence. I question the wisdom of abandoning the eleven-plus system under which I, a kid from a working-class home, son of a trade unionist who voted socialist all his life, got an excellent education. An equivalent education is now only available to those able to pay, and that's certainly not your labour-voting factory worker. There were, though, plenty of others willing to pay so competition for places at Solihull School was fierce but, to our delight, Rory passed the entrance exam and became a public schoolboy. Two kids at fee-paying schools; I would certainly have to keep earning.

I was working and working well but I was sliding off the top rung. Instead of being offered Blackpool, Torbay or Bournemouth, I was offered Lowestoft. The Chuckle Brothers were with me again, also on the bill a young impressionist doing his first ever summer show: '*Bobby Davro, an immaculately groomed impressionist with a baby face and a voice that sounds more like Johnny Mathis than Johnny Mathis.*' It was obvious to me that he'd go far and I'm not wrong about these things. He has indeed made his impact on the British comedy scene. The critics liked me too, I'm pleased to say: '*Unlike many established comedians who saunter on stage expecting appreciation, Don Maclean works hard. Cracking a continuous stream of jokes, he matched the speed of a machine gunner with the accuracy of a sniper and won roars of approval.*'

Despite the success of the show, I was not sure it was the right move for me. Certain other people were to question whether they'd made the right choice; it was during that summer that Prince Charles married Lady Diana Spencer.

I began to feel rather like a top footballer who was slightly over the hill. Should I continue to do what I loved doing but slip into a lower league each season, or should I make one last bid to stay in the Premiership? I was also starting to go grey, just the hair, not all over. Another dilemma: should I maintain my hair colour artificially or should I accept the fact that I was beginning to resemble a racoon? My desperation to be on television was probably working against me, it was certainly affecting my peace of mind. I wasn't sleeping. I'd lie awake for hours and if I did drop off, I'd wake up bathed in perspiration. It was affecting my relationship with Morris Aza, too. He couldn't get me on to TV and I began to blame him. I decided in my own mind that the agents who got their artistes on to TV were those who already had clients working for the TV companies. One such agent was Paul Vaughan in Birmingham. Larry Grayson, Ann Diamond, Chris Tarrant, Nick Owen, everyone he represented was constantly on. Yes Paul Vaughan was the answer, my key to staying in the top league.

Leaving Morris Aza is something I regret deeply. If you pushed me, I'd have to say it's something I'm ashamed of. I don't suppose my career now would be much different but I'd probably feel better.

Initially, though, it seemed I'd done the right thing. Within a week it was reported that Larry Grayson was to leave the *Generation Game* and I was tipped to take over from him; sadly that turned out to have no foundation whatsoever. Paul pushed me, encouraging me to write, something I'd never done before. Within a short time, I'd read four of my own short stories on Radio 4's *Morning Story*. ATV booked me to present a daytime series entitled *Super Savers* about spending wisely and managing money sensibly. I was back on the box.

Paul employed several people, each with their own speciality. He put me with John Tyler, the drama expert, his thinking being: get Don into a stage play, develop him as an actor then try to get him into a television sitcom. Before we could begin journeying down that road, I was again approached by CSE. I told you about that earlier but perhaps I should expand.

CSE was the modern-day version of ENSA which troops in the Second World War said stood for 'Every Night Something Awful'. Likewise CSE stood for 'Crap Show Expected' to modern service personnel. The war in the south Atlantic had been over for about a year. They'd just started sending shows out to the Falklands. Jim Davidson was the first, followed by Harry Secombe; they wanted me to be next. I couldn't wait and neither could John Tyler; he would accompany me.

There were ten of us, performers, musicians and technicians, who boarded the VC10 at Brize Norton *en route* for Ascension Island, the half-way point. Ascension is a volcanic island, a sort of ashtray in the middle of the Atlantic. The black ash gets up your nose, in your eyes and ears, on your teeth if you're daft enough to smile. In two days we did five shows for the RAF refuelling crews there, by which time the show was pretty slick. Now it was time to make our run for the Falklands. We clambered aboard a C130 Hercules, a wonderful shire horse of an aeroplane. It was packed with freight but passenger-wise there was just the ten of us. Needless to say I was straight up on to the flight deck. The crew were extremely blasé.

'How long will it take us to get to Port Stanley?' I asked the pilot.

'Dunno, we've never made it all the way,' came the reply. The Herc couldn't in fact carry enough fuel to make it all the way so we had to rendezvous with a Victor tanker and refuel in mid-air. What a procedure that is! The RAF is fiercely proud of the flying ability of its pilots. If you remember, during the war, a Vulcan bomber had travelled several thousand miles to bomb the airfield at Port Stanley, refuelling not once but several times in the process. A new modern airfield has now been built for the islands but at that time Port Stanley was still the only landing place. If an aircraft was expected it was necessary to ensure that the runway was clear of sheep. This gave me one of my best gags: 'There's only two things here in Port Stanley: sheep and landmines. It's very much a case of "baa, baa, boom!" and the sheep are all over the runway, doing their little jobbies. I thought if the Pope ever visits the Falklands, he'll leave with a nasty taste in his mouth.'

I also wrote a routine about mid-air refuelling, another about the winch men, those lunatics who hang from helicopters on a bit of string, and one about the RAF's navigational expertise: 'I said to the pilot, "How do you find these small islands in this vast ocean? Sonar, radar?" He said, "No, we just follow the empty lager cans in on the tide".' There were cruel jokes too: 'The RAF are saving up to buy General Lami Dozo a glass-bottomed boat so he can keep an eye on his Airforce.'

We entertained at all the now famous battle sites: Mount Kent, where abandoned artillery pieces and burned-out half-tracks still littered the ground; Port San Carlos from where the resting places of HMS Antelope and HMS Ardent could be clearly seen, marked by buoys; and Goose Green, where we performed in the same village hall where the villagers had been held captive as H. Jones and his Paras approached.

We were transported to each place by helicopter. Flying above the flat, tree-less terrain at two hundred feet or less, one wondered how it was possible to coax a living from this land. There was bird life in abundance, every make of goose you could think of and also several varieties of penguin, one of nature's best jokes. On land penguins huddle in a large circle, moving around and chattering away to one another. As they can't fly themselves, they're very interested in anything that can, especially helicopters. Whenever we flew over them, they would look up, keeping their eyes glued on us and, as we passed over them, instead of turning round to follow our progress they would just lean further back until inevitably they fell over. Looking out of the rear of the chopper, you'd see this mass of black and white desperately trying to regain its feet.

Helicopters were essential so soon after the war. Movement on foot or by motor vehicle was still dangerous as the retreating Argentine army had scattered mines in their wake. We did twenty-two shows in fourteen days. Wherever we performed our last show of the day was where we'd stay the night. We slept in tents, in 'bashers', a type of portakabin, and one night, all ten of us were issued sleeping bags and bedded down on the floor of an army kitchen – at least it was warm. The locals were invited to our shows; they'd drive in miles from the hinterland. I made a point of talking to all the locals, they'd each have a war story to tell. An interesting lot the Kelpers, as they preferred to be called: fiercely patriotic and grateful to every living Brit for their deliverance. They were also immediately recognisable by the woolly hats worn by both males and females. The hats earned them the name Bennies, which they were quite happy with until the advent of television brought *Crossroads* to their notice. They were then mortally offended to be likened to Paul Henry's creation of the intellectually challenged Benny. A directive went out to the troops that the islanders were no longer to be referred to by this offensive title. When we got there the lads had taken to calling the locals Stills because, as they explained, they were still Bennies!

The incumbent RRF (Rapid Reaction Force) were the Royal Warwickshire Fusiliers, many of whom came from Birmingham. Before I left home, the *Birmingham Mail* printed an article saying that I would deliver, by hand, any letter or small package from the family of a Brummie soldier. I had a sackful. After each show I'd call out the names of chaps who I knew were in that particular audience. They were shocked as they had no prior knowledge that I was carrying something from their Mom, Dad, wife or girlfriend. It was one of the most rewarding tasks I've ever had to perform, great to see the delight on their faces, even the odd moist eye. I was also asked by ex-servicemen's groups in Birmingham to lay wreaths on their behalf at the beautiful war cemetery, built in the shape of a sheepfold. Like all Commonwealth War Graves they are lovingly cared for and deeply evocative.

I've always been a bit of an action man and every morning, while the others languished in their sleeping bags, I'd be up learning to launch a blowpipe missile or learning to read meteorology reports. I had breakfast underground one morning with the crew of a Rapier battery, I helped pre-flight a Chinook helicopter and I sat in the cockpit of a Harrier. For a few glorious moments I was strapped into the rear seat of a Phantom but the Squadron CO got to hear of it and my only chance of a flight in a fighter jet was aborted. I began to think that maybe I should have been a pilot rather than a comedian.

The final three days we spent in Stanley. We were accommodated in the 'coastel', an enormous floating hotel which would have given a mole claustrophobia. We did a show each evening in the gymnasium which could seat several hundred servicemen and women. After portakabins, tents, gun sheds and a rubber hangar (honest), it was a real bonus to work in a venue that was something like a theatre.

A very posh Volkswagen jeep arrived to take us to the gym.

'Galtieri's personal vehicle this was,' explained the ginger-haired corporal who was driving. 'Had it shipped over from Argentina special, he did.' I took stock. There were bullet holes in the back of the jeep behind my head. There was also a bullet hole that went right through the driving seat and a corresponding hole in the centre of the steering wheel. 'Dangerous job being a driver,' continued Ginger, cheerfully poking a forefinger in the hole. 'Looks like the bloke who sat here before me went home to Buenos Aires in a wooden overcoat.' Callous, you may think, but soldiering is a callous profession.

We were really well received whether working to a dozen Royal Engineers in a tent, to nurses and patients in the ramshackle hospital or to the grand mix of squaddies, matelots and airmen in the vast gym. The trip back to the UK, via Ascension again, was long, noisy and uncomfortable, but we all felt a tremendous sense of achievement at having been privileged to have brought entertainment to the lads so far from home.

John Tyler and I had become firm friends during the tour. I knew he'd work hard on my behalf and indeed he did. There was a new series being planned for BBC2. It was about people who were obsessive about their hobbies. It was to be produced from Pebble Mill and I got the job of presenting it. Originally it was to be called *Nutters*, which I must say appealed to me. The subjects we wished to interview, however, took their interests very seriously so it was decided to use the title *Keen Types* – rather public school don'cha think? I went on to do three series of the programme and met wonderful eccentrics – OK then, 'nutters' if you prefer: Gilbert and Sullivan fanatics, people who bought and drove around in tanks and jeeps from the Second World War, people who spent their weekends playing cowboys and indians or Vikings or knights in armour. That was the attraction really, it was all about dressing up. Only in England would you find people like that, people obsessed. During the summer of 1984, I was to become one of them.

Francis Golightly had for several years been putting the summer show into the Westcliff Theatre, Clacton, where I'd appeared for Bunny Baron in 1967. He asked me to top there that year. I took the Chuckle Brothers with me again so we could do our balancing act; their television potential had not yet been recognised but it would not be long now. I also worked for the first time with Dottie Wayne. Throughout my life I've been blessed with funny ladies, I think she's the funniest.

Several faces from the past turned up at Clacton, including June and John Webb who'd been part of the young set who came to see me every week in Felixstowe, eighteen years earlier. They're such good company that we made sure we'd not lose contact again and we never have. The season was a great success but that's not the reason it's so memorable.

Since returning from the Falklands, the interest in flying which I'd had since I was a small boy had increased. I went to Clacton airfield, a short grass strip at the Jaywick end of town, and signed up for flying lessons. After eleven hours I was deemed ready to go solo. What an amazing feeling! No trepidation, just sheer joy as I pushed the throttle and the Cessna 150 leaped forward, eager to be free of the earth. With only one person aboard it climbed so much quicker. Reaching 500 feet I turned left on to the cross-wind leg of the circuit; at 1000 feet I had to level off, turn left again, so that I was now flying alongside the runway, and call 'down wind'. I could hear singing, I realised it was me. I pressed the transmit button: 'Romeo Oscar down wind, singing Amazing Grace,' I called.

There was a smirk in the controller's voice: 'Romeo Oscar, roger, call finals.'

'Wilco!' I carefully completed the downwind checks. Out over the sea I turned on to base leg and began to descend to 500 feet. There was the threshold on my port wing tip. Stick and rudder together, I turned left again, selected full flap and lined myself up. Over the beach, over the golf course, eyes on the air-speed indicator, don't let your speed drop below seventy knots until you're over the hedge. Pull the power off, keep the nose up, flare out and touch the grass light as a feather. I was down, I'd done it.

I taxied over to the clubhouse where congratulations were heaped on my head by all and sundry. A large bowl of strawberries and clotted cream awaited me, I sat and savoured them. The fourth of July 1984 is another day I'll never forget.

I had a flying lesson every morning and every afternoon. I

took my three written exams and also the practical exam to obtain my radio-telephony licence, and completed my qualifying cross-country during which I had to fly solo from Clacton to Bourne in Cambridgeshire and land, then fly to Andrewsfield, not far from Stanstead, before returning home. On 2 August, less than five weeks after my first flying lesson, having a total of forty-three flying hours, I took my General Flying Test and passed – I was a qualified PPL. Flying is an obsession which is with me still.

Having got my licence I couldn't wait to take up my first passengers. I rented a Cessna 172. Rory sat up front with me, eager to get his hands on the controls. Rachel sat behind him reading a Mills and Boon romance, and Toni who was behind me kept saying, 'Shall we go back now?' In time she'd get to enjoy flying as much as me but that time had not yet arrived.

'A good pilot is any pilot who has the same number of landings as take-offs,' I pointed out to her, as I do to anyone who questions my aerial competence.

Rory was confirmed at the end of the season. I was pleased to see both my children embracing the rites of passage of the faith. He took the confirmation name Sebastian. We had a small tea party afterwards and I presented him with an arrow tie clip which I'd had made in Clacton. He still hated school but had a passion for swimming and rugby football. I was at every gala and match.

John Tyler had heard that there was a tour going out of a very funny play, *Bedfull of Foreigners*. He got me the comedy lead, Stanley, which had originally been played by Terry Scott. My co-star was to be the notorious Mata Hari of the sixties, Mandy Rice-Davies. Here's a claim to fame – I can truthfully claim to be the only man ever paid to get into bed with M.R.D. – twice on Saturdays. Despite her interesting past, Mandy was a delightful person and a woman of great intellect. She spoke several languages, her knowledge of English and European literature was extensive and she was also an extremely competent actress. She'd lived in Israel for some time and had embraced the Jewish faith. Wherever we went with the play, there would be flowers and bottles of champagne awaiting her. Invitations flowed in. Often she'd ask me to go with her, I thought for protection but, on reflection, I have to admit there's probably never been a woman more capable of fending off unwanted attention than Mandy. She was a sex symbol to a generation, many of whom were still out there, eager to see her on stage, hence the success of the tour. I've hardly seen her from that day to this but my life benefited from having known and worked with her. She's now remarried, to a millionaire of course, and lives in Florida, very happily I hope.

The play didn't lead to a sitcom but Paul Vaughan had found a game show for me. Jeremy Fox, son of Paul Fox, had a company called Action Time which specialised in developing game shows. I did a pilot for him of a show called *Mouthtrap*, rather apt as Les Dawson had once said of me, 'He's the only comedian who can get three billiard balls in his mouth at once and still not get a cannon.'

One of the contestants on the pilot was a tall young man with floppy hair. He wasn't just brimming with confidence, he was drowning in it, despite the speech detriment which he made no attempt to disguise.

'And what's your name?'

'Woss, Jonafon Woss.'

'What do you do for a living?'

'I'm a wemoval man.'

'How's business?'

'Picking up.'

He was a great contestant, the pilot was a great success and Anglia Television commissioned a series of thirteen. These would be done in the New Year. In the meantime my acting potential had been recognised, no, not by the RSC, by Malcolm Knight who had long wanted to do a revival of the Ray Cooney success *Chase Me Comrade*. I could have the lead role of Gerry Buss, if I was prepared to colour my hair. 'Gerry Buss is supposed to be early thirties, you could pass for that but not with grey hair.' As I mentioned before, I did consider dyeing my hair, but I then caught a glimpse of Ted Rogers on *3, 2, 1* with sooty black hair and a rusty parting and it put me off completely. The company would pay for me to have my hair dyed dark brown and I'd be touched up (if you'll pardon the expression) every four weeks during the run. What no one had foreseen was that at the end of the tour when I tried to dye my hair back to its original colour I ended up with purple hair for four weeks – the things we do for art!

The tour went well, I was learning much from having a cast of excellent actors around me. Dad, though, was unwell again. He was very worried about the appointment he had with the surgeon who had operated on him five years earlier. I spent my Sunday at home trying to reassure him. The following day I set off for Billingham with the show. Quite early on the Thursday Toni rang.

'Your Dad's been in severe pain all night. I'm just going to collect him and take him to Heartlands Hospital.'

'I'll come home after the show tonight,' I offered.

'Come home now,' she said.

I got into the car and began the long trek from the north-east. Toni picked up Mom and Dad and as she was helping Dad down the path he said to her, 'This is the end of me, you know.' He collapsed against the car, the next door neighbour dashed out to help Toni get him into the front seat. Dad was seemingly unconscious. Toni drove like mad to the hospital where they tried to revive him but his heart had failed. I arrived forty minutes too late. I know he was unconscious but even now I still feel that had I been there to hold his hand, he would have been unafraid as he took his last breath. Does that sound silly?

The show must go on, we're told, and the following Monday we opened in Harlow. Because there were funeral arrangements, etc. to be made, I'd decided to travel home each night after the performance. It was dark and rainy as I started back. Dad was filling my thoughts. When I was a small boy Dad had been my hero. I remember what a disappointment it had been when I grew old enough to realise that he didn't know everything after all. He'd supported all my sporting endeavours and been proud of my academic achievements such as they were. He'd been determined that I'd have all the opportunities he'd never had when he was a boy. Now he was gone. I prayed that God would have mercy on the soul of this gentle man.

I definitely wasn't concentrating. Suddenly the car was spinning through 360 degrees. The wheels hit the central reservation and the car flipped on to its roof. I was hanging upside down. A voice in my head, not my own, was shouting, 'Get out of the car.' I released the seat belt and fell on to my neck and shoulders. The voice was still shouting, though louder now. I kicked with both feet, the windscreen popped out and I crawled through the space where it had been. I was perfectly calm, I had no reaction, no outpouring of relief. When the police arrived and looked at the car they couldn't believe I'd walked away from it without a scratch. I felt the rain on my face and remembered the words of the psalm: 'The Lord is my light and my salvation; whom shall I fear?'

14

My Mom

The thirteen week series of *Mouthtrap* was to be recorded in a ten-day period at Anglia's Norwich studios. It was manic and the studio audiences loved it. I had Howard Imber with me, writing gags and even giving me lines while the show was under way. Anglia had a great track record with game shows. The secret of success was to make sure that the show went out at the same time in every ITV region. Unfortunately, only Anglia and Granada scheduled it for an evening slot; all the others put it out in the afternoon, moving it around time-wise from week to week. The result was a poor showing in the ratings. The national press weren't mad about it either: '*As entertainment it must rank alongside the worst American game show, indeed I feel* Mouthtrap *is the most ill-contrived programme seen for a long time. Host Don Maclean was presented as "the man with the mouth", most apt as he never stopped prattling.*'

There would be no second series. Howard, though, had impressed Anglia. They asked him to write *Lucky Ladders*, which ran for several series. *Mouthtrap* had opened a door but only one of us had passed through. Howard went on to write on *Family Fortunes*, *Punch Lines*, *Bullseye*, *New Faces*. He provided television material for Tom O'Connor, The Krankies, The Grumbleweeds, Bernie Winters, Kenneth Williams; the list is endless. It had been at my instigation that Howard had gone into writing full time and I always felt slightly responsible and concerned that he'd make a reasonable living. Now he was earning extremely well without me. I was pleased for him, especially as we'd heard that *Keep it Maclean* had been axed after three series, much to the disgust of its producer, Martin Fisher, who said openly that it was the best comedy show currently on BBC Radio.

Each week on *KIM* we'd featured a comedy song written by a chap called Gid Taylor. Travelling home from a cabaret date one night, I stopped at a motorway service station where I encountered a coach load of ladies returning from a concert at the National Exhibition Centre. How can I describe them? They looked like a very recently formed weight-watchers group who'd not yet got round to the watching bit. Each one had a white T-shirt stretched over her ample bosom proclaiming the legend 'I Love Barry'. The object of their affection was Barry Manilow and I began to muse how Barry felt when he looked out upon this mass of adoring adipose tissue. Did the idea of being fantasy-provoker to these flauntresses of the fuller figure fill him with dread? The ladies did recognise me but fortunately all their affection was reserved for Barry and 'I made it through the night' back to my car and safety. Next day I rang Gid Taylor and he wrote 'Just Barry', in which the famed heart-throb, fearful of the women he attracts, decides to give up the concert platform and become a welder.

All my life is girls and they seem to overwhelm it.
I'd rather hide my nose inside a smelly welder's helmet.
I'll sell my limousines, buy myself a motor scooter,
Incognito, there will be no, mention of my hooter.

Paul Vaughan fixed a one-record deal with a small label and the record was released. I sensibly didn't put my own name on it; 'Just Barry by Barry Just', read the label. Although Radios 1 and 2 never played it, it was picked up by many BBC local stations and most of the commercial ones. It was said that a few hundred sales would put a single into the top forty. Despite many plays and sales 'Just Barry' failed to make the charts, but Barry Just made quite a few bob and accumulated a bundle of abusive letters from Manilow fans, all on the same theme: 'He's the greatest singer that ever lived and all that people like you talk about is the size of his nose.' Political correctness now forbids us from making jokes about a person's appearance like, 'Put Barry Manilow and Barbra Streisand back to back you'd have a pickaxe.'

– Shame! Fortunately the true identity of Barry Just was never disclosed – until now, that is.

At the same time I wrote a book called *Maclean up Squash*. It consisted of short stories and even shorter gags about the game I loved:

'What's up with you?'

'The wife says that if I don't give up squash she'll leave me.'

'What rotten luck.'

'Yes – I shall miss her.'

Published in paperback, it sold 15,000 copies and meant that I was warmly welcomed into any squash club in Britain.

Howard and I submitted an idea for a comedy quiz to BBC Radio 2. We called it *The Cleverdickathlon*. We did two series of that, with me as resident question master.

Rachel had by now left St Martin's and accepted a place at Sixth Form College to do her 'A' levels. She was determined to get into showbiz as quickly as possible: 'If I can get a job, can I take it and not go to college?'

She already had a junior Equity card, having appeared as Eleanor in *Diary of an Edwardian Lady* on television, she sang well and played guitar to a reasonable standard, but there was no way she'd get a job, I was pretty certain of that.

'OK,' I said. 'If you can get an acting job, you don't have to go to college.' She took herself off to an audition and landed a part in a theatre tour of *Hansel and Gretel*. What could I do? I'd given my word.

'I shan't be like you, Dad, I'm going to be a star,' were her last words to me as she prepared to launch herself on the unsuspecting British public. It made me laugh as I remembered how determined I'd been to achieve stardom. Perhaps what she'd said was in the back of my mind a few weeks later when I drove up to Border Television in Carlisle to be interviewed by Derek Batey for that lovely little series of his, *Look Who's Talking*. I remember nothing about the interview except the final question, 'What are your ambitions now, Don?'

Without a second thought I said, 'To be my son's best friend and the sort of man my daughter would want to marry.'

I hadn't expected the question and the answer I'd given had

obviously been hidden deep in my psyche. I had to admit to myself that ambition was no longer there. For years I'd wanted fame but now, in the words of the great Buddy Holly, 'I guess it doesn't matter anymore.' I decided I was no longer going to look for work. I would do any work that came along to the best of my ability, but I was never going to become a household name even in my own household, so why keep striving.

Rory, in a very short time, had gone from being a small boy to becoming a large young man. In a mere twelve months he grew eight-and-a-half inches. He was six-feet-two and still growing. The bottoms of his trousers' legs looked like concertinas where they'd been let down weekly.

This led to certain problems. What we used to call growing pains now had a name, Osgood Schlatter's Disease. Severe pain in heels, ankle and particularly knees meant that rugby was out for a full season. Swimming, though, was no problem and the extra height meant he was winning all the butterfly and most of the free-style races he entered. Not so good for me; for years my son and I had indulged in regular combat, usually on the floor in the lounge but anywhere would do. I had always triumphed due to superior skill, strength and guile. We were on holiday that year, grappling in a swimming pool. Rory got me in a head-lock and held me under. Should I admit that I was no longer the strongest member of the household or should I drown? I chose the cowardly way and there's not been a lot of fighting between us since.

The following season Rory was to come back to rugby better than ever. He was converted from full-back to play No. 8 for his club and second row for the school. He would shortly have the honour of being chosen for Solihull School's First XV at the tender age of fifteen.

Paul Vaughan had a new chap in the office and he put him in charge of finding me work. Let's refer to him as 'Will' – that's not his real name (sorry about the deception, I'm not doing an Ulrika on you), but trust me, it's for the best. He was a rotund young man and I have to say I didn't take to him at all. He was over-confident and naturally unpleasant, but he had amazing energy for the job and he created a demand for me in the corporate market which was the growth entertainment area in the 1980s. Companies eager to motivate their sales force or reward their customers were organising events all over Europe. I went with Carlsberg to Malta, with Stelrad to Portugal, with Saab to Sweden. The money was great and I enjoyed the travel. Jersey and Guernsey were popular conference destinations. I could fly myself over there as I'd bought a two-seater Piper Tomahawk which I kept at Coventry airport. Seeing the Needles pass beneath your wing as you head out across the waters of the Channel towards Cap de la Hague is a great adventure, believe me.

I worked hard on personalising my material, often spending a day at the company accumulating local knowledge with which to target individuals within the company or ridicule their competitors. My memory was my biggest asset. I would often be asked to do a gag on each member of the board of directors or on every product sold by the company. One company had an Asian chief executive named Parmeeth Chimas, I racked my brain, but nothing would come. In desperation I worked out an anagram of his name, 'Hamish Teemcrap'. This caused great mirth among the workforce and I'm ashamed to tell you that the poor man is known as Hamish to this day.

I did a lot of work for Saab, they were a marvellous company to work for and I became a sort of court jester, invited to turn up at anything from major launches of new models to small office parties. A new MD was appointed. He was Scandinavian and completely unknown to the British contingent. There was a lunch to be given in his honour and I was asked to attend and make a short, funny speech. As I began, the new man lounged in his chair and closed his eyes. As often happens when there's a major player in the audience, the rest of the assembled folks were waiting for his reaction before they themselves laughed. The act was going down the tubes rapidly. In desperation, I decided to recount a trip I'd done for Saab to Gothenburg:

'We sailed from Harwich,' I said, 'on one of those big ferries DFDS which stands for "Danes, Finns and Drunken Swedes".' The MD whom we all thought had dropped off suddenly roared with laughter. He laughed so much that he slid off his chair on to the floor where he continued his convulsions. Everyone else in the room was laughing at him. The rest of the act went superbly well and I'm now a legend in Stockholm! Yes the corporate market was great. My new agent wasn't getting me TV exposure but so what, I was no longer bothered about that, I was content with my lot.

Head of Sport for Central TV was a chap called Gary Newbon with whom I'd long been friendly. He was determined to find a quiz-type programme to challenge the success of BBC's *A Question of Sport*. All sorts of formats had been submitted, none of which caught his imagination. He asked me if I had any ideas – indeed I had. One of the conference-creating companies for which I worked regularly had made a triangular game board for an inter-departmental game show at a big conference. I'd been in at the inception of this game and we'd since adapted it for Comet, for Lyons Maid Ice Cream, for Avis; surely we could adapt it for sport! I contacted Bob Lawrence of *The Electric Picture Company*, together we worked on it and the long-running *Sporting Triangles* was born. Again I saw it as a vehicle for me to compère, but alas, the fresh-faced Nick Owen was seen as a more credible question master and I have to admit he made a very good job of it.

I was trying to stay nearer home, avoiding seasons or tours and concentrating on one-nighters. I'd found my niche. Living in Solihull meant that I rarely stayed away, I'd drive home after a show when the surfeit of adrenalin ensured my wakefulness. Rachel's foray into showbiz had stuttered to a halt. After a promising start with the tour followed by a number one panto at Sunderland she'd gone to audition after audition without success. A bit more perseverance would have paid off, I'm sure, but she just couldn't cope with the rejection – she certainly had the talent but not the resilience. She was back living at home, which pleased her Dad greatly, and working for a large local travel agency. She'd also encountered Guy Pattinson who seemed to be turning up at our house with increasing frequency.

I did have one major worry – that was Mom. She'd seemingly taken Dad's death quite well. I saw her almost daily. On Sundays we all went to mass together and she spent the rest of the day with us. She had two neighbours who were also widows and they visited each other regularly. She then had a couple of nasty falls that left her bruised and battered. We found that often she didn't know what day of the week it was. We bought a blackboard with Monday to Sunday on it and wrote a weekly diary for her. She began to lose weight but assured us that she was eating well: 'I have a cooked breakfast nearly every day.' Toni bought eggs and bacon and put it in Mom's fridge. A week later it was still there, untouched.

It was Wimbledon fortnight and we'd spent a splendidly warm day sipping Pimms, nibbling strawberries and rubbing shoulders with the Duchess of Kent, as you do. We arrived home to find Rory there alone.

'Nan's in the hospital,' he said. 'Rae's with her.' Because we were worried about Mom and we were to be away all day, I'd said to Rachel, 'Check up on your Nannie during the day.' She'd waited for Rory to come home from school and they'd gone to Mom's house together. They could see her sat in her lounge but got no response to either ringing the door bell or knocking on the window. Rory climbed over the back gate and opened the front door for Rachel. Their presence had no effect on Mom, who was rocking backwards and forwards in her chair, hands clasped in front of her. She gave no response to anything they said. Rory found two rashers of bacon and a broken egg on the kitchen floor and thought perhaps his Nannie had fallen, though there was no other evidence of this. Rachel rang Mom's GP, who arrived within minutes.

We dashed to Solihull Hospital where we found a distressed daughter and a sleeping mother.

'Come back tomorrow,' said the nurse. 'We'll know more then.'

The following day Mom was dressed and sitting on the bed, swinging her legs when I arrived.

'Hello, Mom,' I said, but she looked at me without recognition. 'I've brought you a few things.'

She wasn't bothered, she was busy with her leg swinging. 'Have you told our Mom I'm here?' she asked.

'Pardon.'

'Our Mom. They brought me here straight from school. Our Mom won't know where I am.'

'She doesn't know me,' I said to the doctor when he arrived.

'That's because you've not been born yet,' he said. 'Your

Mother has gone back in time. There's absolutely nothing wrong with her physically, she's very healthy for her age, but part of her mind has decided to shut down.'

'Will she stay as she is now?'

'It's unlikely, we'll have to wait and see.'

I went to kiss Mom goodbye but she looked at me strangely and leaned away from me. The next day I took Rory with me. She was pleased to see us and gave us both a big kiss. She was in bed, I sat in a chair and Rory sat on the bed, Mom kept looking at him with such love.

'Isn't he a lovely lad, didn't we do well?' she said to me. 'I'm sorry you're having to come home to an empty house,' she said to Rory, then it was back to me again. 'Are you all right cutting up your own sandwiches for work? You'd better get another loaf on the way home.'

It suddenly dawned on me; as far as Mom was concerned, I was my Dad and Rory was me. Rory realised at the same time. He was completely unnerved and too upset to visit the hospital again.

Over the next few days, Mom's mind returned in stages to the present, or almost.

'Who are you?' she said to Toni.

'I'm Don's wife.'

'Don's wife! You're not married, are you?'

'I am actually, Mom.'

'Well nobody told me.'

We found that quite amusing. Other incidents were far from funny.

'How long have I been here?' she asked.

'A week, Mom.'

'Charlie's not been to see me you know. I thought he'd have come.'

I put my arms around her, 'Mom, Dad's dead. He died last year, don't you remember?'

'Charlie dead! No, please no!' She began to weep, very loudly. It was heartbreaking, as though he'd just died. The nurses rushed to my assistance. She'd calmed down by the time I left, she was just sobbing quietly.

The following day, she was dressed and doing a little bit to help on the ward. She was all smiles when she saw me. After a short while she said, 'Is your Dad all right? He's not been to see me yet you know.'

I walked her down to the empty lounge at the end of the ward and again told her that Dad had died. It was as though she was hearing the news for the very first time. She sank into a chair, her body racked with sobs.

'I can't stand that again,' I said to Toni when I got home. 'If she asks me about Dad tomorrow, I'll just say he's ill and can't get to see her.'

The following day Mom had undergone another change. No smiles, just a black look: 'You've got to get me out of here, I've had nothing to eat or drink and I've not been to the toilet for days.' She'd become obsessed with her bowels, insisting that the nurse must give her strong laxatives. She was functioning quite normally but couldn't remember going.

The hospital, having decided to discharge her, sent a mental health nurse to advise us. Her name was Faye Crofts and the advice she gave was invaluable. Nearly everything she predicted would happen over the next few months did. Mom was expecting to go back to her own home.

'I don't think she's capable of looking after herself,' said Faye, 'but she must be allowed to find that out for herself. Take her home and get her to prepare a simple meal.'

I collected Mom from the hospital.

'We're going home, Mom, and you can cook lunch for us.'

She quite liked that idea. 'What shall we have?'

'Beans on toast would be nice,' I said.

We stopped at the supermarket where she usually shopped. She hadn't got a clue what to buy nor where to find anything. I tried not to help but eventually I had to and we left with bread, butter and a tin of baked beans. I put everything down in the kitchen and sat and waited. It was as though she'd come from another planet. She just stood there helpless. She didn't know what a tin opener was, in fact she didn't realise that the tin had to be opened. She couldn't turn the cooker on and when I did she put the bread inside the oven instead of under the grill. Terrified that she'd burn herself, I did what I'd been told not to do and took over. It was a terrible moment seeing one of the most efficient women that ever lived incapable of a simple, everyday task.

Mom moved in with us. It was a nightmare. She'd lost all concept of time. If we left her for five minutes, when we returned she'd say, 'I've been here on my own for eight hours.' She told us and anyone who came to visit that we never gave her anything to eat, but probably the most upsetting thing was her accusing us of stealing all her money and selling the house that she had bought. We collected her pension and put it, untouched, into a metal cash box which Dad had made years before. We had no intention of selling her house, though it was ours as I'd paid for it.

Life at home was getting very strained. We'd just got to the stage where the kids were independent. We could go out at night socially or Toni could come with me to work and we didn't need to worry about babysitters. Rachel and Rory had stopped arguing, though she still bossed him around a lot. They'd both invite their friends home when we went out. They were enjoying their independence and so were we. Now the independence of all four of us was threatened by the presence of my mother, who couldn't be left for a minute. I was out working most evenings, which meant that Toni bore the brunt. It was my mother, not Toni's mother, she was my responsibility; perhaps I should give up work and care for her?

Faye Crofts suggested that we might like to consider residential accommodation for Mom. There were several places prepared to take people with dementia, she said. I was pretty horrified at first but Mom seemed to like the idea. She trotted round happily looking at various homes. She even stayed for a few nights at one of them. Eventually she moved into St George's which I could reach by car in two minutes from our house. She was surrounded by ladies of her own age and settled in almost immediately. I saw her every day, often taking her out with me if I had a short trip to do. On Sundays we picked her up for church, where Rory took charge of her. She'd once or twice taken communion then, being unable to remember where she'd been sitting, had charged off to another part of the church. Once she'd made straight for the exit. The sight of grandson and nannie receiving the Blessed Sacrament hand in hand became a familiar sight at Our Lady of the Wayside.

* * *

Paul Vaughan called me in to tell me that Will would be leaving the agency; he didn't say why but I got the idea that it was more than a mere clash of personality. I was, however, getting a constant stream of cabaret and conference work so I said that if he was going I'd go too. Paul wrote me a letter: 'Your decision proves to me that you are either innately foolish or insane. The man is an inveterate liar and fantasizer, is the possessor of a prison record and is being pursued by all and sundry for large sums of money. You will be sorry.' It wasn't a threat, more a prediction.

Will was confident, plausible and, when he felt it necessary, totally charming. As a child, he told me, he'd been locked up in a turret room in the house where he lived with his mother because he was uncontrollable. This led to many problems. He ended up in Borstal from whence he graduated to prison. He was now going straight and, with my help, would continue to do so. Everybody should have a second chance I thought – another mistake!

I was flying and playing squash; I played for the Warwickshire Over-45 team in the County Championship; surely I didn't have time for anything else. But I was persuaded to do an 'A' level by Colette Ware, a parishioner at our church, who was head of history at Solihull College of Technology. The course was European History from 1848 to the present with a special study of Nazi Germany 1933–1945. I spent three hours every Thursday evening at the college and I read every book on the period in the local library. In the summer of 1989, I took my Modern History 'A' level and passed with a Grade A. Colette was delighted. Next thing I knew, she'd contacted the University of Warwick where she herself had been an undergraduate and they'd offered me a place to study part time for a BA in Modern Political History.

I continued to visit Mom every day. She would be in the lounge with her two friends, Lucy and Tandy. Often I'd be greeted with, 'Hello stranger, I've not seen you for a long while.'

'I was here yesterday, Mom.'

'Oh were you? That's nice.'

I thank the good Lord that she never forgot who I was, that would have been too much to bear. She was always pleased to see me and would sit playing an imaginary piano on the arms of her chair while I told her about my day.

Several of the residents were in various stages of dementia. One old chap spent all day moving furniture round the large lounge. If I stood up, he'd hurry over and take my chair to another part of the room. 'Ignore him, he's barmy,' Mom would say. She'd lost all inhibition and said what she thought. We'd said hello to a friend while we were out shopping with Mom one day. 'Look at the size of her bum,' she said in a loud voice as the lady turned to leave us.

I'd talk to the other residents when I went to see Mom. Hilda was very confused, always looking for a baby whom she could hear crying. She greeted me with a smile.

'Hello, Hilda,' I said. 'Are you settling in?'

'Oh yes, I'm so glad we've found a new place to live, it wasn't easy finding somewhere suitable for my mother, you know.'

'Oh,' I said. 'Why was that?'

'Well she's been dead for nine years,' came the reply.

One of the few male residents was Jack. He gazed straight ahead, never communicating with anyone.

'Where've you been today?' Mom said to me.

'I've been flying, Mom.'

'Flying!' said Jack. Everyone looked up. Jack had spoken. 'I flew a plane, I flew planes off aircraft carriers.' I sat next to him and for nearly an hour listened fascinated as he told me about his war service in the Fleet Air Arm. He was animated, he laughed. The following day, I was eager to continue where I'd left off but Jack showed no recognition of me whatsoever and had reverted to zero communication as before.

Mom's two friends, Lucy and Tandy, were both as sharp as tacks. At first when I went to see Mom, I'd take her off into a corner to chat to her, but it became increasingly obvious that she was much happier with a three- or four-handed conversation; it took the pressure off her I suppose.

Toni and I with Rory took Mom on a fortnight's holiday to Tenerife. I'm so glad we did that, she had a lovely time though we had to watch her all the while; if she'd wandered off she would have been unable to tell anyone who she was or where she was staying. She was also becoming increasingly institutionalised. She referred to the man who owed St George's as 'the Boss' and, particularly on Sundays, which she'd spend with us, she would become agitated after a few hours saying, 'I'll have to go now, the Boss will be annoyed, I'll be locked out.'

I'd take her home, where the care staff would ask, 'Have you had your tea, Rosie?'

'I've had nothing to eat all day,' she'd reply and, despite having polished off dinner and tea at our house, would tuck into the sandwiches and trifle which had been put aside for her.

I've had several letters to Radio 2 from daughters or sons who've been forced to put a parent into residential care. I understand the feelings of guilt expressed in those letters, that won't go away, I still feel guilty even now; but I believe my mother was as happy as her condition would allow her to be. I also believe that both my children would now remember their Nannie with resentment had she continued to share their home. As it is, they remember her with great fondness.

The 1980s had been a decade of upheaval. My star which had been in the ascendancy throughout the seventies had waned, what did the nineties now have in store?

15

Good Morning Sunday

In March 1990, Guy Pattinson turned up at the house. Rachel was out so it must be me he'd come to see. The lad looked immaculate; his shoes shone and so did his face with a film of perspiration.

'I wanted a word with you,' he began. 'I would like your consent to my asking Rachel to marry me.' I remembered saying the same thing to my future father-in-law and his reply sprang to my lips.

'I'd be delighted to have you as part of my family,' I said, and I still am. Rachel's twenty-first was on 19 March. We'd arranged a party which we were to hold in the garden. The weather was glorious. Guy was the first to arrive. He had with him his mom and dad and a ring. Rachel had no idea what her birthday present was to be. He took her out into the garden and four parents, rather indiscreetly, peered out from the patio window. Guy produced the ring from his pocket and Rachel let out a squeal of delight.

Work continued to pour in for me, and in April I was offered a week at the City Varieties, Leeds – I told you that place would crop up again. Things had changed at that theatre – no more disrobing ladies, just variety with an Old Tyme Music Hall feel and a top of the bill that changed every week. Jan Hunt was in the resident company there. On the Friday evening I received a phone call from Yorkshire Television. Was it true that I was a practising Catholic? I confirmed that I was. In that case they'd like me to go along to the studio, after I finished on stage that evening, to take part in a live discussion programme about religion. I was delighted. I arrived and was introduced to the other participants: a Yorkshireman who had converted to Islam and a Methodist minister, Frank Topping. The presenter was a warm, friendly chap called James Whale; friendly, that is, until the programme started. The red light went on, the floor manager signalled James, who looked into the camera and said, 'Most of you out there are saying to yourselves, "religion, that's a load of b******s." '

Three jaws dropped as one. I hadn't expected anything like that. James then started on poor Frank, who was still gobsmacked by the opening gambit and managed little by way of response. James, with blood-lust dripping from every pore, moved on to his next victim. 'And you Muslims,' he accused, 'you're not interested in religion, all you want to do is get your hands round the throat of Salman Rushdie.' The poor chap was as nonplussed as Frank. I was thankful that I'd had a few seconds to gather my thoughts. When James rounded on me I was ready. 'You Roman Catholics are all obsessed with birth control. Do you and your wife practise birth control?' I quickly remembered every condom joke I'd ever heard and selected one at random.

'I was in a chemist's today and on a condom packet it said "new shape". New shape! Does that worry you James? It's been worrying me ever since.' Everything he threw at me I fielded with a gag. He bullied the other two as he bullied the people who phoned in while the show was on but he didn't try to bully me. He could think quick but I could think quicker.

Asked by a caller if he believed in God, James Whale said, 'Well, yes, I suppose I do; there, that's ruined my credibility.'

I decided to take him on: 'Ruined your credibility, that's the first thing you've said tonight that's had any credibility.' I was taking over but somehow he didn't seem to mind. I went on to explain how being a believer and publicly identifying myself as a Christian was something of which I was proud. I'd never had such an opportunity to stand up for my church before and I was relishing it. The programme finished and James Whale discarded his television persona as though it was an old suit and reverted to the charming chap I'd first met.

I spent the next few days in Athens, fronting a conference for a major computer company. When I returned, Will was in a frenzy.

'BBC radio wants to talk to you urgently. They've rung me three times.'

'What's it all about?' I asked.

'Some religious programme, I've told them you're studying theology at Warwick University.'

'But I'm not, I'm studying history.'

'Well, they won't know, they seemed impressed with the university thing. You've got a meeting with them tomorrow.'

The following day, I had lunch with three people who were to become very important in my life: Michael Wakelin, young, intense, Methodist and the producer of *Good Morning Sunday*; Rosemary Foxcroft, his researcher; and the Rev. Ernest Rea, Head of Religious Broadcasting. They took me to a posh Indian restaurant. I realised I was being wooed. *GMS*, I was told, was the flagship of BBC radio's religious output. For many years it had been presented by ministers of religion, the current presenter, Rev Roger Royle, was leaving and they were looking for someone to take over. Not me, surely? They've all been sniffing glue, I concluded.

Apparently Michael and Ernie had been in discussion for some time about what type of person they needed to replace Rog. The person they both wanted apparently was Roy Castle who combined showbusiness and faith. Roy had television commitments and was also undergoing tests for chest problems which we now know were life-threatening. They wanted a presenter who would make the audience sit up, who would surprise and, dare I say, shock on occasion. Alternatively, they could play safe and find another competent cleric; there were plenty about. They'd made a short list of potential presenters and they were keen to put me on it – well, Ernie and Michael were; Rosemary I felt had some reservations. I admit now that I didn't take any of it very seriously. Questions came thick and fast from three sides. I was quizzed about my faith and my commitment to the mass and the sacraments, but when we got on to sexism, racism and every other 'ism, I couldn't resist the temptation to wind them up a little. Michael told me that I would have to curb my sense of humour and certainly not overstate my Catholicism, which might ostracise listeners of other denominations. 'Oh, come on,' I thought. 'Being a Catholic and telling gags just about sums me up as a person.' Despite that, I was impressed by Michael Wakelin's enthusiasm and I left the meeting having agreed to do the programme for three weeks.

The following Sunday, Toni and I set the alarm for 7.30 a.m. On came Rog, warm, sincere, comforting. A most competent broadcaster is Rog, his 'Old Mother Riley' approach is truly comforting. We listened in virtual silence. At nine Toni turned to me and said, 'You can't do that.'

'You're right,' I said. I'd realised that half way through. 'I'll do the couple of weeks I've been contracted for but no more.'

I arrived at Broadcasting House at six sharp on the Sunday morning. There was no need for me to be worried, Michael was worried enough for both of us. At 7.30 the green light went on and I was off.

'Good morning, good morning, good morning Sunday, this is Don Maclean here with you for three weeks, that's not three weeks in one lump, just ninety minutes to start with.'

I was determined to be breezy and slick and to slip in the odd funny line if the occasion arose. Perhaps that would come during the interview. I had never interviewed anyone in my life before, and believe me interviewing ain't as easy as it looks. The then Governor of the Bank of England was to be my very first interviewee, Robin Leigh-Pemberton: Eton, Oxford and The Guards – we had a lot in common did me and Rob! Michael gave me some good advice:

'Your first question is so important, it needs to set your guest at ease. If it makes him smile, so much the better.' I took this on board.

'My guest this morning is Robin Leigh-Pemberton, Governor of the Bank of England.' I looked him straight in the eye and said in broad cockney 'Good morning, Guv'na.' The poor man was taken aback. There was a long pause then, with a weak smile that failed to expose a single tooth, he said, 'Erm, yes.'

The interview was a disaster, as were the next few interviews I did if truth be told. I must admit though that even now I work hard on finding the right first question for all my interviews. The Rev. Tony Campolo came over from the USA a little while ago; the conversation went like this:

'I have with me now the Reverend Tony Campolo. I

understand, Tony, that you are currently spiritual advisor to President Bill Clinton.'

'Yes, Don, that's correct.'

'Not very good at your job, are you?' Tony laughed loudly and genuinely at my observation. Well, Clinton was a nightmare. No wonder Hillary wore the trousers in their house, he could never remember where he'd left his!

I have a cleric live on *GMS* every week; there are now rabbis, Buddhists, Muslims as well as Salvation Army officers, bishops, nuns and priests. In those days they were all Anglicans who knew and felt comfortable with Roger Royle, they were quite taken aback by me.

Although the early interviews and the interactions with visiting clergy were a struggle, I was pleased with other aspects of the show, particularly the prayers. I'd said from the outset, 'If this is a religious programme, why is nobody praying?'

'Never thought of that,' they replied. 'What a good idea.'

Thus began the topical prayers which I write every week, sometimes relating to the relevant part of the church year or to the special guest or to happenings in the news.

Having presented *GMS* for three weeks, I sat back and listened to the other potential presenters. Dana I felt was too gentle but the three male 'contestants', Canon Colin Semper, Ian Gall and the aforementioned Frank Topping, were all excellent, far more competent than I'd been. I accepted with good grace the fact that I would not be the one chosen. *GMS* generated quite a lot of post and after my very first appearance most of it was negative. We received thirteen letters objecting strongly to my denomination:

'What are the BBC thinking of allowing a Roman Catholic to present a religious programme?' asked one listener from north of the border. A lady from down south asked me,

'Do you really expect God to listen to a prayer delivered in such a dreadful Midlands accent?' And you thought I was a bigot!

I'd enjoyed my foray into radio presenting, in fact I'd got a bit of a taste for it, but I honestly felt it would go no further and now I had other things on my mind. Rory's 'A' levels loomed. Having put together an impressive GCSE performance, I'd had high hopes when he'd opted for English, History and Religious Studies at 'A' level. He'd not enjoyed the sixth form. He was still very shy, though he fought against it. Playing for the school First XV and competing for the school in the National Relay Championships and other swimming matches kept him sane, but academically he was not putting the work in and I was unsure how hard to push. Rory never went through the 'Kevin stage'; at home he was cheerful and communicative.

I'd had a bit of bother with Rachel when she was fourteen and she'd decided that no one in the house was worth talking to. The silence had lasted nearly a week.

'I just don't know what to do,' Toni had said.

'Don't worry, I'll fix it.' That morning I loaded the kids into the car. Rory in the back was keeping up a non-stop conversation as usual, Rachel was silent in the seat beside me. St Martin's was the first stop but I sailed straight past – that got her attention,

'What are you doing, you've driven past the school?'

'Yes. I said to myself this morning, "If Rachel has spoken to me by the time I get to her school, I'll stop, otherwise I'll carry on." '

'You can't do that, I'll be late.'

'Exactly.'

We drove on to Solihull School where Rory, still talking, left us. Rachel, face like thunder, sat beside me. 'You've not spoken to either your mother or me for several days. What you need to realise is that I am your sole source of income. If you wish to carry on your silence, that's fine. I will honour my obligations, I'll feed you and clothe you and allow you to live in my house but there'll be no pocket money, no clothes other than school uniform, no transport apart from to school. If this is what you want then carry on as you've been doing but if you'd like to play happy families as before, when I pick you up tonight, say "hello, Daddy" give me a big kiss and we'll be back to normal.' She folded her arms defiantly and stared out of the window. I started the car and headed for St Martin's. Once there, she slammed the door so hard I thought the car would turn over on its side and strode off without a backward glance. That afternoon, I arrived early, parked in the road at the side of the school and stood by the car waiting. Rachel was the first girl out of school. She ran to me, threw her arms around my neck, kissed me and said, 'Hello, Daddy,' and that was the end of all our problems.

This experience, though, was of no help in the present situation, with Rory returning from each exam in despair. At university, I was studying modern history while Rory was studying medieval; I could be of little help with his revision. We'd just have to wait and see.

While we were waiting, a letter arrived from the Rugby Football Union, Twickenham: 'You have been selected for the Potential England Colts Week at Trent College, Nottingham from 22–27 July 1990.' There followed a list of names. Rory had been selected for the Warwickshire Colts' squad who would contest the County Championship next season. Unknown to the lads they had been assessed at every practice match or training session and Rory, together with three others from Warwickshire, had been chosen to go to Trent. I don't know who was more thrilled, him or me.

I was shortly to be thrilled again when, after all the other presenters had finished their try-out period, the BBC offered me the job of presenting *Good Morning Sunday* permanently. On reflection, I have to put the whole thing down to divine intervention. Having embarked on the part-time degree course at the University of Warwick, I'd begun to investigate the possibility of the diaconate. This was open to married men. The first ones, several of whom I knew, had been ordained in June 1989. If accepted, after a period of theological study, I would be ordained deacon and attached to a local church where I'd assist the parish priest with his duties. Perhaps the Lord despaired at the prospect of my becoming a deacon; it was almost as though He said, 'You'd be no good at that, Don, I'll find some other way for you to serve me,' and along came *GMS*. You're probably thinking that's a pretty conceited view of things but when you look back through history and see the deadbeats and hopeless cases who have been called by the Lord in some capacity, it's not such a self-compliment.

'As far as Religious Broadcasting is concerned, you're not just a breath of fresh air, you're a blast of fresh air.' Not the Lord's words, the words of Michael Wakelin. He was to be a great support to me as was the Rev. Ernie Rea, Head of Religion, the Rev. John Newberry, his deputy, and Frances Line, the Controller of Radio 2. Believe me, I needed all the help I could get. I knew that doing a weekly show would mean changing my life somewhat. My main concern was churchgoing. We went to mass as a family, which I felt was important, but I was soon to find that, if I left Broadcasting House straight after the show, I could easily make it back to Our Lady of the Wayside in time for eleven o'clock mass.

I was to start *Good Morning Sunday* on 16 September. Six weeks earlier my Mom had fallen in St George's and broken her leg. Although the leg appeared to heal well, Mom herself deteriorated. Toni and I were sitting at her bedside when suddenly she sat up.

'Look at those angels,' she said, staring at the far wall. 'Aren't they beautiful?' She also saw her mother and her brother, George, who had died a couple of years earlier. I remember being quite upset that she hadn't seen my Dad.

We brought her home from hospital. Fr O'Mahoney, our parish priest, gave her the last rites and came daily to pray at her bedside. She lost consciousness and we were told it was just a matter of time. On the Tuesday, I sat with her until six o'clock when I set off for London where I was to appear in cabaret. My place at her bedside was taken by my good friend Ernie Greer, who you'll remember built our house. When I left, Ernie was holding Mom's hand. It was a defining moment for Ernie, his faith was re-awakened and he is now an extremely devout, practising Christian. I like to think that something of my mother passed to Ernie, who was deeply moved by the experience.

Nothing in life prepares you for the moment when you look down on your mother in her coffin. Being an only child is hard work and a great responsibility but the benefit is that you don't have to share your mother's love with anyone else. Mom had lavished all her love on me. She'd also given me the most precious of all gifts, my faith and my Catholicism. I had her energy, her impatience, her speed off the mark. Now here she lay, still and cold. Something fell on to the front of Mom's shroud. What was it? It happened again and I realised it was water from my eyes. I can't call it tears, there was no sobbing involved. I stood motionless as the water poured from me on to the white silk garment. There was no way to turn it off; I still can't believe there was so much water in me. I was glad I was alone; crying is not something I would ever wish to share.

I spoke to Michael Wakelin; he said that he thought I should present *GMS* the following Sunday. I did. I spoke very openly about Mom and about her dementia, as I'm trying to do now in this book. I didn't attempt to hide my sadness, I shared it. The response from listeners surprised me. Many wrote to say that what I had said had helped them in some way.

Our Lady of the Wayside was packed for the funeral. We had a full set of cousins there, which was a great comfort. It's also wonderful when not just your own family but your church family turn out to offer their support. I gave the homily, Rachel and Rory both did readings, and Fr O'Mahoney spoke of Mom with true affection. I always try to remember Mom as she was before Alzheimer's robbed her of her memory. I pray that a cure will be found for this cruel disease. In the end I think Mom actually forgot how to live, it was as simple as that. Doctors tell us that many of the problems we experience in later life are inherited. Every time I go into a room and say, 'What did I come in here for?' I panic.

Alzheimer's Awareness Week every year encourages us to remember sufferers and their carers. To mark the occasion one year I was sent the prayer of the dementia sufferer: 'Dear Lord, I don't know who I am, I don't know what I am, I don't know where I am, but please love me.'

Rory had passed three 'A' levels and been offered a place at Lancaster University which he promptly turned down.

'Wrong course for me, and I don't want to go to uni anyway,' he said.

'Too far away from Mommy,' said I, and I was probably right. He applied for a job at Eversfield, a local prep school, where he helped to coach sport and maintain the swimming pool. My university term started, I had plenty of cabaret and after-dinner work and I was settling nicely into the broadcasting. Just as well there was no panto; I'd never cope with that on top of everything else.

At the end of October, the Birmingham theatres announced their Christmas programme: a musical at the Alex, a children's play at the Rep and the Royal Ballet at the Hippodrome.

'The first time in over 100 years there's not been a panto in Brum,' screamed the headline in the *Birmingham Mail*. 'Save our

Panto!' They began a campaign, thousands of letters, petitions a-plenty poured in. I received an invitation to a meeting from the council. Could I put on a panto at this short notice? I had the scripts as I'd written an *Aladdin* and a *Cinderella* which I'd directed and performed in at Torquay and Wakefield – but where was there a venue? The council owned the Old Rep, a 400-seat, fully equipped theatre used mainly nowadays for amateur productions. So, I had a venue but where would I get a cast? Earlier that year, we'd celebrated the centenary of Birmingham becoming a city. The *Mail* had asked their readers to vote for their favourite living Brummies. Three of us headed the cast, singer Maggie Moone, comic and great friend of mine, Malcolm Stent, and me of course.

'*All Brummie cast save pantomime for our city,*' said the *Mail*, which was indeed true, everyone in the show was a native. Local radio, television and the *Mail* got right behind us. We ran for five weeks, twice daily. It was a great success though I still don't know how we pulled it all together.

The first night was a bit dodgy. The *Birmingham Post* critic wrote, '*This panto replaces visual clout with skilful playing and inspired naffery. It's a rollicking evening of family fun. With its torn scenery, held up with string, this could become a cult show. It's all quite unique and without pretension, I hope to go again. This is panto perfection.*' Probably the best crit I've ever had, and all the more valued because I'd written and directed as well as performed. Quite by accident I had become an impresario. I'd enjoyed the experience and would promote a few stage shows in the future with my mate Malcolm Stent.

There was, though, one very disturbing evening during the run when Birmingham Social Services booked most of the stalls, 200 seats, for underprivileged children. All went well until the chase routine. It was quite simple: I ran down the steps at the side of the stage, chased by Pong, one of the Chinese policemen. Along the front we ran, between the pit rail and the front row, then back up on to the stage via the corresponding steps. Once Pong made it back on stage, Widow Twanky and I pushed him into the washing machine and proceeded to shrink him. As I scrambled back on to the stage that night, Twanky was looking into the audience in horror. Pong had been tripped and was surrounded by children who were punching and kicking him as he tried to regain his feet.

Not only that, children were leaving their seats and streaming down to the front, eager to join in the massacre. We jumped off the stage and with the help of most of the band managed to save Pong and get him on stage but he was shaken and badly bruised. The children were under the 'care' of three social workers. I told the theatre manager to find one of them and bring her round during the interval as we wanted no repeat of this in the second half when both Abanazar and I went into the audience at one point.

The social worker, wearing sensible shoes and a defiant look, said, 'I accept no responsibility; it's entirely your fault.'

'How on earth do you work that out?' we asked.

'You dressed that man as a policeman and to all of these children the police are the enemy.'

What a tragic view of life!

I'd enjoyed that panto run but at the end of it I said to Toni, 'That'll be my last pantomime.'

'I can't believe that,' she said. Well, I could. One critic had described me as 'a middle-aged Wishee Washee'. The writing was not just on the wall it was in the papers – time to go.

'I'm too old to play Wishee Washee, Idle Jack, Simple Simon and certainly Buttons. I can't stand there with white hair saying, "I'm in love with Cinderella", the kids'll think I'm a dirty old man.' It was a tough decision. After all, I'd had what was probably my most memorable panto moment while playing Buttons a few years earlier at Birmingham Rep. At the end of the show, when the glass slipper had fitted and Cinders had gone off to get married to Prince Charming, I was left alone on stage, a picture of misery, about to sing a sad song when a high-pitched, clear voice rang out,

'I'll marry you, Buttons.' I looked into the auditorium and there stood a seven-year-old brownie, tears streaming down her face and both arms stretched out towards me.

That's the magic of pantomime and I would miss it, but I accepted what I thought was the end of my panto era with good grace.

16

Something to Shout About

Rory seemed to have found a job he really enjoyed and was getting increasingly noticed in rugby circles. Having played all of the county championship games for Warwickshire, he was selected to represent Midlands Colts in the Divisional Championships. There are four divisions; North, South-West, London and Midlands. Amongst the names you'll know who played that year were Lawrence Dallaglio, Mark Regan and John Sleightholme. The England Colts squad was selected but, much to the amazement of the Midlands selectors and his father, Rory didn't make the final twenty-two. He was, however, called into an England select XV at the end of the season to play against Argentina Juniors. It was a proud moment for us both when he pulled on the white jersey with the red rose.

There would shortly be a wedding to arrange. The date set was 7 September. We included the listeners in the preparations, inviting them to send in 'advice for newlyweds'. Anyone whose piece of advice was read out would receive a piece of wedding cake after the wedding. This was Michael's idea and a very good idea it was. Hundreds of letters flooded in. Many said the same thing, 'Never go to sleep on a quarrel,' but there were some very original ones and also funny ones directed at Guy.

'Never raise your hand to your wife; it leaves your groin exposed.'

'Remember that wives are like wheelbarrows, difficult to push around but very easy to upset.'

Toni was having a lovely time sending invitations, making arrangements. The wedding seemed to be her only topic. It never took her less than thirty minutes to describe the wedding dress.

How many things can you say about a dress? It's white and it's long, what else is there? It's only a dress, for goodness sake!

As the day approached I became more and more melancholy. Difficult to explain; I was happy that my daughter had found someone she genuinely loved and I liked Guy enormously, but he was about to take my little girl away. Sons grow up but, to fathers, daughters are always little girls. I tried very hard to be as happy as everyone around me but I was sad; that's the only word I can find – sad.

The moment I was dreading came. Everyone had left for church except us, just the two of us, waiting for the wedding car to arrive. We held hands as we often did and still do. The car arrived. I have always been very close to my daughter but during the next few minutes, as we made the short journey to church, we were closer than ever before. I smiled as I knew I must: 'Don't spoil the day, Don.' She was a beautiful bride but whenever I looked at her I saw a little girl with pigtails sticking out at odd angles, with braces on her teeth or covered in rosettes won at rabbit shows.

The wedding itself was lovely. My school friend, Fr Paul Chamberlain, married them as Fr O'Mahoney was very ill and had to cry off. I was, outwardly, the picture of the delighted father at the reception. My speech went well:

'As Rachel and Guy left the church all of you looked at one another and said, "There goes a grand couple." Toni and I looked at one another and said, "There goes a couple of grand." '

At the end of the evening I arranged all the guests in a great big circle. Bride and groom, moving in opposite directions, shook hands and kissed everyone goodbye. We then formed an arch which they went through and away. Toni and I and Rory left for home, only round the corner. As we opened the front door, the phone was ringing. It was Rachel in floods of tears,

'Daddy, I didn't kiss you goodbye, I kissed everybody except you.'

'It was my fault, I was too busy organising your exit. Don't worry, there'll be plenty of time for you to kiss me in the future.'

'I'll always be your little girl,' she said as she put the phone down and I realised that she'd read my mind. All the time she'd known my thoughts.

* * *

I was flying more than ever and thoroughly enjoying my time in the air. Imagine my horror, then, when a national daily newspaper carried the headline: 'Air-raising escapes of Desperate Don'. The article claimed that a Birmingham Air Traffic controller had said, 'This man is a cross between Frank Spencer and Biggles when he is airborne.' It then listed several things which I had supposedly done, making me sound like a 1920s barnstormer. The article then emphasised my Christianity and said I should stop flying before I caused my own or someone else's death.

Within hours of the article appearing another tabloid rang offering me £1000 if I would take their reporter up in my aeroplane. He would then write an article entitled 'I flew with Don Dare'. Naturally I refused but the paper kept ringing and, by the evening, the fee on offer had reached £5000. I decided to take the paper on through the courts if necessary. It was easy to disprove all their claims, and a quick call to the SATCO at Birmingham confirmed that they had received no enquiry about my flying and had certainly not made the statement attributed to them. I contacted a solicitor. The newspaper seemed quite happy to settle out of court and to print a lengthy apology, finishing with the statement: '*We wish to withdraw any suggestion that Mr Maclean is a menace in the skies or unfit to hold a pilot's licence. We apologise to Mr Maclean for any embarrassment.*'

Honour was satisfied but I now view the press very differently. I certainly no longer believe what I read or what people are reported to have said. Can I suggest you do the same?

For the first Sunday of Advent, the Rt Rev. Roy Williamson, the new Anglican Bishop of Southwark, came into the studio. Since I'd taken over the programme, all the clerics who appeared had already established themselves during Roger Royle's time, they were Roger's men. Bishop Roy, I felt, was mine. With his soft Ulster accent he was an instant hit, and he and I formed a real bond. I was embracing ecumenism with enthusiasm.

Prior to taking over the programme, my Christianity was deeply rooted in the Catholic tradition. I had little experience of any other denominations and none of other faiths. When I was nine, I had been due to take part in a parade of local Wolf Cub packs which was to end up with a service at an Anglican church. My

mother had taken the precaution of asking the dispensation of
our parish priest before allowing me to attend. My association
with *GMS* has opened my mind and my arms to embrace all
other denominations and I now consider myself a Christian first
and a Catholic second. I was impressed by the intellect of the
hierarchy of the Church of England and particularly the incoming
Archbishop of Canterbury, Dr George Carey. He had presence,
holiness, but there was something about him that I can only
describe as 'ordinary'. This meant that no one was afraid to
approach him, everyone knew they would be welcomed. He was
treated badly by the press and media on many occasions. I think
this made him wary, but he was never wary of me and went out
of his way to accommodate *GMS* if ever we requested an interview
with him. His wife, Eileen, is a devoted listener to *Good Morning
Sunday*, I'm pleased to say. I trust that, in retirement, he himself
will have time to listen with her. He impressed me so much that
no matter who holds the office in the future, as far as I am
concerned George Carey will always be *the* Archbishop of
Canterbury.

Panto-free Christmas enabled us to do *Good Morning Christmas*
from our house. We invited all the neighbours, and listeners who
lived locally also turned up. There were over a hundred of us
packed into the house. We had the Sparkhill Salvation Army
band on the drive and a splendid black gospel group in the
lounge. Jasper Carrott popped in to help eat the mince pies and
drink the Bucks Fizz. Toni and the kids did the prayers, and
listeners, particularly those living alone, wrote in afterwards to
say that they had felt part of it all and were glad to have been
included.

The programme over we dashed off to eleven o'clock mass at
Our Lady of the Wayside. Fr Gerry had asked me to do the
readings that day so we sat in the front pew. We came back from
receiving Holy Communion and I was knelt in prayer when
Rachel tapped me. I looked up to see a man standing in front of
me with tears pouring down his cheeks. I stood and put my arms
around him, I didn't know what else to do. He seemed unable to
speak and after a moment he made his way back to his seat.

'Watch where he goes,' I said to Rae. I caught up with him at
the end of mass; he was standing at the crib. He told me that he'd

not been to church for about twenty years. He'd nursed his wife for many years and she'd recently died. He'd heard me say on the radio that morning that I was going to eleven o'clock mass and he decided to come too. He later wrote a letter to me which I still have:

'When I went to the crib to ask for solace, I was not alone because I felt the arm of an angel around me to share my grief. That angel was no less than Don Maclean. You will never know the comfort you gave me that day. You are wholly responsible for bringing me back to the church though spiritually I never left it, so amid my tears I felt happiness too.'

I can't tell you how proud I felt that God had used me as an instrument to reach that man.

Early in 1992, I was approached by a computer genius named Colin Johnson. Colin lived in Stratford and worked for IBM. His hobby was competing in and compiling quizzes. He'd devised a television game show called *First Letter First* but had no idea how to get it on TV. Neither had I, but as soon as he showed it to me I knew it was a winner. I rang Dave Ross who headed up the BBC's quiz division: 'All I want is ten minutes of your time in a room with a 13-amp plug in it,' I said.

Within days, Colin and I were sitting in his office at Elstree. It didn't need me to sell it, it was such an original concept. Dave Ross commissioned a series for daytime television, gave us recording dates starting 3 August and put Andrea Conway, the highly competent producer of *Mastermind*, in charge of production.

I was becoming increasingly worried about Will. The work was still coming thick and fast but he had moved into a suite of offices and kitted it out with a new computer system, he had a brand-new sports car and his wife had an expensive estate car. He came to where I was working one night, and there was a smartly dressed woman with him.

'This is my bank manager,' he said, by way of introduction. 'I've told her that you'd be prepared to stand surety for a loan, I'm thinking of buying a house.'

In the dressing room she outlined the situation. 'Have you got something for him to sign?' asked Will.

'Not at the moment,' she said. They stayed to see me work and afterwards the bank manager slipped me a card. 'Ring me,' she said.

The next morning I did just that.

'You realise that should your agent decide not to repay for any reason, you would be liable for the full amount of the loan and we would recover that immediately.'

'You're telling me not to agree to this, aren't you?'

'I'm not in a position to offer you advice,' she said. 'I'm merely trying to ensure that you fully appreciate the obligation you're being asked to undertake.'

I thanked her and realised that she was another of those angels who pop into your life occasionally. I'd had a few disturbing reports about my agent telling others that I would do anything he told me to, that he controlled me. I'd dismissed them as gossip but now I began to reconsider. All the money I earned was collected through him, he subtracted his commission and sent the balance to me, as is normal practice. He'd never been too prompt in paying me but I accepted this as many of the companies we worked for took three months to pay. I'd had no money for quite some time except for the Radio 2 cheques which arrived weekly. Suddenly they dried up too. I smelled a rat.

'No money from the BBC for three weeks,' I said.

'They're having trouble. The computer at BH has gone down.'

Easy to check that, it only needed a phone call. There were no computer problems. 'Contracts' confirmed that payments had gone out to my agent as normal. I rang Will and told him to be at my house within the hour. He arrived and, standing in our kitchen, told us he had money problems. No surprise there.

'I shall take you to court,' I said.

'If you do that, I'll just go bankrupt,' he said with a smirk on his bloated face. 'I'll pay you £400 a week until I've paid all I owe you.' We actually received just one payment then he went bankrupt anyway. There was no point pursuing him through the courts, the VAT & the Inland Revenue would have first call on him as he'd not paid them for ages either.

The legal system of our country is geared to enable fraudsters to get away with it. He'd simply decided that the money I'd earned was his and he spent it, £12,500 in total. No one can afford to lose twelve and a half grand, I certainly couldn't, but I was determined not to be consumed with hatred for this morally bankrupt person who'd betrayed the misplaced trust I had invested in him. Regret yes, revulsion no! I've not seen him from that day to this but I've since learned that money from two large charity concerts he organised, when I and several top name acts gave our services free, never reached the charity concerned, he'd pocketed that too – swine! Paul Vaughan's warning should have been heeded. 'Never give a sucker a second chance,' said W. C. Fields, and I never would again!

Having been an extremely reluctant pupil at every school he attended, Rory had taken to teaching like a duck to water. The headmaster of Eversfield school suggested to him that his future lay in education and Rory applied to three universities, all within cycling distance of home. Rory was a simple soul. He opened a fridge and there was always food there. He left his dirty washing, including muddy rugby gear, in a bin in the laundry room and when next he saw it, it was clean and folded in his drawer. He had no idea how these minor miracles were accomplished but he had a sneaking feeling that they would not happen if he left home. He was offered a place by Birmingham University and was to spend the next four years at Newman College studying for a degree in Physical Education and Sports Psychology with Qualified Teacher Status. That's a bit of a mouthful isn't it?

Rory had been spotted by Moseley, the senior rugby club in Birmingham, and was playing for their Under-21 side. In March 1992, he was picked as reserve for the Moseley first team who were playing Northampton. An injury to the open side flanker gave Rory the chance to make his debut. Within three minutes of coming on to the pitch, he broke away from a set scrum, took an inside pass from the scrum half and raced over for a try, handing off Buck Shelford, the New Zealand international, in the process. The crowd was stunned, I was euphoric and my nineteen-year-old-son was a legend for at least a week. Local newspapers were generous with their praise:

Don Maclean regularly tunes in to his son's rugby career. At 19, Rory is the youngest player to appear for the Moseley first team this season. He scored a try on his debut against Northampton with his first touch of the ball after coming on as a replacement. When Rory makes his full Courage League debut, it's doubtful whether two million Radio 2 listeners will ever hear the end of it.

The Scottish RFU, who scour the globe for players who might qualify for Scotland, rang to enquire if Rory, as his name implied, was Scottish. He revealed that his grandfather had been and they invited him for a trial for the Scottish Exiles, players who qualify for Scotland but live in England. Needless to say I went along to watch. There were about fifty young men there. After a rigorous training session, two sides were picked; Rory was in the 'Possibles'. He started very strongly and after a few minutes took a difficult pass, threw an outrageous dummy and scorched thirty yards to score in the corner. The game was stopped and Rory was switched to the other team. He was now playing for the 'Probables'. They kicked off and again he got himself into space and avoided several tackles to score under the posts. I could see that the group of selectors were impressed with him and so was I; there were a lot of quality players on show but Rory had made his mark.

More trials followed, then training sessions during which Bill Cuthbertson, the former international lock, took Rory under his wing and taught him more about rugby in a few weeks than he'd learned in the previous twelve years. Rory played against the Welsh Exiles and the Irish Exiles, then the inter-divisional championship began. Each player was assessed during each game; Rory got top marks every time. Cuthbertson labelled him the best young flanker since John Jeffrey. On Wednesday 2 December, the Exiles played against Glasgow, refereed by Jim Fleming, Scotland's top referee. After the game I was in the bar waiting for my clean son to emerge from the dressing room. As he walked in, a chap approached him, handed him an envelope and said, 'Congratulations'. The letter inside said he'd been selected for the Scottish Under-21 team. He had to report to Murrayfield the following Saturday.

On Friday we saw him off at Birmingham Airport. That night he was to play a match at Kelso then stay overnight in Edinburgh. It was after midnight when I returned home from a cabaret. Toni was waiting up for me. Rory had rung. He'd been stretchered off the pitch at Kelso with a broken leg. I rang him immediately. He was in tears, in pain and far from home. I've had many disappointments in my career, as you'll know if you've read this far, but none affected me as badly as this disappointment which had befallen my son. He'd worked and trained so hard, but now there would be no Scottish Under-21 cap and the doors that would have opened for him rugbywise would remain shut. It's far from being an isolated incident; this story is repeated many times each year, promising young athletes get injured at the wrong time and never reach their potential.

After six weeks in plaster, the bone had healed and Rory was running around again but the big chance had gone never to return. Stupid to waste time thinking of what might have been but I tell you now that's a disappointment I'm not fully recovered from a decade later.

Having been recorded in August, *First Letter First*, thirty-two of them, were transmitted early in the new year. It was revolutionary, being the first ever computer-driven quiz show. It went out four afternoons a week and built up an extremely good audience. The contestants were bright and found the questions and the format a worthy challenge. By the time the last programme went out, a second series had been pencilled in for next year. Colin and I were confident that it would run for years – another mistake.

My skills were being stretched, expanded and added to by *GMS*. I'd become a competent interviewer. I was at home with politicians, evangelists, prison governors, trade union leaders. I'd interviewed the Astronomer Royal, The Dalai Lama and the England Football Manager. Both Eartha Kitt and Brooke Shields had *asked* to come on the programme when they visited England and we'd got the only interview with Cliff Richard for his fiftieth birthday.

In October 1992, I interviewed General Norman Schwarzkopf, the man who'd commanded the US forces during the Gulf War. He said to me afterwards, when we'd stopped recording, that history would see George Bush as the worst President of the twentieth century because he'd not finished the job. 'We let Napoleon off the hook and eventually had to defeat him three times; it'll be the same with Saddam.' I get a chill every time I remember those words.

During the Gulf War, *GMS* had been extended from ninety minutes to two hours. Frances Line, the Controller, asked us to retain the extended slot. We instituted the Bible quiz and the Dawn Chorus – that's when we invite you, the listeners, to sing two good old hymns with us.

The programme was progressing and more and more people were tuning in. It was also becoming a forum for people to air their views. 'Let the Laity have their Saity' was a popular feature. We invited your opinion on many a subject: 'How do you feel about offering the sign of peace to those around you during the service on Sunday?' we asked. Reaction poured in, with many of the older generation being less than enamoured of the practice, summed up by one elderly lady who wrote, 'I object most strongly to the sign of peace. I go to church to praise God, not to be friendly.'

By far the biggest postbag we received was generated by the Church of England's decision to ordain women to the priesthood. The sacks of letters were so heavy we feared we might need to buy the postman a truss. What tickled me about the argument was that those in favour and those against found evidence in the Bible, particularly the writings of St Paul, to verify their point. The trouble was that those in favour and those violently against were using exactly the same biblical passages to prove themselves right. Ah, the Holy Bible! Was there ever a book more capable of being misquoted, misinterpreted and misused by readers for their own ends? And, as I've said before, I don't really trust that St Paul – too clever by half he was!

The ordination of women gave rise to the magnificent *Vicar of Dibley* – what a great sitcom – not to mention a few good gags:

'What's the difference between a registry office wedding, a Catholic wedding and an Anglican wedding? In the registry office, the bride is pregnant; in the Catholic, the bride's mother is pregnant; and in the Anglican, the priest is pregnant.'

Probably the best gag came from Fr Paul Lockett, a high Anglican priest I'd known for some time:

'We had a meeting of all the local vicars. This woman stood up and said, "I am delighted that I can now be ordained to the priesthood and do you know why?" We all said, "No". She said, "Because I shall now be able to anoint the sick and the dying with the oil of salvation and do you know why I was not allowed to do this before?" And we all said, "No". She said, "Because I haven't got a penis." We all looked shocked except for one old priest in the corner who whispered, "that's funny, I've always used my thumb." '

Being a radio regular gave rise to a few spin-offs. I went round the country in a van as Pudsey Bear's representative for Children in Need, calling in live to several daily programmes including *Wake up to Wogan.* What a great exponent of radio that man is, don't ya just love him? I only wish his listeners would write to me too, the wit in those letters amazes me.

I rarely get a *really* funny letter, though I do remember mentioning one week that church sharing, you know, more than one denomination using the same building for worship, struck me as a good idea. The following week a letter arrived from someone claiming to be a minister, though I rather doubt he was:

'Church sharing, I'm sad to say, didn't work for us, probably because while we were inside singing "All Things Bright and Beautiful" the other lot were in the car park sacrificing a goat.' If only I could get a few more of those.

I was also asked to get involved with *Songs of Praise.* I quickly realised that the programme with its karaoke hymns wasn't really my bag, and that it would benefit little from my contribution. Pam Rhodes, calm, assured, that's what you want for *Songs of Praise.* I always refer to Pam as 'The Ever Fragrant One' because you know that no matter where she went she'd come back smelling of roses. The title has caught on. I think she likes it.

Someone else who's benefited from a christening of mine is Field Marshal Forrest. Definitely the most ambitious and fearless of producers, John was responsible for doing *Songs of Praise* from Old Trafford.

'I need someone to stand in the middle of the pitch and command 50,000 people, you're the only person who can do that,' he said. Flattery does work and I revised my views on being involved with the show. The Field Marshal pulled off the logistically impossible not once but three times, the others being

Goodison Park, Liverpool and the Millennium Stadium, Cardiff – but more about that one later.

Funny, though, how things you don't particularly want come beckoning. Dave Ismay had become my agent. A friend of long standing and a stand-up comic himself, Dave was a contemporary of mine, we'd worked the clubs together. Who better then to represent me and I needed someone scrupulously honest after my experience with Will.

'Paul Elliott wants to see us, I've a feeling he wants you for panto.' A real man of the theatre is Paul, his company E&B was then producing every major panto in the UK.

'He won't attempt to cast me as Buttons or Simple Simon, he's too shrewd for that,' I mused, 'it'll be Baron Hardup or Alderman Fitzwarren that he'll have in mind for me.'

'I've always seen you as Dame,' said Paul as soon as we stepped into his office. I was horrified.

'Me in a frock? I don't think so!'

'It's in Birmingham, you'll be at home.'

'No,' I said, heading for the door. 'I could never play Dame, it's just not me.'

Dave Ismay was quite upset but didn't attempt to change my mind. Just as well, I was not going to play Dame and that was final. I'd reckoned without the perseverance of Paul Elliott. He rang Dave, he rang me – eventually we were called to his office in the Aldwych again.

'I know what I'm talking about,' he said. 'You could become the best Dame in the country, believe me.' Every objection I put forward, he shot down in flames:

'I've never done a Dame make-up.'

'I'll employ a make-up artist to make you up until you feel confident to do it yourself.'

'With all those changes, I don't want to be too far from the stage.'

'You can have the dressing room nearest to the stage.'

'What about wigs? I can't dress my own wigs.'

'I'll have a hairdresser who'll dress them each night after the performance.'

I'd run out of arguments, I was about to become Dame Trot and my beanstalk-climbing son would be the shy, retiring Su Pollard.

Radio 2 agreed that I'd be able to do *GMS* from Pebble Mill. The prospect of being in the studio at 5.30 a.m. and then having two panto performances to contend with filled me with insomnia. 'You can cope, Don,' I told myself, but could I cope with playing Dame? I'd seen so many really good comics play Dame really badly, I was determined that, if my performance didn't come up to my own high standards, I'd never play Dame again.

Who was the nicest Dame I'd ever worked with? Frankie Desmond of course. He would be my blueprint. I was horrible during rehearsals (I'm usually horrible during rehearsals), the splendid cast put up with my rampant insecurity which increased as opening night approached. I had invaluable help from the Hippodrome's chief executive, Peter Tod, a man whose opinion is worthy of respect. He watched my every performance, coming round afterwards with words of advice and encouragement. The press too were encouraging:

> *Maclean effortlessly demonstrates how a panto dame should be, a genuinely funny comic who never loses sight of the old bag character. We could have savoured much more of him.*

> *Don Maclean wore a dazzling array of garish costumes and no one can deliver a large dose of comedy and gags better than he.*

They seemed to think I'd been playing Dame for years, surely they could tell it was my first time? I worked hard to improve my motherliness, though always remaining 'a man in a frock'.

On the last night – bear in mind I'd had nine weeks to hone the character – Paul Elliott burst into my dressing room.

'I am a genius,' he proclaimed. 'I have discovered the best Dame of his generation. You can play Dame for me every year from now until you die.'

And I've been playing Dame for him ever since.

17

G-DONI

During the last week of the pantomime, my lovely mother-in-law, Bet, who had been taken ill over Christmas, was called to her eternal reward. Pat had come over from Australia so all four of her girls were at her bedside. She had loved me like a son, as she'd loved her other sons-in-law. Each of us will tell you, 'I was her favourite,' but don't believe the others, she loved me best.

Her face wore a beautiful smile and with good reason, she knew she was off to join her beloved Tom. We often spoke about the afterlife Bet and I; she'd been without Tom for eighteen years and she couldn't wait to see him again.

First Letter First had sadly not been given a second series. Janet Street-Porter, Shergar with glasses, had been made head of quizzes at BBC Television. Why? You might ask and so did I. She new-broomed her way through the department, sweeping aside several programmes including ours, then within months, damage done, she moved on to become 'Head of Yoof Programmes' for some other unsuspecting network. I'm still amazed to this day that no one at the BBC stood up to her and made her reconsider. *First Letter First* was a good format and maybe in the future someone will blow the dust off it and give it a second airing.

I settled for radio. I was younger and far better looking on radio than I'd ever be on the telly. Michael Wakelin had moved on within the BBC, he's a bit of a high flyer you know. I had several different producers, some of whom tried to tighten the reins on me. The BBC was changing. Political correctness was the in thing and nowhere was it more eagerly embraced than in the BBC. Big Brother was watching you, though in our case it was Big Sister. I picked up a letter during one show. The writer's name was Marian Moore.

'Ah, Marian Moore,' I remarked. 'That was Robin Hood's most oft-repeated phrase.'

'You must not use the programme to express sexual innuendo,' came the reprimand.

Introducing a record the following week I said, 'This is what you'll hear if you're surrounded by small Japanese children: little arrows, "arro, arro, arro".' Racist bigotry that.

'I took the wife on the QE2. When the captain saw the amount of luggage she had he said, "If I'd known you were going to bring that much I'd have got a bigger boat."' Female stereotyping, another slap.

A few weeks later *Songs of Praise* was to feature two brass bands. I felt I should alert my listeners to this. 'Tonight, *Songs of Praise* presents the Black Dyke Mills Band and the Fairy Aviation Brass Band. In these days of political correctness that's the last time you'll hear the words Black, Dyke and Fairy mentioned in one sentence on the BBC.' All hell broke loose!

My thoughts on political correctness are pretty unprintable. It's so silly that I really thought it would be laughed out of existence in a very short time. Instead it gets stronger. People campaigned and even died for freedom of speech; that freedom has been taken from us. It amazes me that TV companies are perfectly happy to have four-letter words used with increasing frequency on their programmes yet 'handicapped', 'fat' and any word other than 'gay' to describe a person of alternative sexual behaviour will land you in serious trouble. Whatever happened to 'Sticks and stones may break my bones but names can never hurt me'?

PC was something I would have to learn to come to terms with. I remember being extremely disturbed when I went to a London hotel to interview the Rev. Jesse Jackson. He had with him another black American minister who told me in no uncertain terms that I was a racist. He'd only just met me, he'd had no time to assess me but I was white and therefore I must be a racist. I couldn't quite follow the logic of that.

My young granddaughter recently encountered a couple at the Rugby Club. The lad was Asian and his wife English, they had a small son. Gracie waited until the lady was alone then said to her,

'You're pink and they're rather brown. Did they go on holiday and leave you behind?' The couple concerned have been dining out on that story ever since but no doubt our American minister would brand my innocent granddaughter and anyone who found that story funny as rampant racists. How long I wonder before we're forced to deny our Christianity for the same reasons?

Religious broadcasting, though, was still in the safe hands of the Rev. Ernie Rea. He and I had become great friends and we had a lot in common, though that didn't include two first-class university degrees – Ernie's definitely the bloke you want with you if you enter a quiz. We shared a love of rugby and I introduced Ernie to skiing, which is a passion we indulge in together every year. In July 1995, Ernie asked me to be his best man. He was to marry Gaynor Vaughan-Jones who had been head of BBC Radio Wales. Both Ernie and Gaynor had been married before and Ern wondered if I, as a Catholic, might have a problem with that. I've not. Divorce is something the Roman Catholic church is taking very seriously nowadays. Each diocese has a marriage tribunal, with priests and lay people working long hours to investigate failed marriages and, where appropriate, to adjudicate on annulment. I know many Catholics who have divorced and remarried and although they attend mass every week, they do not receive Holy Communion, which is a great source of pain to them. It's a source of joy for me to see my two good friends, Ernie and Gaynor, in a wonderful, love-filled marriage, something neither of them achieved the first time around. Divorce, though, was something that affected other people's families and would never affect ours, or so I thought.

In August, Radio 2 wanted to do a programme to mark the fiftieth anniversary of the dropping of the atomic bomb on Hiroshima. Toni and I, together with producer Denis Nowlan, researcher Rosemary Foxcroft and sound engineer Phil Booth, boarded a plane for Tokyo. Japan is another world. Hardly anyone speaks English and all road signs and directions are in Japanese; get lost at your peril. Hotel rooms and especially hotel bathrooms are extremely small, probably because the people themselves are small. It's quite uncanny walking through a crowded shopping centre and being able to see over the top of everyone else. I could tell you that Disney decided not to build a Disneyland in Japan because, had they done so, not one of the indigenous population would have been tall enough to go on any of the rides, but perhaps that's stereotyping too.

Denis is a very interesting bloke and wherever we went he knew someone. The rest of us referred to these people as FODs (Friends of Denis). Denis wished to pre-record the famous tea ceremony for inclusion in the programme; of course he knew someone who could help. This turned out to be Eliot, a small American robot from New York. He was a FOD but in his case it stood for 'Friend of Dorothy'.

He explained the ceremony in detail. Apparently, wealthy Japanese have a hutch in their gardens. Every so often they 'do tea!' They invite a person they know, who in turn invites four others. On arrival, the five, dressed in old dressing gowns with external cummerbunds and sling-back flip-flops, slide back a small hatch on the side of the hutch and crawl in. They are awaited by the host who has before him a ceramic bowl made by an arthritic potter with cataracts, which he is trying to get to stay upright. He fills the bowl with pond water and the five have to drink it. The four sub-guests can speak to one another but not to the host. Having been ignored for four hours by the person who asked them to come in the first place, feeling the onset of lumbago from being bent double and in danger of cholera from the pond water, they risk Dutch-elm disease in each knee, crawl back out of the tea chest and shove off home. What a way to spend an afternoon!

We were then invited to 'take tea' – there was no way out, the doors were locked. To refuse the tea is an unforgivable insult, as is failing to drain the bowl; however, if you finish your bowl of tea, your host is obliged to fill it up again for you.

Toni and I found not just the tea but also the food a challenge. Japanese restaurants are built without kitchens, everything comes up raw. After two days of starvation we found a place offering fish and chips. Can't go wrong with that. The dish was placed in front of us. Before I could start, the fish opened one eye, winked at me and began to eat the chips. We each lost half a stone in seven days.

The programme, though, was a triumph. The Roman Catholic Peace Cathedral which was built with donations from all the belligerents of the Second World War was the venue. I began the programme by saying:

> The cathedral in which we now stand rose from the charred heart of Hiroshima. Today we remember all those Japanese men, women and children who perished as a result of that most indiscriminate of all weapons, fifty years ago. We pray for the governments of the world, that in future they will follow the way of truth not deception; of justice not violence; of love not hate. We remember the words of the gospel 'Blessed are the peacemakers for they shall be called the children of God.' The British, Commonwealth and American servicemen who died as a result of four years of war in the Pacific are being remembered by relatives and comrades today. We're remembering too, Chinese, Filipinos, Koreans, Burmese and Indians. Men forced to work as slave-labourers in mines and factories, and women forced into sexual slavery. Forty thousand such people died in the Hiroshima bomb blast. We pray for understanding and tolerance between nations. From this day forth we ask You, Lord, to make us all instruments of Your peace.

On our return from the Far East, Rachel and Guy invited us round for Sunday lunch, just me and Toni and Liz, Guy's Mom. Rachel stood and raised her glass.

'Mrs Pattinson would like to take wine . . .' she began.

'What is she up to now?' we thought.

'. . . with all those people who are going to become grandparents next April.'

The two mothers decided to weep, Guy sat there looking smug and I was stunned. What was she trying to do to me? I was far too young to be a grandfather, and apart from that there was no way I was going to sleep with a grandmother! Did this mean I would finally have to admit that I was getting old?

I approached the onset of grandfatherhood much the same as I'd approached the onset of fatherhood; I didn't think much about it. I'd had no feelings for Rachel until the moment she was born, as I've explained, and I had no feelings now. We'd just settled down to watch *Apollo 13* on the telly when the phone rang.

'Hello, Grandmother,' said Guy's voice when Toni answered.

I headed for the front door. Gracie was beautiful, it was just like seeing Rachel again, and again I was smitten. I wrote a poem which I read the following week on *GMS*:

I was lost from the moment I first saw you.
You were small, you were wrinkled, you were tired.
As I bent to plant a kiss upon your forehead,
Your eyes flicked open and you smiled.

As you grew up each day was an adventure.
When your front teeth dropped out you still looked good.
After school you would run at me and hug me,
We spent all the time together that we could.

Like a flower, you blossomed into beauty,
And the time you had for me grew less and less
Till that day you hung on my arm so tightly
In your veil and your long, white, flowing dress.

Without you the house was sad and silent,
I couldn't bear it, even though I knew
That you must leave my home and live your own life.
Even so, my heart was broke in two.

Early this evening came your phone call.
You said, 'Daddy come quick as you can.'
You were lying there with something small beside you,
I reached down and touched a tiny hand.

She was small, she was wrinkled, she was tired.
I looked down upon her little face and then
Her eyes opened wide and she smiled at me.
From that moment, my heart began to mend.

Radio 2 were going off the idea of trips abroad but we thought we'd float the idea of a *Good Morning Sunday* pilgrimage to the Holy Land. Would listeners be interested? We were overwhelmed. In no time at all we'd got over three hundred takers and had to close the bookings. A pilgrimage to the Holy Land is something every Christian should undertake if possible. To walk in the footsteps of our Blessed Lord, to look down and think, 'I'm standing here where He stood,' is truly mind-blowing. Breaking bread on the shores of the Sea of Galilee and seeing all the places that, until then, had just been names in the Bible will truly give your faith a boost. I think the most poignant moment for me was attending mass in the Ecce Homo church. The arch which forms part of the altar was the same arch under which Jesus stood when Pilate said, '*Ecce Homo* – Behold the man.' I still go all shivery every time I think about it.

We were to take two more Holy Land pilgrimages, in 1998 and 2000. Three hundred and fifty listeners accompanied us in 2000, eight coach loads. Sadly, I fear, it'll be a long time before we go again. The people of the Holy Land, Muslim, Christian and Jewish need all the prayers you have.

There are so many moments that stand out from our pilgrimages. Let me pick a couple for you. In 1998, a devout woman named Gill Smith conned her husband, Alan, into coming by telling him she'd booked a golfing holiday. When the taxi arrived to take them to the airport she said,

'You won't be needing them,' as he picked up his golf clubs.

'No golf clubs?'

'Not in the Holy Land,' she replied.

Alan went because he knew it was too late to get a rebate on the ticket but something happened to him while he was on the pilgrimage; he gave his life to God and, from being a non-believer, is now a devout, practising Christian.

Norma and Bernard came with us too. Bernard had been told that, as the cancer from which he'd been suffering had now spread throughout his body, it would be unwise to travel. He looked ill and was in obvious pain, but he coped and received help and comfort from the other pilgrims. On the plane coming home, I sat with Bernard. He was content, he'd made his pilgrimage, he'd made his peace with God and he told me he was going home to die.

In 2000, Bernard was with us again on our next pilgrimage, no sign of cancer; he was as fit as a flea. No, I'm not suggesting that everyone with a life-threatening illness should jump on the next El

Al flight. Bernard was certainly not seeking a cure when he went the first time, but I know he went the second time to give thanks.

I've jumped ahead, so back to 1996. As soon as we returned from Israel, it was off to Clacton. Summer season at the Westcliff yet again. Toni drove and I flew. I'd bought a new aeroplane, a Grumman Tiger – four seats and a powerful engine. I managed to get the registration G-DONI which is half DON and half TONI but you'd probably worked that out for yourself.

During that summer, Toni and I flew all over the south of England. We flew to the Isle of Wight to pre-record part of *GMS* from the Garlic Festival; a good job we were in a Tiger not a Vampire. Toni had learned how to navigate. She knew how to handle the navigation instruments, I'd give her a map and a ruler and she was away. She was enjoying flying as much as I was. It had become *our* hobby.

Francis Golightly excelled himself that year with scenery, costumes and casting. Resident heart-throb Andrew Robley was back again. We referred to Andrew as 'Impossibly' because he was once described in a newspaper as 'impossibly handsome'. Dottie Wayne, that funniest of funny ladies, was our comedienne and the comedy was assured by Gordon and Bunny Jay with whom I'd worked at the very start of my career. It was an exceptionally funny show, in fact I'll stick my neck out and say that it was the funniest and happiest summer season I've ever done. Yes, the show was great, the business was great, our daughter and granddaughter spent their holiday with us, it was a really super time.

Rory graduated from Newman College and in September took up his first teaching post at St Bernadette's RC Primary School in Birmingham. He was the first member of the family to obtain a degree. I'd only managed half of the degree course at Warwick; BBC commitments meant that I was unable to put in the necessary time. That and the fact that many of the events we were studying in modern history had happened in my lifetime hastened my decision to call it a day. Help was at hand however. An envelope came through the post marked 'Strictly Private and Confidential'. It was from the Senate of the University of Birmingham. They were proposing to confer on me an honorary degree. I was thrilled – Rory was furious. However he agreed to come along on the day.

I'd been told that I'd be called upon to make an acceptance speech. I sat down and wrote a comedy act aimed at the majority of the audience who were of course the parents of the graduates.

'Like you, I have recently had a child at Birmingham University. We took out a bank loan to see our son through his four years, it wasn't enough. We calculated board and tuition correctly but forgot about bail. Like you we received the letter "Dear Mom and Dad, send me a cheque so I know that you're all right." They come home; not only do they bring vast amounts of laundry, when they've gone back again you have to look round the house to see what's missing. It's like having your own personal burglar. Most students live away from their place of learning in what's called student accommodation. For eighteen years you bring up your child in a warm, clean, tidy home then they end up living in something that resembles Bosnia on a bad day. You visit them and realise that you've actually wiped your feet on the way out and, as you shut the door on this squalor, you hear someone inside say, "It's a good job we tidied up." '

I also treated them to a couple of verses of 'The Vatican Rag'. Afterwards the Pro-Vice-Chancellor said to me, 'It's the first time anyone's sung at a degree congregation in the Great Hall of Birmingham University.' Mind, he had a greater shock in store when Toni treated him, the Principal and the Recording Officer to her version of *Riverdance* in the atrium. She's amazing; from the waist up she's as good as Michael Flatly, if only she could get the legs right!

The following year we were invited again to the degree ceremony. As an honorary MA, I was to process with the great and the good and observe that year's honorary graduate receiving his degree. The cameramen who film each graduation ceremony dashed over to me.

'We've come to thank you,' they said.

'Thank me for what?'

'We sold over twice as many copies of last year's video than we've ever sold before.'

* * *

A few years previously, I'd appeared in a Royal Performance at the Birmingham Hippodrome. Sir Harry Secombe had topped the bill and afterwards he asked me if I'd be his support act on a few concerts in aid of the Army Benevolent Fund. The first of these was at the Barbican in London. Harry, the Band of the Women's Royal Army Corps and me. I opened the show.

'I've not told anyone at home that I'm working with Sir Harry,' I confided to the audience. 'We don't like the Welsh in Birmingham and with good reason; I'm sure they wee in our water!' Harry opened the second half with a magnificent Puccini aria, after which he acknowledged the applause, took a drink from the glass of water on the piano, spat it out and boomed,

'That Don Maclean was right you know folks!'

We kept the gag in for future gigs together. I wish there'd been many more; he was a comedy hero of mine was Harry.

Because of my appearances on behalf of the Army Benevolent Fund I was invited to Buckingham Palace to present the Duke of Edinburgh Gold Awards. The Duke makes an appearance at the ceremony of course, the awards are very close to his heart, but the actual presentations are made on his behalf by half a dozen people of whom I was to be one. Toni was terribly excited at the prospect of going to the Queen's pad. We drove up the Mall which was full of people *en route* to the Palace for the awards ceremony. Toni became very concerned,

'All the women are wearing hats Don.'

'So?'

'I've not got a hat.'

'Not *all* the women are wearing hats.'

'Well, I've not seen a woman without one yet.' I decided to ignore her, which wasn't easy, as she was getting more panicky by the minute. We went in through the main gates as our pass allowed. Toni waved regally and several Japanese cameras flashed.

'Is that the Queen?'

'I don't know, they all look alike to me.'

Once in the courtyard, the police checked underneath our car with a mirror on a stick but Toni had no interest in matters of national security, she was still trying to find just one hatless female. We were shown into the green drawing room. Every lady there sported a vast piece of headwear.

'What am I going to say if someone asks me why I'm not wearing a hat?' She was getting distraught.

'You'll think of something,' I replied through clenched teeth but she was unconvinced. We were led into the Grand Ballroom where all the recipients were gathered, as were their proud parents. A long podium stood at one end with twelve seats for those about to present and their spouses. The Band of the Grenadier Guards played a selection from *The Sound of Music* and the hills were alive with the sound of Toni moaning about hats. They moved on to *My Fair Lady* – 'Why can't a woman be more like a man?' Why indeed, I thought as, together with my bareheaded wife, I was shown to my seat. I turned to my right to engage in conversation an elderly general while Toni turned left to be confronted by a marchioness wearing on her head what can only be described as an empty cushion cover. She looked at Toni and the first words out of her mouth were, 'How did you get in here without a hat?' I have never been so proud of my wife. She raised her eyes, clutched at her hair and said in shocked tones, 'Has it gone?'

A few years later we would again be invited to the Palace, Toni would certainly have the dress code right then, but that was well in the future. She's been a great source of humour to me over the years. During the *Crackerjack* days, my agent announced that a company was to open several toy shops in the south of England and they wanted a children's television personality to perform the openings; it would be a very lucrative contract. They were, however, considering not only me but also the current Doctor Who and someone from *Blue Peter* – stiff opposition. They wanted to meet me for a chat.

'Why don't we invite them to lunch,' suggested Toni. They duly arrived at our house in Twickenham, a well-built couple who looked as though they enjoyed their grub, as indeed they did. They tucked into the starter and the main course with a will, which pleased Toni who has always taken great pride in her culinary ability. The four of us were getting on famously.

'I'll just get the sweet,' said Toni, disappearing into the kitchen. I heard a crash and a muttered oath.

'Won't be a minute,' I said, excusing myself. Toni had slipped while removing the cherry pie from the oven, there were pastry and cherries all over the kitchen floor.

'What are you going to do?' I whispered.

'Give 'em another glass of wine,' she instructed. 'I'll think of something.'

I did as I was told and five minutes later my wife appeared in the doorway. 'Cherry crumble anyone?' she beamed.

Both our guests had second helpings, they'd never tasted anything so good; and yes, I did get the contract, neither *Blue Peter* nor Doctor Who stood a chance against my wife's crumble.

It was now 1996 and things were changing at Radio 2. The Controller, Frances Line, a woman loved by all who knew her, was to retire. This posed three questions. Who would take her place? Would the new controller decide that religion was unnecessary on the station? Would I get the sack?

The new man was Jim Moir, a larger-than-life character who had been a television light entertainment producer/director during my *Crackerjack* days and had gone on to be Head of Light Entertainment. I knew Jim and always thought that he'd have made a very good living as a stand-up comic. Jim is a devout, practising Roman Catholic so religious-output was safe, but he immediately began to make interesting moves, moves which we now know were to result in Radio 2 becoming the nation's favourite and most listened-to station.

GMS was to be slimmed down. Instead of two producers alternating, there was to be just one producer responsible for the programme every week. That person was to be Rosemary Foxcroft. Her elevation to producer status the following January came as no surprise to me; no one knew more about *GMS* than she did. Rosemary is far too complicated a person for me to describe in print. The widow of the Church of England clergyman and broadcaster Robert Foxcroft, she was a tenacious researcher. She procured all our interviewees, no one ever got away from her, she never took 'no' for an answer. Carl Lewis tried to run away from her but she chased after him and caught him – yes, even a triple Olympic sprint star could not escape a rampant Rosemary. Not only did she know the programme better than anybody, she also cared about it passionately, as I did, so it was a great appointment.

Listening to Wogan, I realised how Pauli Walters, his producer, had become an important part of the on-air persona of their show. Now I had just one producer, could I do something similar? I began mentioning 'Mrs Foxtrot', telling listeners how she was giving me a bad time, controlling my life, correcting my political incorrection. The listeners latched on immediately: 'Why can't you be kind to Mrs Foxtrot?' 'That Mrs Foxtrot must be a saint to put up with you.' Well, that's taking things a bit too far. Rosemary and I are the total antithesis of one another. I accuse her of being a beatnik and a hippy, she tells me I'm an old reactionary Catholic. Being a *Guardian* reader she accuses me of getting all my opinions from the *Mail* or the *Telegraph.* She will forgive seventy times seven while I find forgiveness totally beyond me. Our tastes in music are poles apart; she loves Bob Dylan, Van Morrison, Stevie Wonder, I prefer blokes who can at least sing a little bit.

Something we do have in common is that neither of us bears a grudge; we have disagreements, sometimes heated, but it never affects our relationship. The only thing that matters to us both is the end result, a good programme. Rosemary is the final arbiter and has several times saved my career by censoring a gag or a remark. Despite her vigilance, I still manage to upset listeners on a regular basis. The advent of e-mail means that irate listeners can register their 'disgust', 'horror', 'total disappointment' within minutes. You'd be amazed how many e-mails to me begin with 'Call yourself a Christian!'

If a letter is written in red and green biro, it gives you a clue to be wary of the writer but e-mail has a disturbing anonymity. On 4 November I happened to say, 'Well, tomorrow is bonfire night when people go out and set fire to Roman candles. I'm staying in, it'd be just my luck to bump into a dyslexic Protestant.' Within three minutes Rosemary had received an e-mail saying, 'It's people like Don Maclean who are perpetrating the sectarian violence in Northern Ireland.'

The Sunday following England's limp exit from the World Cup courtesy of ten-man Brazil, we played a song which contained the words 'Reach just a little bit higher', and as it finished I said, 'I dedicate that record to David Seaman.' The e-mails flooded in.

'Call yourself a Christian!'

The biggest mass of electronic communication came last year

when I was asked to announce that it was 'National Breastfeeding Week'. Who designates these weeks? The one that kills me every time is 'Breast Awareness Week'. Don't these people realise that, for the average heterosexual male, that's fifty-two weeks of the year? Back to the aforementioned Week. The aim is to promote breastfeeding in public. 'I can do without that,' I commented. 'I don't want some mother trying to choke her infant while I'm having a sandwich.' The computer nearly crashed – over two hundred e-mails before the programme ended. I was accused of all sorts of things including being in the pay of Nestlé who apparently make powdered milk. I got severely slapped by Radio 2 but I would say that the breastfeeding campaign got more publicity than it could possibly have hoped for.

Within a few months of taking charge Mrs Foxtrot was to be tested to the limit. On 31 August 1997, Toni and I walked into the studio in Manchester at 5.30 a.m. It was a hive of activity, three people on three phones.

'Morning,' we chirped.

'You've not heard have you?' said Rosemary.

'Heard what?'

'Princess Diana is dead.'

Rosemary had moved like lightning. She was in touch with Controller Jim Moir and she'd already spoken to Cardinal Basil Hume, who'd said that he'd be waiting by the phone for our next call. Nobody knew where the Archbishop of Canterbury was – well, it was holiday time after all – but she'd managed to track down Bishop Roy Williamson and he was on his way. Canon Noel Vincent, having heard the news, had taken it upon himself to head over from Liverpool cathedral, and weren't we glad to see him! She'd also located Roger Royle and we'd be able to talk to him by phone. Jim said that he wanted *GMS* to be the first programme, apart from the news, to go live on R2 that morning; the music, though, needed to be selected very carefully.

Just to give an example of how easy it is to offend, the first record we'd had programmed for the morning's show was 'Knock, knock, knocking on heaven's door'. We didn't have time to play every record through, so we had to rely on our memories of lyrics and hope we'd overlooked nothing. We finally went live at 9 a.m. We gave our listeners a reflective programme with prayers that were particularly comforting for a nation in total shock. When we finished the programme at eleven, I stood up and my legs buckled under me, I'd expended so much nervous energy I had nothing left. 'Rest in peace,' we say when someone departs this life. Sadly the Princess of Wales has not been allowed to rest in peace. Any mention of her will bring forth a flood of letters.

After the wonderful Commonwealth Games opening ceremony in Manchester lots of people contacted us to say that the Queen was dismissive of the little girl who carried in the baton. Without exception, every letter of complaint made some mention of Diana. There are many people out there determined to use Diana as a stick to beat our Royal Family with – how sad!

Christmas 1997, and Paul Elliott was to launch his biggest panto yet – *Goldilocks*. As with all brand new panto productions, it would begin at the Birmingham Hippodrome, the country's number one panto house. He wanted me as Gertie Gemmill, the Dame, and Frank Bruno was to headline. Frank had been in panto before but he'd always been expected to play an existing character. This was different. *Goldilocks* is set in a circus, and Frank was to be the Ringmaster or 'Master of the Ring'. Keith Simmons had written a perfect vehicle, playing to Frank's strengths; not too demanding dialogue-wise and incorporating a choreographed skipping routine which would stop the show. Sportspeople have been featuring in pantomime for years. I've never had a problem with that. If a boxer, cricketer or athlete attracts a big audience – great, all the more people for me to entertain.

There is, though, a well-documented tale of an Olympian being booked to play the Genie in *Aladdin*. He buttonholed the Dame, a well-known panto veteran, and said, 'Look, I really like this acting lark, I'm thinking of giving up sport and going on stage full-time, what do you think of my chances?' Now he was probably the worst genie ever to pull on a turban but the Dame, being a kindly soul, wanted to spare his feelings.

'Ooh, I shouldn't do that, love,' he began. 'Anyone can act but you have a gift given to very few. There's hundreds of people in showbusiness who'd love to have been able to swim like you do.'

Much to the Dame's surprise, the genie said, 'Name one!'

The Dame thought for a second and said, 'Natalie Wood.'

Frank Bruno, though, was a different prospect from that. Audiences loved him and his basso-profundo laugh. I stayed with him in that particular production of *Goldilocks* for three years.

Pantomime is a British institution, a theatrical art form as important as opera and ballet, and should be recognised as such. Pantomime is a living, evolving animal, that's why producers like Paul Elliott and Nick Thomas work hard to advance it, bringing in sports personalities, gladiators, power-rangers, spidermen and any other current trend.

I am now an elder statesman of panto and I revel in the role. I feel so proud of the younger element who have made panto their own: Bonnie Langford, probably the finest musical performer of her generation, Brian Conley, the current king of panto, and Bobby Davro who's extremely close on his heels. They've learned from people like me and, in time, they'll graduate to playing Dame and watching younger men and women coming through to take their place. It's important for those with years of panto experience to pass on the knowledge to the next generation; panto routines that we have devised must not be lost.

Rory had become engaged to Andrea. She was a pretty girl who lived locally and worked for a law firm in Birmingham. I went out of my way to emphasise to them both that engagement was a period for them to discover whether they were right for each other.

'A broken engagement is sad, but a broken marriage is a tragedy,' I quoted. The two of them argued quite a lot, something Toni and I have never done, and they did indeed break up on occasion, once for quite a spell, but much to my surprise they got back together again. I'd always told myself that I must try to treat my daughter-in-law the same as I treated my daughter but I knew that wouldn't be easy with Andrea. She was a morose girl with a pessimistic outlook. There's only so much you can say to your children about their choice of partner; I restricted my comments to 'Every bloke needs a happy woman; it's a great compliment if your wife's always happy.'

Rory, though, seemed content. The decision had been made to marry in 2000 but Andrea then brought the wedding forward to

August 1999. It was a splendid wedding, Andrea's mom and dad, who were delightful people, really went to town. The bride was unsmiling but we put this down to nervousness. Pam, the bride's mother, had arranged a barn dance for the reception. What a great idea; everyone joined in. Rory danced all night and had a great time but Andrea felt unwell and sat out.

Rachel had been very pregnant at the wedding, insisting on standing sideways for all the photographs. A month later, Francesca Rose arrived. She was beautiful with luscious, kissable lips. As often happens in families, she's very different from her older sister. She's now a real character with a highly developed sense of the theatrical; she sings well and loves getting laughs. Is there to be a next generation treading the boards? One thing's for sure; Cheska will only do what Cheska wants to do.

The third year of *Goldilocks* was to be at Woking but it was the Millennium and Radio 2 wanted me in Vatican Square on Christmas morning. Not only that, Field Marshal Forrest was planning the biggest ever *Songs of Praise* live from the Millennium Stadium, Cardiff on Sunday 2 January 2000. He told me in no uncertain terms that he couldn't do it without me. I therefore told Paul Elliott that I would have to give panto a miss that year.

'Nonsense,' came the reply. 'You'll do pantomime at Woking but on Christmas Eve and on 2 January you will be replaced by your understudy.' Why hadn't I thought of that?

The event at the Millennium Stadium was amazing. Seventy thousand people packed in to declare their Christian faith to the nation. There were choirs, bands, massed harps; Daniel O'Donnell and Bryn Terfel sang. Sir Cliff gave us 'The Millennium Prayer' and I shared the presenting duties with the ever fragrant Pam Rhodes and BBC Wales' Roy Noble. I was in charge of keeping the crowds happy as they were coming in.

'Tell them that they have to stand for every hymn,' instructed the Field Marshal.

'You can't do that,' said the authorities. 'The top tier is too steep. If people stand they're liable to topple over and fall. Can't do that look you, isn't it!' This gave rise to my catch phrase, 'Everybody stand *but not the top tier*'. By the end of the warm up I had the whole stadium chanting '*but not the top tier*'. We went live at 3.30, the atmosphere was electric, and everyone in the place knew they were making history. Prince Charles was due to arrive with his sons towards the end of the programme and as I had been given the job of announcing him, I was very proud.

After about twenty minutes, while Laura-Michelle Kelly, the star of *Whistle Down the Wind*, was on stage singing Andrew Lloyd Webber's 'Prayer for the Third Millennium', John Forrest beckoned to me from the side of the pitch. I ran over. The conversation went like this,

'Don, the princes have arrived.'

'Oh good, they're early.'

'As soon as Laura-Michelle finishes singing, I want you to announce them and they'll enter the Royal Box as arranged.'

'I can't announce them, they're not due here for another twenty minutes.'

'You can't keep the Prince of Wales waiting for twenty minutes.'

'Can't you give him a sandwich or something?'

'Announce him as soon as she finishes.' John was getting agitated.

'Do I then announce the massed harps?'

'You can't announce the massed harps,' he said, his voice having risen two octaves. 'They're not on for another twenty minutes.'

'Well, neither is the Prince of Wales and they follow him.'

'Listen, do you want this programme to finish twenty minutes early? Announce the princes then announce "How Great Thou Art", understand? I'll decide how we get into the harps later.'

'Right,' I said. 'But how do you want me to announce "How Great Thou Art"?'

'You'll think of something,' said the Field Marshal, turning on his heel. I hurried back to the centre of the pitch as Laura-Michelle sang her last notes.

'Ladies and Gentlemen, can I ask you to be upstanding, *including the top tier,* to welcome our honoured guests, Prince Charles, Prince William and Prince Harry.' The entire stadium went wild. The princes sat just in front of my Toni. She was ecstatic but I was busy thinking what to say next.

'Your Royal Highnesses,' I began, still making it up as I went along, 'you'll be delighted that the hymn you're about to hear is the favourite hymn of your Grandmother, sir, and your Great-grandmother, young sirs – "How Great Thou Art".'

I trust the good Lord won't hold me to account for that teeny weeny lie. The Queen Mum obviously didn't mind, as I received no letter of complaint from the Palace.

18

Flying High

I love interviewing, I've become really good at it (he said modestly). If Parkinson or Des O'Connor need a break, I'm the man to take over. I work hard at framing my questions, determined to ask my subjects things they've not been asked before, keen to get a different angle.

I enjoy people. Having done well over seven hundred interviews, I can count on two hands the people I've not really liked. In March 2000, though, I was to do my most disastrous interview. I was sent a preview copy of Lord Longford's *Prison Diaries*. The publisher was very keen for the author to appear on *GMS*. Rosemary set up a pre-record. My interviewee didn't take to me at all. At one point he told me that I should be ashamed to call myself a Roman Catholic and that Myra Hindley was a better Christian than I would ever be. I've spoken to eccentrics before; he was something different – he was driven. At the beck and call of several mass murderers whom he considered his friends, he would travel to various prisons, by public transport and at his own expense. These people would play him like a fish on a line, often refusing to see him when he'd arrived at their behest. He despised the prison system and believed that no one should have their liberty taken away from them.

'What if a murderer or rapist is released and then immediately commits another rape or murder?' I asked.

'That's a risk we have to take,' came the reply.

'What do you say to the relatives of the victims of crime, those people whose lives have been ruined by the violent death of a loved one?'

'You can't talk to such people, all they want is revenge,' said the great man.

I'd more or less decided by then that I couldn't talk to him either. Rosemary and I agreed not to broadcast the interview; it would have provoked a storm had we done so. Lord Longford, prisoners' friend, died shortly afterwards. Is he in heaven yet? He certainly believed that he was doing God's will. He was indeed holy but, in my opinion, wholly misguided. He was shortly followed from this life by Myra Hindley; may God have mercy on both their souls.

As I get older I get increasingly emotional about violent crime, especially if it involves children. I was terribly upset by the murder of Sarah Payne and the killings of Holly and Jessica and also Milly Dowler. I just couldn't get out of my mind the terrible fear and suffering of those children's last hours. I know that their fathers will spend the rest of their days in total despair that they were unable to save their daughters from these nightmares. What sort of society do we live in if we are unable to protect our children? Is society as we know it breaking down? It would appear to me that there is a concerted attack on the family. We've negated marriage and made illegitimacy socially acceptable. Marriage and the family are the bedrock of society yet we are bombarded with alternatives which we're told are equal to marriage. Men can marry men and women can marry women now, not in the sight of God but in the sight of Ken Livingstone – where will it end?

We returned to Clacton in 2000 for the Millennium summer show. Francis Golightly and Roy Cloughton had again pulled out all the stops. I specified that I wanted Dottie Wayne in the cast so that we could repeat some of our previous successes. One of these involved Dottie, as an elderly dowager, being wheeled round the stage in a wheelchair by me. We then turned upstage where a film was projected on to a screen so that from the audience it appeared that the wheelchair was negotiating the road at high speed – get the picture?

I was running on the spot, or so I thought. In actual fact I was moving backwards with each step. Suddenly I fell off the front of the stage, closely followed by the wheelchair containing Dottie. Her head hit the floor with a sickening thud. Despite having fallen nearly five feet myself, I was unhurt. I scrambled over to Dottie and tried to support her head. I could feel a huge bump. The audience was unsure of what had happened, some of them thought it was part of the sketch. What an opening night!

Dottie was taken to hospital in Colchester where she remained for several weeks, flat on her back as she'd damaged her spine. She was unable to return to the show. I can honestly say it was the worst thing that's ever happened to me on stage in over thirty years. I'd had a few accidents myself but to have been involved in an injury to a fellow performer was much worse. I'd been so looking forward to the season but that ruined it from the outset. Yes that was awful but other problems were on the horizon.

Rory and Andrea had been married for nearly a year. Rory who was one of the happiest people ever to draw breath had changed; he was becoming increasingly morose. We saw little of the newlyweds and when they did call on us, Andrea would sit on the sofa and immediately fall asleep. We were never invited to their home and if we called on them we always felt most unwelcome. Something was seriously wrong. Rory had had a good rugby season, gaining promotion with Birmingham Solihull yet again and scoring several tries in the process. He could look forward to playing at the very top level in National Division One. That didn't make him happy and he seemed to have lost interest in teaching too.

We came back to Birmingham on the first Sunday of August to attend the SPGS Colts' Reunion – you know about that. We'd be returning to Clacton the following day. That night we were asleep in bed when the doorbell rang.

'I've got to talk to you,' Rory called. We let him in and he sat in our bedroom for two hours telling us how his marriage had gone wrong from day one.

'I think you'd better stay here tonight,' I said. The next morning he went back to his own house, collected his clothes and other personal belongings and moved back in with us. We, of course, had to return to Clacton. It was a sober journey with much heart searching. After a few days, Rory joined us there. He was altogether brighter having made the decision to abandon the marital home. We went to mass together. 'You do realise I'll not be able to take communion if I'm divorced,' he said to me. That's not strictly true. A person who has divorced and then remarried is denied the sacrament unless the first marriage has been annulled by the Church.

Their civil divorce was achieved extremely quickly, meaning that they could both get on with their lives. I confess that I found it most disturbing. Andrea's parents, too, were most upset. I believe that both Rory and Andrea knew they were doing the wrong thing when they married but went ahead regardless – why? Had they called it off on the day there would have been no recriminations from Toni and me.

Our son continued to live with us but was very unsettled. Eventually he announced that he'd been offered a job by a holiday company as a children's entertainer in a Spanish resort. We both thought this was a good idea – change of scene, change of climate. Just before he set off for the Costa del Sol he bumped into a girl whom he'd fancied strongly in the past. Her name: Melanie Westley. You may recall that she'd been in the same class as Rachel at St Martin's. Previously she'd spurned Rory's advances as, despite being six foot three, he was Rachel's little brother; but time contracts age, doesn't it?

Rory set off for Spain with a heavy heart at leaving Mel behind and Mel set off for the travel agent to arrange a couple of short visits to see him. I have to confess that I took to Mel straight away. There was so much about her that reminded me of Rae. She was lively, highly intelligent – dynamic wouldn't be stretching it too far. After about four months of getting sunburned and entertaining not just children but adults as well, Rory returned and shortly afterwards got engaged to Mel. Legally they would be able to marry but not in a Catholic church as the Diocesan Marriage Tribunal were still deliberating on the annulment.

On 2 June 2002, the Queen celebrated her Golden Jubilee, Toni celebrated her birthday and Melanie Westley became Mrs Rory Maclean in a civil ceremony at the Birmingham Botanical Gardens. I was asked to say grace which ended with the words: 'We've got at last, you will observe, the daughter-in-law that we deserve and we pray, without meaning to offend, this is the last wedding of Rory's that we attend.' 'Amen' echoed the assembled.

I still can't tell you exactly how I felt about the day. The bride was beautiful and, what was more important, happy. She was also totally in love with my son and he with her. I just wish the marriage had taken place in a church.

You'll be pleased to know that the annulment eventually came through, and now the marriage can be 'blessed and approved' by the Roman Catholic Church in a small ceremony which will probably take place on their first anniversary – Thank You, God!

Towards the end of the Millennium year a most official letter came through our letter box. 'From the Office of the Prime Minister,' it said. I panicked. What had I said about our leader on last week's show? Was it a complaint? Was I to be thrown in the Tower? No, I was to be made a Member of the Most Excellent Order of the British Empire, for services to religion and inter-faith dialogue. Well you could have knocked me down with a damp lettuce.

I wanted to ring everyone I knew and tell them but apparently if news leaks out before it's officially announced to the press on New Year's Day, the award may be withdrawn. I couldn't tell anyone! How could I possibly keep this quiet? But I did.

You're allowed to take three guests with you to Buckingham Palace. On 1 May we set off early, Rory in his best suit, me in my morning suit, Rachel and Toni in big hats; she wasn't about to make that mistake again. We arrived in London earlier than anticipated so we went to Westminster Cathedral to offer up a few prayers of thanks, light a few candles and collect our thoughts – as you do.

The police and the army were on duty at the Palace gates. Again they had a mirror on a stick to view the underneath of our vehicle. They allowed Rae to use it to adjust her hat. Once inside the Palace, I was separated from the family but Rachel was in her element, guardsmen everywhere – she loves men in uniform. The briefing was very amusing and the wait interminable but eventually my turn came. I was so excited that I forgot to bow to the Queen as I stood before her.

'I was listening to your programme on Sunday,' she said. Oh joy! Her Maj listens to Radio 2. I was half expecting her to add, 'Please don't mention that, it could ruin one's credibility,' but she didn't. Having received my award I was taken to the back of the ballroom where the family was seated. We all stood as Her Majesty left via the centre aisle. Both Toni and Rae beamed in her direction. Never having seen so many teeth on display at once, she beamed back.

'Did you see the Queen smile at me?' asked Toni.

'She didn't smile at you, she was smiling at me,' said Rachel. They had to be separated by Rory. As we were driving out after photographs had been taken, a police sergeant held up his hand for us to stop. 'Mr Maclean,' he said, 'very many congratulations. My wife and I listen to you every week without fail, your award is very much deserved.' Do you know, I think that was the icing on a perfect day.

We went off for a splendid lunch, then set off for home where Gracie was waiting to view the medal.

'I think I should take that to school tomorrow, don't you Poppa?'

'No chance!'

My very good friend Ernie Rea had decided to resign as Head of Religious Broadcasting. No, I don't know why, he's never told me, but I do know I was mortified. Ernie had appointed me, he'd listened to every single edition of *GMS* and commented on it, he was also a man who believed that religious radio deserved equal status to that of religious television. Most of the department feel 'If it aint got pictures, it aint worth bothering about'.

Ernie was an ordained Presbyterian minister from Belfast, a theologian with a mind like a razor. He'd not just kissed the Blarney stone, he'd swallowed half of it. Who on earth would they get to replace him? The chosen one was Alan Bookbinder, a brilliant programme maker whose first act on being appointed was to declare himself an agnostic. I thought to myself, 'It's like one of those Hollywood disaster movies where the pilots collapse and someone who has never flown before takes over the controls and is expected to save all the souls on board.' I have to say, though, that Alan Bookbinder has certainly fought his corner, and has retained the 'slots' occupied by religious output. He's made programmes, some controversial, which believers and non-believers want to see, but he's made sure that they've gone out at times when they are watched not just by insomniacs and bats.

The eleventh of September 2001, or 9/11 as the Americans call it, was to change all our lives. Tom Foxcroft, Rosemary's son, works in the financial district of New York. With all the phones being down, she spent an anxious seven hours waiting for news. The following Sunday we linked up with Major Mollie Shotzburger who was one of the senior Salvation Army personnel at Ground Zero. It was then decided that we'd go over there for Easter 2002. Ground Zero would be our resurrection story.

I was deeply moved by all the people we spoke to, some of whom had lost loved ones in the atrocity. All the fire stations in the city were unrecognisable as they were covered with letters of thanks and pictures drawn by children from all over the USA. National flags flew from nearly every building and car aerial; it was interesting to be in a place where love of country is not frowned upon.

The USA is a nation made up of all nationalities, faiths and skin colours, yet they come together under one banner and have pride in *their* country. Major Mollie had access to the very centre of the area where the Twin Towers had stood and I interviewed her there. We had to stop several times as she was overcome emotionally. Rosemary, Phil Booth, our engineer, and I were each affected in our own way. As soon as I got back to the hotel, I wrote the following.

I've been to Ground Zero, I'm glad I went. The area where the Twin Towers once stood is now a void. The two great piles of rubble which we saw so often on our TV screens have been cleared and painstakingly sifted through. Further digging has created a large crater, known as 'The Pit' to those working in it. To one side are gathered several lumps of unearthed metal, grotesquely twisted, only the wheels giving indication that they were once cars parked in the underground car park. All the pieces of steel which liberally litter the site and everything around it are blanched a dirty white, presumably from the intense heat. I'm informed that the core temperature was still 2400 degrees a month after the atrocity. Bodies are cremated at 1500 degrees, so what hope is there of finding anything of those who died? But hope they do and as I watch, a mechanical shovel, like a JCB only much bigger, drops two shovels full of earth taken from the pit on to the ground – 'Holy Ground' as Major Mollie calls it.

With great skill the operator combs through the earth with the teeth of the shovel, spreading and gently flattening it before withdrawing. Immediately, five New York fire-fighters in helmets, masks and gloves and armed with long rakes move on to the earth and begin raking through it. Frequently they stop, bend and pick up something to examine it more closely. They're looking for body parts, by which they mean bones or a personal effect, anything which might have survived: a ring, a wallet, a policeman's shield. Ten of those who perished have been identified in such a way during the past few days. There's a priest or a minister of religion on hand at all times in case body parts are uncovered. God is in evidence here. Overlooking the Holy Ground stands a cross made from two girders found in their cruciform shape among the rubble. Beneath the cross a small sign says 'Holy Mass here every Sunday 10.30'. To one side someone has recently placed an Irish flag, underneath it, the handwritten inscription 'Lt Bobby Wallace, I love you Mommy' and a date 17 March 2002.

I nip into a wooden hut, 'The Hard Hat Café', where Salvation Army volunteers provide coffee and soup for those working their twelve-hour shift in The Pit. Young men sit staring into their coffee or straight ahead. The knees of their trousers are worn through, the toes of their boots are worn away too, exposing the steel beneath. On the walls of the cabin are several photos of smiling fire-fighters, written beneath each the word 'found' and a date.

I'm struck by the lengths to which those searching and those supporting them will go and by their obvious regard for human life compared with the perpetrators of this vile act who had no regard for life, not even their own. The tallest building in the vicinity, still standing though sorely damaged, is swathed in black netting from roof to ground level. On the side facing The Pit, it boasts an enormous Stars and Stripes flag.

Of all the people I met, I was most moved by Bill Butler, a retired fire captain. He'd been there since 13 September without a break. He's looking for his fire-fighter son, Tom, himself the father of three small boys all under six. He refuses to give up hope.

'I just want to take him home,' Bill said to me. I pray that one day soon he will.

I've been to Ground Zero – I'm glad I went.

We returned from New York on Easter Saturday with a finished programme ready for transmission. In actual fact it was transmitted three weeks later because at six that evening the announcement came from Windsor that the Queen Mum had been called to her eternal reward. Rosemary never got to bed that night, she was busy putting together a programme from scratch. She contacted Robert Lacey, the Queen's biographer, who, needless to say, had been approached by every other programme, but he decided that *GMS* was the one programme he really wanted to contribute to – bless him! Roger Royle was with us too. He was a great fan of the Queen Mother and she of him. Her passing was very different from that of Princess Diana, the element of shock was absent, but again the nation united in grief and we were pleased through *GMS* to be able to pay tribute to one of the great figures of the twentieth century.

Another consequence of 9/11 was that Religious Broadcasting's obsession with multi-faith was instantly multiplied. I accept the argument that we are BBC *Religious* Broadcasting not BBC *Christian* Broadcasting and that we must reflect the beliefs of the country as a whole but, for the moment, Britain is still a Christian country. Whether or not it will be a Christian country fifty years from now is open to debate. Yes, it's essential that we as Christians learn as much as possible about the other great world faiths: Judaism, Hinduism, Sikhism, Buddhism and particularly Islam. Each year in Britain we have 'Muslim Awareness Week'; each year we get several letters asking, 'Where in the Muslim world is there a Christian Awareness Week?'

I would not dream of trying to stop anyone from worshipping God in whichever way they see fit. In Birmingham, you'll find mosques, synagogues, gurdwaras and Buddhist temples, you can

buy a copy of the Koran in most bookshops, yet there are
countries around the world where conducting a Christian service
or just owning a Bible will result in instant imprisonment. The
persecution of Christian minorities continues in territories of
the former Soviet Union, several African countries, Pakistan,
Indonesia, China. This may come as a surprise to you because it
is rarely reported in the national press.

I have several clerics from other faiths as regulars on my
programme: Rabbi Y. Y. Rubenstein, Krishna Dharma, Indarjit
Singh, Iftikar Awan. They have become my friends, I respect
their views and hopefully they respect mine. When speaking to
someone of another faith, I'm advised that I should be sensitive
with their position as a minority living in a largely Christian
country and I can understand that. 'Don't ask any searching
questions, Don.'

If, however, my guest is an Anglican bishop: 'Make sure you
bring up the question of homosexual clergy, Don.' If I'm speaking
to a Roman Catholic: 'Make sure you ask about paedophile
priests, Don.'

Yes, the questions of homosexual priests, same-sex marriage,
female bishops are relevant, as is the disgusting situation
of paedophiles in the priesthood. I am so angered that my
denomination is being undermined by these perverts who
become ordained so that they can gain access to children. I do,
however, find it interesting that *only* Christianity is laid open to
question, and that Christianity is the *only* religion you are allowed
to ridicule on TV.

Occasionally, not often, all of us involved in the programme
plus a few movers and shakers from Religious Broadcasting have
a *GMS* meeting. One in particular became heated, or rather I did.

'*GMS* is a multi-faith programme,' someone stated.

'No it's not,' I countered. 'It's a Christian programme which
readily embraces people of other cultures and other faiths.'

'But is that what we want in the present climate?'

'Tough! That's what you've got. The programme's called *Good
Morning Sunday*, for God's sake. If it was *Good Morning Friday*, it'd
be Muslim, *Good Morning Saturday*, it'd be Jewish, but it's *Good
Morning Sunday*, it has a Christian presenter and it's a largely
Christian programme.'

The place went very quiet following my outburst but Michael Wakelin backed me up and confirmed what I had said that *GMS* was indeed a Christian programme and would continue to be so.

I have to ask myself the question, 'Would I have walked out had I not received that assurance?' This is the one thing I constantly pray about: should I leave if BBC policy goes too far away from what I believe? I'm sticking with it mainly because it's impossible to change things from without; only as an insider do you have the opportunity to ensure that your own faith is fully represented.

Having said that, I have to admit that presenting *GMS* has opened up all sorts of new insights for me. When I was being brought up as a Catholic in Birmingham I had little opportunity to learn about other faiths. I am grateful to *GMS* for helping me to experience all that we share in common with our non-Christian brothers and sisters as well as those things on which we differ. The two things that the great Abrahamic faiths, Christianity, Judaism and Islam, have in common are a bedrock of moral, biblical values and a conviction that God can and does change even the most apparently hopeless of human lives.

Well, I've done enough reflecting, it's time to look forward. I'm rapidly approaching three score, the age at which everything you've got aches and if it don't ache, it don't work; the age where people constantly ask, 'When are you going to retire?'

The way things are at the moment with the Chancellor having spent all our pension money, I'll have to keep working till I drop. I'm about to appear in a musical play called *Go and Play Up your Own End*. It's written by my good mate Malcolm Stent, it's about growing up in Birmingham in the 1950s and we've got high hopes for it.

I've just finished a most successful panto with the highly talented Bobby Davro and, provided I keep fit, I can play Dame for years to come. Arthur Askey was still playing Dame when he was eighty, you know.

'But how long can you survive as a stand-up comic Don?' I hear you cry. A few years ago I was prepared to turn my back on the thing I enjoy most, standing there alone, getting laughs. I felt the comedy scene had left me behind. Comedy has become so blue. Four-letter words, bodily functions, bladders and bowels, comediennes explaining the joys of menstruation, I couldn't compete with that material; surely it was time to call it a day? But suddenly I began to get more work than I could cope with. Friends of mine like Tom O'Connor, Jimmy Cricket and Bernie Clifton have had the same experience; people who book us know that their audience will not be offended. Comedy, though, follows television's lead. If you switch on the box after nine any evening, you'll be amazed not only by the frequency with which vile language is used but also by the subjects covered. Lesbian and homosexual practice is not just accepted, it's glorified; don't you dare speak out about it, though – we tolerate anything except intolerance. Heterosexual men are held up to ridicule as is anyone prepared to speak up about our liberal, hedonist society.

When I was in TV in the 1970s, programme makers had come from a theatre background, they knew about entertainment; they also had self-censorship. Nowadays programmes are made by floppy-haired, business studies graduates. Television needs creative people with heads full of ideas, not number crunchers who talk of bottom lines and balance sheets.

Radio, though, is king. I have no intention of leaving *GMS*. I do realise that, despite surviving the appointment of a new controller of Radio 2 and a new head of religious broadcasting, my position is in no way safe; if they'll sack Jimmy Young, they'll sack anyone! In fact when this book is published and read by them I may well get my marching orders. If I survive to fight another day, I shall continue to fight for what I believe, to be honest and to let you the listener into my life. I'll tell you what I truly think, not tell you what I think you want to hear. I'll continue to walk the edge, not take the wide middle road where the bland lead the bland. I'll also persevere with my campaign to prove that faith and fun do mix, that religion can be humorous, that you can laugh in church.

Recently one of our parishioners was giving the first reading, which was from the prophet Isaiah. Three times he had to say the phrase 'camels in throngs' and each time he said 'camels in thongs'; we were in bits.

One Sunday a parishioner stood at the lectern and announced the second reading as being from the book of Elasticus instead of

Ecclesiastes, and a few weeks previously, following the gospel of the ten bridesmaids, five of whom had oil in their lamps and five who didn't, the priest in his sermon actually said, 'Would you rather be in the light with the wise virgins or in the dark with the foolish ones?' No, I couldn't believe it either.

I started presenting *GMS* before Rowan Williams became Archbishop of Canterbury, before Cormac Murphy-O'Connor was made Cardinal, before Joel Edwards became General Director of the Evangelical Alliance, before Jonathan Sacks was made Chief Rabbi and before Alex Ferguson became Manager of Manchester United. Does this make me the longest serving purveyor of faith in Great Britain?

Toni and I have grown up together and now we're planning to grow old together. The family will help to keep us young. I'll make sure I watch every rugby game in which Rory plays. Rugby football has been the cement which has held together the very strong relationship I have with my son. His achievements and the way he has dealt with his disappointments have been a great source of pride to me.

I'll watch Rachel's every dramatic performance. She recently played Anita in *West Side Story*; she was so good I almost burst with pride. And then there are the granddaughters. They do say that grandchildren are God's reward for not killing your own kids. I'm not a boring grandparent like many of my friends. I don't carry around photos of them – well, they don't carry photos of me. When Gracie says to someone she's just met, 'Would you like to see a photo of my Poppa?' I may reconsider, but not until then. I do love spending time with Gracie on my own, just the two of us, especially in the theatre where she displays a theatrical awareness well beyond her years.

If you've read this far you'll know that I've done a lot of silly things in my life, I've made many mistakes but I've accepted responsibility for all of them. I've never attempted to blame anyone else for anything I've done – I'm not seeking compensation. I do recognise that I get more like Victor Meldrew with every passing day but do any of us successfully move with the times?

I'm glad I was born when I was, when young lads like me were taught discipline and self-control, when people had a strong sense of morality, when the way you lived your life afforded you more kudos than the size of your car and your bank balance,

> When lovers really fell in love to stay
> And stood beside each other come what may,
> When promises were something people kept
> Not something they'd just say,
> When families really bowed their heads to pray
> And daddies never walked away.

What an old romantic I am!

I'd like to have written a best-selling novel, had a number one hit record, played international rugby, competed in the Olympics and flown as one of the Red Arrows; but apart from that I've had a life supremely blessed. I thank the Good Lord for it and I only hope He feels I've used the talent He's given me for the glory of His name.

If you've managed to stick with this book to the very end, I offer you a sincere thank you and the sincere wish that the Lord will continue to walk with you and keep you safe.

Don's Highlights

1943	Born 11 March
1961	Entertainments manager at Northney
1962–64	Joins Birmingham Theatre School
1964	Summer season at Skegness' Pier Theatre
1964/65	Pantomime in Southampton at the Gaumont Theatre
1965	Summer season at Skegness' Pier Theatre
1965/66	Pantomime at Kidderminster Playhouse
1966	Summer season at Felixstowe
1966/67	Pantomime at Weston-super-Mare's Knightstone Theatre
1967	Married Toni 11 February
1967	Summer season at Clacton's West Cliff Theatre
1968	Billy Cotton Music Hall – live BBC television
1968/69	The White Heather Club tour
1969	Rachel Heather Maclean born 19 March
1969	Summer season with The White Heather Club in Llandudno
1969/70	Pantomime at Bradford's Alhambra Theatre
1970	Summer season at Blackpool's North Pier Pavilion
1970	London's Palladium Theatre

1970/71	Pantomime at Oxford's New Theatre
1971	Australia during the British summer season
1971/72	Pantomime in Birmingham at the Birmingham Hippodrome
1972	Rory Gregor Maclean born 24 June
1972	Summer season at Blackpool's Opera House
1972	*Crackerjack*
1976/77	Pantomime at Wolverhampton's Grand Theatre
1977	Summer season at Scarborough's Futurist Theatre with the *Black and White Minstrels*
1979	*The Cheapest Show on Telly*
1981	ITV's *Super Savers*
1981/82	Pantomime at Birmingham's Repertory Theatre
1983/84	Pantomime at Swansea's Grand Theatre
1984	Falklands trip to entertain troops
1985	Touring with stage play *A Bedfull of Foreigners*
1985	*Mouthtrap* for Anglia Television
1986	Touring with stage play *Chase Me Comrade*
1990	*Good Morning Sunday*
1994	Played Dame in pantomime at Birmingham's Hippodrome Theatre
1994	Summer season at Clacton's West Cliff Theatre
1995/96	Pantomime at Southampton's Mayflower Theatre
1996	Summer season at Clacton's West Cliff Theatre
2001	Made an MBE on the New Year's Honours list
2003	Invested as a Knight of the Holy Sepulchre at Southwark Cathedral